D1192677

THE Language OF Medicine

THE Language OF Medicine

Its Evolution, Structure, AND Dynamics

Second Edition

John H. Dirckx, M.D.

Library of Congress Cataloging in Publication Data

Dirckx, John H., 1938–
 The language of medicine, its evolution, structure, and
dynamics.

 Includes index.
 1. Medicine—Language. 2. English language—Etymology.
I. Title. [DNLM: 1. Language. 2. Nomenclature. W 15
D598L]
R123.D57 1983   610'.1'4   83-8863
ISBN 0-03-063961-1

Published in 1983 by Praeger Publishers
CBS Educational and Professional Publishing
a Division of CBS Inc.
521 Fifth Avenue, New York, New York 10175 U.S.A.

Second edition © 1983 by Praeger Publishers
First edition © 1976 by Harper & Row/Lippincott

3456789 052 987654321

Printed in the United States of America
on acid-free paper

Preface

Despite its somewhat pretentious subtitle, this is not a systematic treatise. Any author so imprudent as to attempt an orderly and thorough examination of the whole subject of medical speech and writing would surely exhaust his readers long before exhausting his subject matter. It has been my purpose, rather, to present a sampling of what is most characteristic and most fascinating about medical language in as informal and diverting a manner as is consistent with accuracy. Though I have sketched out and generally kept to a logical scheme, I have often deliberately abandoned the well-trodden highway of dictionary and textbook language to wander along the lanes and byways in search of the quaint and the curious, of unusual word origins and quirks of usage.

The language of modern American medicine is an amalgam of words and roots from dozens of ancient and modern languages, a distillate of 3,000 years of cultural and linguistic evolution and of almost as long a period of scientific and technical progress. For all that, it is predominantly English, and I have chosen to set the stage for a consideration of medical language with a chapter on the history and chief characteristics of lay, nontechnical, or "plain" English. The reader who is interested only in medical terminology may prefer to skim this first chapter.

Similarly, the last chapter may not be particularly appealing to the reader who is impatient of orthographic and grammatical restrictions, who converses by choice in the banal and turbid idiom of the six o'clock news, and whose taste in reading matter runs to Medicare handbooks and advertisements for proprietary headache remedies. At first I had no thought of introducing any critical observations, much less of offering prescriptions for the clear and effective use of language. But as soon as I began to gather material, I was struck by the number and variety of faulty or objectionable usages current in medical speech and writing. And when I had put the most flagrant of them together and ventured to suggest how they might be rectified, the result was the longest chapter of all.

Though the nonphysician will find here both instruction and entertainment, this book is addressed in particular to members of the medical profession. The physician who would ply his art with a steady and tranquil mind, preserving his equanimity in spite of his blunders and failures and never losing sight of the essential worth and dignity even of God's most pusillanimous and exasperating creatures, must become something more than a scientist and a technician: he must be a philosopher and a humanist as well. Of all the manifestations of the grandeur and profundity of the human spirit, none is more ubiquitous, none more revealing, than language—the miracle of interpersonal communication through articulate speech, the no less wondrous phenomenon of writing, the staggering diversity of the world's tongues and the timelessness of their literatures.

Thomas Mann wrote that speech is civilization itself. Just as we can learn much about a person's character and attainments by carefully observing how he speaks and writes, so can we gain valuable insight into the mind and soul of a nation, of a race, of mankind itself, through the study of language. If we take seriously the old Greek exhortation, Know thyself, what better language to start with than our own?

Preface to
the Second Edition

For this second edition of *The Language of Medicine*, the text has been entirely rewritten, and much new matter has been added. Since my chief aim in revising the book was improvement rather than enlargement, much has also been deleted.

It is a pleasure to acknowledge the corrections, criticisms, and suggestions so generously and tactfully proffered by Drs. Harry L. Arnold, Jr., David L. Dunn, Herbert J. Kaufmann, Edward Kupka, Eugene G. Laforet, Morris Leider, J. Graham Smith, Jr., and Lawrence W. Way.

I am grateful to the *American Journal of Dermatopathology* for permission to reprint material first published in its pages and to the J. B. Lippincott Co. for relinquishing its rights to the first edition of this book.

Finally, my warmest expressions of appreciation must go to Drs. A. Bernard Ackerman and Morris Leider, without whose advice and encouragement this second edition would never have appeared.

Contents

THE Language OF Medicine

CHAPTER 1

Plain English

History

The English language, it should be realized, is not a wayside tree that has grown up wild; it is, rather, a highly cultivated plant which has been crossbred with other languages, which has for centuries been grafted and pruned, and which has been forced in its growth in a soil fertilized by classical culture. Surely the stages in its growth and the processes employed in its development deserve to be more widely known.

George H. McKnight
Modern English in the Making

The first mention of what is now called England in the work of a professional historian occurs in Julius Caesar's *Commentaries on the Gallic Wars*. Better known to posterity as a maker of history than as a writer of it, Caesar himself led Roman troops across the Straits of Dover in 55 B.C. to begin the military subjection of Britain. The aboriginal inhabitants of this island at the western extremity of the known world, whom Caesar called *Britanni*, belonged to the Celtic race, of which the Welsh are the only representatives surviving today.

1

Though the Celts have now all but vanished, they were once a flourishing and widespread people. Before invading Britain, Caesar had put down a series of local uprisings in Gaul, which comprised virtually all of continental Europe west of the Rhine and north of the Pyrenees. Since the people of Gaul were also Celts, it is not surprising that Celtic place-names live on all over the European continent (Paris, Vienna, Rhine) as well as in the British Isles (Kent, York, Avon, Thames, Bryn Mawr, and probably London). Galicia in Spain and Galatia (to which one of St. Paul's epistles is addressed) in what is now Turkey were originally colonies of "Gauls."

Surviving Celtic languages are Welsh, spoken today by perhaps a quarter of the population of Wales; Scots-Gaelic; Irish; and Breton, spoken by about a million inhabitants of Brittany on the French coast.

Around the middle of the first century A.D., during the reign of Emperor Claudius, extensive Roman colonies were established in Britain. In time the native islanders found themselves totally subjugated to Roman rule and their territories annexed to the empire. Though many of them learned the language of their masters and absorbed some of their culture, the Romanization of Britain was never quite complete. The Picts and Scots, half-savage tribes that inhabited what is now Scotland, retreated into the bleak and desolate highlands, where the invaders saw no point in pursuing them.

During the fifth century the Romans, their continental empire tottering on the brink of collapse, abandoned Britain. Although this meant that Rome no longer exacted tribute or imposed its legal system upon the Britons, it also resulted in the withdrawal of the powerful defensive machinery that had kept the Picts and Scots at bay. When these marauding tribes from the north found that their forays were no longer opposed by Roman troops, they grew bolder and began to migrate southward.

In vain the Britons pleaded with Rome to send back a few legions for their protection. Their only recourse was to enlist the aid of the hardy, rough-and-tumble seafarers who appeared on their coasts from time to time from across the North Sea. These visitors, natives of northern Germany and Scandinavia, were a Teutonic people very different from both the Celts and the Romans. Large-limbed and blond, hardened by the northern climate, they farmed little, rode without saddles, and settled their differences with clubs. Like their cousins the Vikings, they were inveterate wanderers and skillful navigators.

As might have been expected, these formidable Teutonic allies soon became invaders in their own right. The first of them to make trouble were the Jutes, a tribe from the upper Rhine Valley or, less probably, from modern Jutland. At the invitation of Vortigern, one of a long series of self-appointed rulers of Celtic Britain, an army of Jutes led by Hengist and Horsa crossed over to England in 449 and successfully beat back the daring and rapacious Picts and Scots. By way of reward, Vortigern ceded to them the Isle of Thanet, but they soon grew dissatisfied with this small territory and eventually took control of all the land from the Thames estuary south to the Straits of Dover, founding the kingdom of Kent.

In 477 a party of Saxons under the leadership of Aella arrived from northern Germany and established themselves west of Kent. In time their domain came to be called Sussex (southern Saxons); the distinction was necessary because in 495 other Saxons arrived under Cerdic to settle further west (in Wessex), and subsequent invasions by still other Saxons led to the conquest and colonization of part of the eastern coast of Britain north of the Thames estuary (Essex).

At about the same time, other hordes of Teutons from what is now Schleswig-Holstein were swarming into northern Britain. These people, the Angles, eventually gained control of by far the widest territories, and their three kingdoms—Northumbria, East Anglia, and Mercia—extended from the Saxon frontier all the way into Scotland.

The seven kingdoms of the Anglo-Saxon heptarchy must not be thought of as political units with fixed borders, coexisting in peace and harmony. The various parties of Germanic invaders had much less difficulty in snatching territory from the natives than in keeping it out of each other's hands, and a more or less continual state of war existed for about three centuries.

Before long the invaders had expelled the Britons from all of England except the barren but mineral-rich western districts of Wales and Cornwall. Parties of refugees who reached the French coast from this area in the sixth century were responsible for the introduction there of the Breton dialect. After this date little trace was left in

Britain of either the original Celtic language or the Latin spoken by the vanished Roman invaders, for throughout most of the island the only languages spoken were Teutonic dialects imported from northern continental Europe, which would one day evolve into modern English.

It is true that several words (*clan, galore, plaid, slogan, smithereens, Tory, whisky*) have come into English from modern Celtic languages in comparatively recent times. Though a few others (*iron, gravel*) seem to have been picked up from native British Celts by the Teutonic invaders, the total number of such remnants in modern English is extremely small. Apparently the only traces of Latin left by the Roman occupation of Britain are in place-names. For example, *castra* 'camp' survives in *Winchester, Lancaster, Leicester,* and *Exeter*; *strata via* 'paved road' in *Stratford* and *street*.

Though each of the invading tribes had its own Germanic dialect, all shared the same grammatical system and had many words in common. When, early in the ninth century, the seven kingdoms finally resolved their territorial disputes and formed a single nation, they accepted Egbert, who ruled Wessex from 802 to 839, as their first king. Though a Saxon kingdom thus achieved political dominance, the Angles occupied by far the greater part of Britain, and it was they who gave their name to the new nation: Angle-land or England. So also the designation *Englisc* 'English' was given to the West Saxon (Wessex) dialect, which became the common language of Anglo-Saxon learning and literature.

Before I examine some of the characteristics of this Anglo-Saxon language, or Old English, let me put it into perspective. Though the ancient British Celts and their Roman and Germanic invaders had no suspicion of it, all of their languages were related. The modern linguist can demonstrate beyond any doubt that these languages had a common parent tongue, which died out long before the dawn of written literature. In fact, the family of languages to which these three belonged, the Indo-European, embraces nearly every tongue spoken today in the Western world.

Sanskrit, the oldest known representative of the Indo-European family, is the ancestor of modern Hindustani and the other Indic languages. We have already met three other large groups within the family: the Celtic (Welsh, Gaelic, Irish, and Breton), the Germanic (German, Dutch, Swedish, Danish, Norwegian, Icelandic and English), and the Latin or Romance (Latin, Italian, Spanish,

Portuguese, French, Provençal, and Rumanian). But this does not nearly exhaust the list, for the Indo-European family also includes the Slavic languages (Russian, Bulgarian, Czech, and Polish), the Baltic (Lithuanian and Latvian), Armenian, Greek, and Albanian.

Not only is the common parent of all these modern tongues lost, but many of the intermediate languages and dialects have also disappeared. A lost language—one for which no written records exist—can never be brought back to life in anything like its original form. The most painstaking research can produce, at best, a reconstruction that is hopelessly tentative and incomplete. Yet a substantial body of information about some of the characteristics of primeval Indo-European—its broad features of phonetics, grammar, and vocabulary—has been assembled after nearly two centuries of study.

Partly because many of the earliest and most brilliant pioneers in this kind of linguistic investigation were German (Adelung, Bopp, Schultze, and the brothers Grimm), the Germanic languages have been analyzed with particular thoroughness. The Germanic family is usually divided into three large tribes, though the distinctions among them are not as clear as one might wish. The West Germanic languages include High and Low German, Dutch, Frisian, Anglo-Saxon, and thus modern English. The North Germanic languages, all derived from Old Norse, make up the Scandinavian group: Swedish, Danish, Norwegian, and Icelandic. Though all members of the East Germanic group (Burgundian, Vandal, and Gothic) are now extinct, these languages made vital contributions to the vocabularies of western European tongues, particularly Spanish, during the Teutonic invasions.

The distinction within the West Germanic branch between High and Low German is important and often misunderstood. The names notwithstanding, Low German is not a debased form of High but a separate dialect—or, more accurately, a family of dialects—that developed along a different track. High German, the literary language of modern Germany and Austria, evolved during the early Middle Ages from a group of south German dialects. Though it is the language taught in German schools, it is often pushed aside in popular speech by local dialects.

The dialects of northern and western Germany together make up Low German or Plattdeutsch. This language branch is essentially identical to Holland Dutch and Belgian Flemish, but different spelling rules have been fixed for each country, and slight variations of vocabulary and pronunciation occur from one village to the next throughout northern Germany and the Low Countries. Since the Teutonic invaders of England came from this part of the Continent, and since Low German has changed much less in the past 15 centuries than High German, it may be said with perfect truth that Saxon survives on the Continent as the core of Low German and Dutch. Anglo-Saxon contained many words and usages that are presently found in both modern English and Plattdeutsch, though there is no trace of them in modern High German. Thus, *brain* (*brein*), *he*, and *pot* appear in English, Plattdeutsch, and Dutch-Flemish, though the corresponding words in High German are *Gehirn, er,* and *Topf.*

In spite of differences like these, all of the Germanic languages and dialects are easily recognized by the linguist as the evolutionary products of a single Germanic parent tongue, long extinct. Around the time that this primeval Germanic speech split off from the Indo-European mainstream, it underwent two phonetic shifts that would from that time forward characterize all its many offspring. The first of these was a softening of initial consonants, whereby, for example, an initial *p* was muted into *f*. Thus the root *PED* 'foot' appears in Sanskrit as *pádah*, in Greek as *pous*, and in Latin as *pes*; but German *Fuss*, like English *foot*, begins with an *f* sound. As another example, an initial *k* sound (*kapalam, kephale, caput*) was softened into *h* (*Haupt, head*).

It should be borne in mind that when I speak of an Indo-European parent tongue and a primitive Germanic tongue, I am referring not to written but to spoken languages, which have been partly reconstructed by scholars working backward from the earliest available records. The second important phonetic change, which remains today as a distinctive trait of all Germanic languages including our own, was a shift of stress or accent to the first syllable of a word. In a compound word such as *countryman, daylight,* or *weekend* the first syllable is naturally stressed even though it is not the most important part of the word. Nouns and verbs in Germanic languages that are not customarily accented on the first syllable are usually loan-words from other languages. Even these may eventually have their accents shifted forward. The process is presently at work on *address, adult, detail, research,* and many other English words from non-Teutonic sources.

By the sixth century the Teutonic colonists in Britain had learned from Christian missionaries to read and write. Though Ulfilas's translation of the Gospels into Gothic was made before 381 (with a Gothic alphabet probably invented by himself), and Scandinavian poetry written in runic characters is still older, Anglo-Saxon literary remains are among the earliest records of any Germanic language written in Roman letters. The considerable body of literature that has survived from the Anglo-Saxon period enables us to study in detail the primitive tongue from which our modern English is directly descended.

Anglo-Saxon was a highly inflected language. That is, it made extensive use of small phonetic changes in words to show changes in meaning or function. Though the language has now lost most of its inflections, a few vestiges remain: the *s* that we add to nouns to make them plural; the '*s* by which we show possession; and the *-ed* added to a "weak" verb to indicate the past tense. I might also mention the irregular plurals *oxen* and *children*: biblical words such as *hast, hath, doth*, and *saith*; and changes in pronouns such as *he, his*, and *him*.

These are all instances of external flection, that is, they are changes or additions at the end of a word. Most Anglo-Saxon inflections were of this type, though like modern German the Anglo-Saxon language also had internal flections in which the stem itself underwent a change, usually a vowel shift. We have remnants of this process is modern English in a few irregular plurals (*mice, geese, men*) and in the past tense of "strong" verbs (*came, taught, fell*).

A notable trait of Anglo-Saxon was its freedom in forming self-explanatory compounds like our *handbook, horseshoe*, and *shoemaker*, a feature that yet today typifies the Germanic languages. Anglo-Saxon was extremely rich in synonyms by which to express delicate shades of meaning. In *Beowulf*, one of the classic verse compositions in Anglo-Saxon, there are 36 words for 'hero'.

Much of the surviving literature in this vigorous and versatile idiom is poetry. Prose works of note include *The Ecclesiastical History of the English People*, written in Latin by the Venerable Bede around 730 and early translated into "English," and the *Anglo-Saxon Chronicle*, prepared under the direction of King Alfred, who reigned from 871 to 899. From these two records much of the historical material in this chapter is ultimately derived.

Here is a brief passage from the close of the *Anglo-Saxon Chronicle* that relates the death of Alfred:

901. Her gefor Aelfred Athulfing, syx nihtum ær ealra haligra mæssan. Se wæs cyning ofer eall Ongelcyn butan thæm dæle the under Dena onwalde wæs, ond he heold thæt rice othrum healfum læs the .xxx. wintra. Ond tha feng Eadweard, his sunu, to rice.

(899 [in modern chronology]. Here [that is, in this year] died Alfred, son of Athelwulf, six nights before the feast of All Saints. He was king over all the English nation except the part that was in the power of the Danes, and he reigned a year and a half less than thirty years. And then began Edward, his son, to reign.)

It is plain from this example how much Old English differs from modern. Only four words (*under, he, his, to*) have come down to us with spelling unchanged. (Anglo-Saxon *the* is not our definite article but an obsolete form of the relative pronoun *that* and the conjunction *than*.) Some words do not differ greatly from their modern counterparts (*her, wæs, ofer, ond, sunu*), while others are barely recognizable (*cyning* 'king'; *healfum* 'half'). Though there is scarcely a word here that has no descendant in modern English, the general impression is that one is looking at a "foreign" language. Indeed, the English-speaking reader can find passages more intelligible to him than this in any book in modern Dutch ("Kees is juist de best vriend in de wereld") or even Danish ("Moder puttede to ægs i en pænde").

The reader will have noted that the domain of King Alfred was said not to have included the part of England under Danish rule. Around 787, even before the consolidation of the English nation under Egbert, a new wave of Teutonic invaders, the Danes, appeared on British shores. As they found most of the country already occupied by the Anglo-Saxons, they established only a few independent settlements in what is now Lincolnshire. But they made repeated assaults on the eastern coasts (notably in 850, 991, and 994), ravaging, plundering, and infiltrating, until at length they had the whole nation under their control. Though in Alfred's time the Danish territory, or Danelaw, comprised only the northeast corner of England, between 1016 and 1042 three Danish kings in succession sat on the English throne.

Old Norse, the language brought by the Danes into England, was very much like Anglo-Saxon, but because there was already a substantial literature in Anglo-Saxon, one can accurately judge which words came into English at the time of the Danish invasions and which were already there. Though Old Norse did not contribute a great many words, it gave us some of our most common ones, including *are, call, die, egg, flat, get, give, hit, ill, law, lift, low, scab, scalp, skin, skull, take, their, them, they, trust, want, weak,* and *window.* Old Norse is the origin of English place-names ending in *-by* and *-thorpe* (both meaning 'village'), of the final *s* of a third person singular verb in the present tense (*she drinks*), and probably of our practice of omitting the relative pronoun from a so-called contact clause: "The book *I saw* was the one *you wanted.*"

The Danes also introduced a few variant forms that appear in some of the interesting cognate doublets that so abound in English: from Anglo-Saxon came *no, shirt, shriek,* and *whole*; from Old Norse, *hale, nay, screech,* and *skirt.* A number of words in the Scots dialect (*bairn* 'child'; *maun* 'must') are of Danish origin.

Only 24 years after the Anglo-Saxons regained control of England under Edward I (the Confessor), an event occurred that was to exert a much more profound influence on the language of England than the Danish occupation. In 1066 Edward died without an heir and was succeeded by Harold on the decree of the witan, or common council. Edward's cousin William, Duke of Normandy, pretended to believed that he had a legitimate claim to the throne, and when he could not secure it by diplomacy, he invaded England at the head of an army and took it by force, becoming William I of England.

Normandy was and is a district of France around the mouth of the Seine, but the Normans were not of French stock. Late in the ninth century a band of Scandinavian wanderers led by Rollo had drifted into northwestern France. By 912 these Northmen, or Normans, had so completely taken possession of the area that King Charles the Simple ceded it to them. Never content to stay at home and lead the simple life, the Normans went on in their roving, adventurous ways. At about the same time that William was winning the Battle of Hastings, another party of Normans under Robert Guiscard was subduing southern Italy.

The outcome of the Norman Conquest was in sharp contrast to that of the Teutonic invasions of five centuries earlier. Whereas the Angles and Saxons had practically exterminated the Celtic Britons, the Normans were content with merely enslaving the English. Although, like their new vassals, the Normans were of Teutonic origin, their language was a dialect of French that soon became the medium of education and culture in England, and continued so, with a strong influence on the Anglo-Saxon still spoken by the unlettered majority, until the fourteenth century.

During the 1,100 years since Julius Caesar had first carried the Latin of Imperial Rome onto British soil, that language had undergone a remarkable series of changes. Once a fairly uniform idiom throughout the vast Roman Empire, it had gradually acquired regional peculiarities, breaking up into numerous dialects. The decline of Rome was paralleled by the increasing corruption of its language. Though the *sermo vulgaris* 'popular speech' of the average Roman citizen was at no period so elegant (or artificial) as the highly polished diction preserved in the writings of the Augustan poets, with the disintegration of Roman culture Late Latin fell upon evil days and was eventually debased and corrupted out of existence. By the end of the Dark Ages, Latin was nobody's mother tongue. In its place remained five distinct families of dialects, each bound to a geopolitical or ethnic group: Italian, Spanish, Portuguese, French, and Rumanian.

Between the third and fifth centuries the Romanization of Gaul gradually extinguished nearly all traces of the Celtic language formerly spoken there. Though the oldest specimen of written French is the Oath of Strasbourg (842), the French language already existed in the fifth century as a "Gallic" dialect of Late Latin. Gallic influences still discernible in French are the "front" pronunciation of *u* (also heard in Spanish) that replaced the long Latin *u* still heard in Italian, a stronger tendency to drop or soften a consonant coming in the middle of a word than is found in the other Romance languages, and a few relics of the Gallic vicesimal system of counting. This system, which counts by twenties instead of tens, survives in French *soixante-dix* ('sixty-ten') for *seventy, quatre-vingt* ('four twenties') for *eighty*, and so on.

During the fourth century the Franks, who eventually gave their name to France, appeared on the banks of the Rhine. Ostensibly allies of the Romans, or at least mercenaries in the service of Caesar, they were chiefly interested in plunder and in extending their frontiers into more temperate latitudes, for like the Angles and the Saxons, the Danes and the Normans, these were yet another Teutonic people. First united under Clovis in 481, the Franks proceeded to conquer most of west central Europe, including what is now France and Germany. Though they imposed their rule on the people of Gaul, they did not impose their language. Still, the developing French tongue borrowed a number of Frankish words, of which *garçon, guerre,* and *hangar,* whose meanings are familiar to most speakers of English, may be mentioned.

By 500 A.D. primitive French displayed two rather distinct dialects. The northern one was characterized by a shift from the *a* of Latin to *e* or *ie*: Latin *mare* 'sea' and *canis* 'dog' became *mer* and *chien.* In the southern dialect, spoken by people closer to the Italian peninsula, this shift did not take place. The two dialects are distinguished by their respective words for *yes,* the southern being known as Languedoc (the language of *oc*) and the northern as Languedoïl (the language of *oïl,* modern *oui*). Languedoc formed the basis of Provençal, the language of the medieval troubadours, which survives as a group of dialects still spoken in southern France.

By the tenth century Languedoïl had further differentiated into Parisian or Île-de-France, Picard, Burgundian, and Norman. Though Norman appeared to be in the ascendant around the thirteenth century, standard modern French is actually derived from the Île-de-France dialect. It was Norman, of course, and not Parisian French that served as the "official" language of England during the eleventh and twelfth centuries.

Though the House of Normandy retained possession of the English throne for less than a hundred years, ceding to the Plantagenets in 1154, the first Plantagenet king, Henry II, inherited control of much of France. Even after Henry's son and successor John, by one of the diplomatic blunders that earned him the epithet "Lackland," had lost control of Normandy and the other French possessions of the English crown early in the thirteenth century, Norman continued to be spoken in England by the wealthy and the literate.

Indeed, it survived as the language of law until the sixteenth century, and many modern legal terms are relics of "Law French": *acquit, arraign, bail(iff), entail, escheat, felony, indictment, malfeasance, mortgage, plaintiff, tenant, tort,* and several dozen more. Medical words that came into English during the Norman period and survive today include *balm, contagion, debility, leper, malady,* and *palsy.* Speakers of English still use French versions of many names of persons (Anne, Horace, Jeanne, Jerome, Julie, Louis) and places (Venice, Florence, Rome, Cologne, Prague, Seville).

Though the Anglo-Saxon language was eclipsed for several centuries by Norman French, it never died out. Having continued to be the medium of daily speech among the common people, it began to flourish again as a written language in the fourteenth century, when the first great writers of English—Langland, Gower, Chaucer, and Mandeville—used it as a literary vehicle. But though Anglo-Saxon had survived the long Norman interlude, it had not survived unchanged. In fact, when we rediscover it in the works of these fourteenth century authors, it has undergone a remarkable metamorphosis: it has absorbed thousands of Romance words and roots from French, lost most of its inflectional system, and evolved so far in the direction of our modern English that we can now make shift to read it without much difficulty. The English of this period is called Middle English to distinguish it from Anglo-Saxon or Old English and from modern English.

The following passage is taken from the Prologue to Chaucer's *The Canterbury Tales*. Except for the use of modern letters in place of the old symbols for *gh* and *th*, the lines appear exactly as they were written in 1387, more than a century before Columbus discovered America. Besides displaying very well the character of Middle English, this is an excellent specimen of Chaucer's droll wit.

> With us ther was a Doctour of Physik:
> In all this world ne was ther noon hym lik,
> To speke of physik and of surgerye;
> For he was grounded in astronomye.
>
>   . . .
>
> He knew the cause of everich maladye,
> Were it of hoot, or cold, or moyste, or drye,
> And where they engendred and of what humour;
> He was a verray parfit praktisour.
>
>   . . .
>
> Of his diete mesurable was he,
> For it was of no superfluitee,
> But of great norissyng and digestible.
> His studie was but litel on the Bible.

The history of the English language after the time of Chaucer is essentially the history of England itself and of its rich and varied literature. By the end of the fourteenth century the language had already received its distinctive character as a blend of two disparate linguistic strains, the Teutonic and the Romance, in an incredibly happy marriage destined to be blessed with many offspring in the languages and dialects of England, Scotland, Ireland, Australia, Canada, and the United States.

Space will permit only a brief notice of three further influences on the shape of modern English: the great vowel shift of the fifteenth century, the rise of grammarians and lexicographers in the seventeenth and eighteenth centuries, and extensive borrowing from other modern languages.

Not long after Chaucer's death in 1400 a crucial and inexplicable change took place in the pronunciation of English. Just when spelling had begun to be stabilized by the development of printing and the spread of literacy, vowel sounds shifted. Fairly accurate information about changes in pronunciation can be gathered by careful and extensive study of rhyming poetry from various periods. During the great vowel shift, low vowels (those pronounced with the tongue low in the mouth) were "raised," so that continental *a* as in *father*, short *e*, and short *o* became *i*, *u*, and long and short *a*. Meanwhile, high vowel sounds were further raised to become diphthongs. It is largely because spelling practices held fast despite this wholesale transformation of sounds that modern English spelling is so inconsistent in representing words as we now say them. Moreover, the vowel shift itself was inconsistent. *Break* and *great* preserve the long *a* sound that they had in Shakespeare's time, while *bread*, *tread*, *clean*, and *speak* have undergone varying degrees of raising. *Blood* and *flood* remain low, *book* and *foot* are intermediate, and *boot* and *food* are high. Modern usage has not yet decided on a single vowel sound for *root* and *roof*.

During the seventeenth and eighteenth centuries the urge to analyze and codify the English language spread like a fever among men of learning and culture. Each felt not only qualified but obliged to express himself on pronunciation, grammar, spelling, and usage. Addison and Swift waged war on neologisms, fad words, and foreign imports. Clergyman and chemist Joseph Priestley lectured on the theory of language and published *Rudiments of English Grammar* (1761). Most of the grammarians, while paying lip service to Horace's maxim that usage is the *jus et norma loquendi*, based their theories and rules on ancient prejudices derived from the classical languages and on the affectations of the social and cultural elite. Ignoring the Germanic origins of English, they sought to determine its grammar by the yardstick of classical Greek and Latin, and, having pruned away all its defects, to fix it for all time in a state of petrifaction like that of these dead languages.

Their "reasoning" on the subject of usage went something like this: "*To whom, as if I were, older than he* are correct, and *to who, if I was, older than him* are wrong, because the former are used by the best and most cultivated speakers and writers, and the latter are avoided by them. The best and most cultivated speakers and writers can be recognized by the fact that they say and write *to whom, as if I were, older than he*, and avoid the variant usages."

To this period belong a great number of spelling "improvements" that are still with us. The tendency of French to drop a consonant between vowels had turned Latin *debita, dubitare,* and *recepta* into *dette, doute,* and *receite.* Long after these words had been imported into English, certain pedantic busybodies declared them corrupt and restored the unpronounced and unpronounceable consonants: *debt, doubt,* and *receipt.* Other meddlers put the *s* in *island* and the *h* in *rhyme* without any justification other than a mistaken analogy with other words.

Despite their prejudices and the narrowness of their horizons, the Stuart and Georgian grammarians made many positive and wholesome contributions to our language. They codified or invented our most rational, useful, and simple rules, and they paved the way for the great lexicographers. Samuel Johnson, who was immortalized by Boswell's famous biography, produced almost single-handedly the first great English dictionary, which was published in 1755. In the United States, Noah Webster's dictionaries of 1806 and 1828 recorded American usage, pronunciation, and spelling. The *Oxford English Dictionary*, the most exhaustive and scholarly dictionary in existence in any language, was completed in 1928 after half a century of herculean toil by a succession of editors and subeditors. Whatever one may think about the proper role of a dictionary, or the usefulness of those presently available, there is no denying the vast influence exerted by dictionaries on our language and culture.

Both the shape and size of modern English have been appreciably affected by the vast influx of new words from foreign tongues. Though in framework and tone the language is still Germanic, a sentence of English may be a rich mosaic composed of bits from many lands and cultures—Gothic, Arabic, Slavic, African, and American Indian. Britannia, Mistress of the Waves, either warred or traded with every other nation on earth and greedily absorbed words from them all, often recasting them in its own mold. Thus, Spanish *cucaracha* became *cockroach*, French *écrevisse* evolved into *crayfish*, and the Arabic chess expression *shah mat* ('The King is dead') appears in English as *checkmate*.

A foreign import may be attracted by a word already in the language to become its homonym, as when Malay *kampong* turned into colonial English *compound* 'residential enclosure'. Latin *ros maris* 'sea dew' fused with the English proper noun *Rosemary* as the name of the kitchen herb. (An aviator in distress is understood the world over if he radios the French plea *m'aider* 'help me', but speakers of English write it *Mayday*.)

During the past century England has been repaying its debt to other languages with interest. Most western European languages have adopted or adapted English *club* ('association'), *jockey, football* (what Americans call 'soccer'), *interview, revolver,* and *whisky*. France has passed legislation, for the protection of consumers, forbidding the use of "Franglais" in legal contracts.

Having brought the chronology of our language to the present, let me now step back and view it from a different direction, pretending, like the grammarian and the lexicographer, that English is an abstraction, frozen in time.

Physical Examination

The English language is a methodical, energetic, business-like and sober language, that does not care much for finery and elegance, but does care for logical consistency and is opposed to any attempt to narrow-in life by police regulations and strict rules either of grammar or of lexicon.

Otto Jespersen
Growth and Structure of the English Language

Most of the features that make our language unique can be traced to the same cause: English is a hybrid tongue, a blend of the best and the worst of two widely differing linguistic strains, the Teutonic and the Romance. The traditional contrast between the fair, taciturn, stubborn, saturnine, warlike Teuton and the dark, voluble, mercurial, genial, passionate Latin may be a little overworked, but like most clichés it contains a generous share of truth.

The Germanic invaders of Britain were a shrewd and practical people who probably viewed their way of talking purely as a means to an end, like using an axe or an oar. Though the language they brought with them was a highly articulate one with a complex inflectional system and a rich lexicon, it had undergone important phonetic changes since splitting off from the Indo-European parent language. Some of these have already been mentioned. It was formerly held, on insufficient evidence, that primitive Germanic was largely composed of monosyllables. The present view is that early forms of Germanic were rich in polysyllabic words and that only later did the language break up into shorter fragments. Be that as it may, the group of dialects brought into Britain by the semibarbarian Teutonic invaders were rugged, harsh, monosyllabic, and guttural.

By contrast, the Romance languages and dialects were born and bred in the countries of the Mediterranean littoral, whose climate and other physical features allowed the inhabitants leisure to cultivate conversation as an art form. These peoples had already developed a literature rich in epic, lyrical, and elegiac poetry and drama at a time when Teutonic "literature" was limited to the rude effusions of hunters and warriors gathered at the tribal fireside. Primeval Latin, like Greek, was fluid, melodious, and polysyllabic.

The contrast between English words of Teutonic origin and those of Romance origin can be seen in the following pairs of synonyms: *house–domicile*; *show–demonstrate*; *trust–confidence*; and *fair–equitable*. These examples are offered by way of illustration rather than proof. Admittedly, the demonstration is a little contrived. So completely have the two elements mingled in modern English, and so far has the language evolved and matured, that with a little effort one might select a list of synonym pairs that seemed to prove the opposite thesis.

Romance (predominantly French) elements have been so completely assimilated into the basic language that only a linguist can distinguish them from native (Germanic) stock. Some words taken from medieval Norman are spelled in English exactly as are their equivalents in modern French: *age, air, large, place, point*. Others have been recast in the Anglo-Saxon mold, losing all traces of their Romance origins: *abridge, budge, curfew, haughty, powder, wig*. Naturally, English has taken no more pains to preserve the meanings of French imports than to retain their pronunciations and spellings. The Frenchman calls his pantry an *office* and his office a *cabinet*, but since he had these words first, it would be unseemly for us to argue with him about their significance.

English has freely formed compounds of French and Anglo-Saxon words and affixes: *atonement, commonwealth, courtly, defrost, napkin, roughage, starvation, underestimate, vengeful.* The useful and nearly inevitable practice of thus joining lexical elements without regard for their "national" origins has its counterpart in the numerous hybrids of Greek and Latin to be found in modern scientific terminology.

Words of purely Teutonic descent tend to be more vigorous, masculine, and explicit than Romance words. In fact, though about half of the words in an English dictionary are of Romance origin, most of those that we use in everyday speech are Teutonic. Nearly all English pronouns, prepositions, and conjunctions are from Teutonic stock, as are a substantial majority of nouns, verbs, and adjectives referring to common and concrete things. When we shout in anger or mutter in agony, we use an almost purely Anglo-Saxon English.

Even before the flood of terms borrowed or adapted from classical Latin to meet the needs of developing science and technology, words derived from Romance roots had seemed more suitable for the expression of subtle, abstract, or complex ideas in the physical sciences, philosophy, and art. Nowadays, Romance words are apt to predominate in sophisticated (also snobbish or pompous) speech and writing. Euphemisms are quite regularly selected from Romance resources, since these usually seem more genteel, or less blunt, than their Germanic counterparts. Thus, the physician would rather ask a patient whether he has a family of history of *seizures* than inquire about *fits*, and he would rather discuss a *malodor* than a *stench*. Premeditated insolence, satire, and the mock-heroic all make heavy use of Romance words.

English is unique among Germanic languages in not forming most of its compound words out of native stock. The noun corresponding to *go down* is *descent*, borrowed (along with *descend*) from French; we have no synonym built up from Anglo-Saxon material. Similarly, our noun for *going away* is *departure*; for *going up, ascent;* for *going in, entry*. Other Germanic languages use their native resources to form compound words for many concepts that English can hardly express at all without availing itself of Romance borrowings. Compare German *Erziehung* and English *education; wiederholen* and *repeat; verschieden* and *different; ausschliesslich* and *exclusively.* Many German composite words, particularly those standing for abstract notions, have been "translated" almost syllable by syllable from corresponding words of Latin provenance: *ablehnen–decline; Nachschrift–postscript; unabhängig–independent.*

Though similar pairs occur in English (*outcome–event; predict–foretell; afterthought–repentance*), in most instances the Anglo-Saxon version has died out. Even for simple Anglo-Saxon verbs in everyday use, English customarily makes the corresponding nouns and adjectives from Romance material—*get–reception; see–visible; can–possible; have–possessive; be–existence*—which is one of the chief reasons why a speaker of English has much less difficulty in acquiring a working vocabulary in a Romance language than in learning the same number and kind of words in German, Dutch, or Swedish.

The diversity of origin of our words makes for a diversity of sounds. Not only is the relation between English spelling and pronunciation erratic, but English has a broader range of acceptable or "correct" pronunciations than most languages would tolerate. This is true even if we disregard geographic and dialectal variations. Compare pronunciations listed in various dictionaries for *envelope, gaseous, harass, lamentable, nausea,* and *route.*

A novelist who wishes to create a stark and grim atmosphere uses Anglo-Saxon words like *stark* and *grim.* If he wants to convey an impression of languorous ease or pensive tranquility, he resorts to Romance words. A poet in need of another syllable can generally find a suitable alternative word that contains it. Indeed English poetry displays a much wider diversity of rhythms and rhyme schemes than that of any other language. German, French, and Italian each have their characteristic cadences, and the poetry of each is ineluctably bound to its phonetic heritage. One may characterize Italian and Greek as melodious, German and Dutch as guttural, French and Portuguese as nasal, and Russian and Polish as sibilant, but English is all of these by turns.

With its rich and varied heritage of words and roots, English has more different ways of saying things than most languages. Foreign students of Shakespeare are dazzled and often completely baffled by the opulence of his vocabulary. By contrast, speakers of English who study the works of Shakespeare's contemporary, Lope de Vega, in the original Spanish perhaps never quite get over their disappointment in the "poverty" of his language nor understand how the fullness of his genius could express itself with so small a store of words.

The mingling of Romance and Teutonic lexical material is not a sufficient explanation for the remarkable number and diversity of English words. Forces inherent in the genius of the language have long been at work to augment our supply of words and alter or extend their meanings. English is not only a greedy borrower but a busy inventor. Linguistically irregular compounds such as *chortle, electrocute, happenstance, paratrooper,* and *telethon,* in which word fragments have been arbitrarily slapped together, abound in modern English. Moreover, the language freely tolerates the invention out of thin air of such words as *blurb, contraption, gremlin,* and *quiz.*

Like its forebear Anglo-Saxon, English is full of compound expressions and epithets like *butterfingers, numbskull,* and *to pussyfoot.* English prefers brief, vigorous forms to the prolixity and circumlocution favored by some languages and likes to shorten words to give them more force and poignancy. Thus, *bus, fan,* and *pants* have completely displaced *omnibus, fanatic* (in this sense), and *pantaloons.* But more often than not, the original word survives along with the cropped form or corruption—*bursar* with *purser, etiquette* with *ticket, humane* with *human, maneuver* with *manure, patron* with *pattern.* The freedom of English in generating variations and corruptions, then tolerating them, and finally legitimizing them is thus combined with a tendency to retain and exploit worn-out or supplanted material.

The whole history and character of a language can be worked out from a study of doublets such as those given above. Homonyms are two or more words that look or sound alike but have different meanings; thus, a *mole* may be either a mammal or a skin lesion or a breakwater or an abnormal product of conception. (The Oxford English Dictionary lists two other meanings, now obsolete.) In other languages, homonyms are generally sets of words from different origins. For example, Dutch *pijn* means both 'pain' (from Latin *poena*) and 'pine' (from Latin *pinus*), and French *palais* means both 'palace' (from Latin *palatium*) and 'palate' (from Latin *palatum,* altered to *palatium* in Gallic Late Latin by attraction to the preceding). Though English has plenty of homonyms of this type, there is also an abundance of imperfect homonyms generated from a single source.

Discreet and *discrete* as well as *passed* and *past* are pronounced the same and are in fact substantially identical, but by convention each spelling has its own meaning. *Crooked* and *blessed* each have one meaning when pronounced as one syllable and another when pronounced as two. *Bereaved* and *bereft* and *hanged* and *hung* show too much divergence to be called homonyms in any sense.

Another source of doublet formation is the borrowing from different languages of words formed from the same Indo-European root. We have already seen some Danish and Anglo-Saxon pairs like *hale–whole*. Another type is seen in *guard* and *ward*, both formed from a Teutonic root starting with *w*. Since the initial *w* sound was foreign to the primitive Gauls, they changed it to *gu*; hence *gu* forms like *guard* have come into English by way of French, while the corresponding *w* forms descended from Anglo-Saxon.

When a Latin word has a direct descendant in English—that is, a learned coinage or borrowing—as well as one that has passed through French, another kind of doublet results: *deception–deceit; fact–feat; fragile–frail; legal–loyal; rabies–rage; redemption–ransom; secure–sure*. Sometimes there is only a "pure" Latin form (*preparation, construct*), and at other times there is only a Gallicized form (*comparison, destroy*). In a few cases three stem forms coexist: *recognition* from Latin, *reconnoitre* from Middle French, and *reconnaisance* from modern French. (The displacement of the Parisian diphthong *oi* by Norman *ai* did not become definitive until the late eighteenth century.)

Words derived from Latin active participles preserve their Latin stem vowels when used as adjectives (*dependent, confident, repellent*) but take the French participial suffix *-ant* when they become nouns (*dependant, confidant, repellant*). During the Renaissance the French language lost many old native derivatives of Gallic Late Latin and replaced them with learned words borrowed or coined from classical Latin. Many of the words thus rendered obsolete in French had long been part of English, and still are. Hence, a French reader may need to be told in a footnote the meanings of words in the works of Rabelais and LaFontaine that are readily intelligible to the English-speaking reader.

Besides doing away with most of its inflections, English has discarded many other useless grammatical features. Ours is the only Western language in which the gender of a noun refers strictly to its meaning, never to its form. To a German, a girl (*Mädchen*) is neuter. If he makes her his *Weib*, she is still neuter, and so are all their *Kinder*. In contrast, French, Spanish, and Italian have no neuter nouns at all.

English has a nearly unique ability to diversify the function of a word without changing its form. Since we have dispensed almost entirely with inflections, we must rely on clues supplied by word order to determine what function is served by *down* in each of the following expressions: "It's fourth down, fans!" (noun); "I'll down him with one blow," (verb); "Take the down escalator," (adjective); "Jack fell down," (adverb); "Pour it down the drain," (preposition); "Down, rover!" (interjection).

All languages, of course, form various parts of speech from the same root, but they generally do this with a regular system of affixes or inflections. Usually the spelling of an English word offers no hints as to its function, though there are some exceptions. Similarly, pronunciation is seldom of use in this regard, except for a large group of words derived from Latin in which the placement of the accent distinguishes between nouns (COMplex, CONduct, INfluence, PROtest) and adjectives or verbs (comPLEX, conDUCT, inFLUence, proTEST). Nowadays even this distinction is becoming blurred.

These are some of the features of everyday vernacular English that make it unique. It is this general language that forms the foundation or framework of technical English, the matrix in which specialized terms are inserted as needed. The formation of a technical term, its derivatives and compounds, the scope of its meaning, and its operation as part of a sentence are all governed by the structure and dynamics of the basic language. Now I am going to show you what happens when the English language and the science of medicine come into contact.

References and Readings

Baugh AC: *A History of The English Language*, 2nd ed. New York, Appleton-Century Crofts, 1957.

Bede: *A History of the English Church and People*. Harmondsworth, Middlesex, Penguin Books, 1955.

Bloomfield L: *Language*. New York, Holt, Rinehart & Winston, 1933.

Bodmer F: *The Loom of Language*. New York, W. W. Norton, 1944.

Caesar CJ: *The Gallic War*. Cambridge, Harvard University Press, 1958.

Chaucer G: *The Works of Geoffrey Chaucer* (W. Pollard, ed.). London, Macmillan, 1899.

Chaurand J: *Histoire de la Langue Française*. Paris, Presses Universitaires de France, 1972.

Earle J (ed.): *Two of the Saxon Chronicles*. Oxford, Clarendon Press, 1892.

Grimme H: *Plattdeutsche Mundarten*. Berlin, Walter de Gruyter, 1922.

Jespersen O: *Growth and Structure of the English Language*, 9th ed. Riverside, New Jersey, The Free Press, Macmillan, 1968.

————: *Language, Its Nature, Development and Origin*. New York, W. W. Norton, 1964.

————: *The Philosophy of Grammar*. London, George Allen & Unwin, 1924.

Johnson S: *A Dictionary of the English Language*. London, 1755.

Lounsberry J: *History of the English Language*. New York, Henry Holt, 1907.

Matthews B: *Essays on English*. New York, Charles Scribner's Sons, 1921.

McKnight G: *The Evolution of the English Language from Chaucer to the Twentieth Century* (Original title: *Modern English in the Making*). New York, Dover, 1968.

Meillet A: *Introduction à l'Étude Comparative des Langues Indo-Européennes*. Reprinted: University, Alabama, University of Alabama Press, 1967.

The Oxford English Dictionary. Oxford, Clarendon Press, 1933.

Potter S: *Modern Linguistics*. London, Andre Deutsch, 1967.

Schlauch M: *The Gift of Language*. New York, Dover, 1955.

Trench RC: *English Past and Present*. London, George Routledge & Sons, 1855.

————: *Lectures on the Study of Words*, 17th ed. London, Macmillan, 1878.

CHAPTER 2

Medical English

Nouns

What's in a name?

William Shakespeare
Romeo and Juliet

No matter how thickly our speech and writing are strewn with technical terms, the foundation or substrate is still "plain" English. Moreover, a great many technical terms used by speakers of English are native to the language rather than importations or coinages from the learned tongues. Since technical terminology consists largely of nouns, my first and chief concern will be with them.

Many of the terms used in gross anatomy are taken from the English vernacular: *arm, back, breast, ear, hair, hand, head, neck, rib, scalp, skin, skull, tongue.* Physicians almost never call these structures by any other names. For some parts of the body there are no "polite" English words, so that the anatomist and the physician use either a Latin term (*anus*) or an English one adapted from Latin (*testicle*). Some English anatomic terms, though acceptable in polite speech, are by convention applied only to animals. Thus, the physician speaks of his patient's *pancreas*, not his *sweetbreads*; of his *esophagus* rather than his *gullet*; of *cartilage* instead of *gristle*. Though *flank* is usually reserved by laymen for references to animals, it is common enough in the language of medicine.

Most internal organs and tissues have native English designations: *gallbladder, liver, spleen, blood, bone, fat.* The anatomist is obliged to use non-English terms for only two kinds of structure: those whose existence was not generally known during the formative period of the language and those for which the available English word is not specific enough. *Adrenal, ovary,* and *prostate* are in the first category, as are all the structures first revealed by the microscope.

To the second category belong such terms as *duodenum, jejunum, ileum,* and *colon* (more specific than the general word *bowel*), and *tendon, ligament,* and *nerve,* all of which were designated by Anglo-Saxon *sionu.* Though modern English *sinew* is seldom used in a literal sense, its cognates, German *Sehne* and Danish *sene,* now mean 'tendon', while Dutch *zenuw* means 'nerve'. Since *nerve* is ultimately from Greek *neura* 'bowstring', it would have been more logical to restrict this word to tendons, but there is no going back now.

The English *womb,* now applied only to the uterus, in the sixteenth century could also mean 'abdomen', 'stomach', or 'intestine'. Its more specific meaning may have arisen from its use as a euphemism for the female reproductive system, just as *loins, reins,* and *thigh* are biblical euphemisms for the male genitalia.

The sensitive, hence "live" tissue under the nails is called the *quick,* from Anglo-Saxon *cwic* 'living'. This sense of *quick* is seen also in *quicklime, quicksilver,* and *quickening* in the obstetrical sense. Much English anatomic terminology shows the same tendency to apply figuratively the names of common things that will be seen in Latin and Greek in the next chapter. In fact, many anatomic terms such as *canal, chamber, column, floor, vault,* and *wall* are simply translations of the corresponding Latin ones. *Eardrum* is a literal rendering of Greek *tympanon.*

Among numerous anatomic metaphors borrowed from lay speech may be mentioned *arch* (of the foot), *eyeball, shoulder blade, nasal bridge, taste bud,* and *kneecap.* The *calf* of the leg is supposed to resemble the belly of a calf. *Apple of the eye* (cf. French *prunelle,* literally 'little plum') has now been replaced by the more concise *pupil,* itself a figure of speech. Similarly, the *cockles of the heart* are now called *auricles*, from the Latin word meaning 'little ears'. (To complete the cycle of metaphors, the resemblance between the ear and a cockle is commemorated in German *Ohrmuschel* 'ear mussel' for the external ear.) *Chest* and *trunk*, as applied to the human body, are also metaphors. In the nomenclature of microscopic anatomy and pathology one finds figurative expressions of more recent adoption, including *goblet, sickle,* and *target* cells.

Here I may note also the practice, found in all languages, of attaching names of body parts to other things: the *eye* of a needle, the *hands* of a clock, the *teeth* of a saw, the *tongue* of a shoe. The carpenter's *nail* is named after the fingernail. An *ear* of corn, however, has no linguistic relation to the organ of hearing, nor is *gum* 'gingiva' in any way connected with *gum* 'vegetable exudation'.

Names of common symptoms and of diseases that were recognized before the era of scientific medicine are usually English: *ache, measles, sore, wound. Sore,* noun and adjective, is Anglo-Saxon *sar.* During the past two centuries the corresponding word in German, *sehr,* has shifted in meaning to become the equivalent of English *very.* Though *sore* once showed a similar tendency (*sore beseiged, sorely needed*), that has now reversed itself.

Cough, croup, and *hiccup* are onomatopoetic or echoic words, whose sounds are supposed to imitate the sounds of the things they represent. The *whoop* of *whooping* (originally *hooping*) *cough* is another example. *Cough* is from Anglo-Saxon *cohhian; croup* is from Danish *hropja. Hiccup* was spelled *hicket* or *hickock* when it first appeared in the sixteenth century. *Hiccough* is an ancient misspelling, based apparently on the analogy of *cough.* German *Schluckauf* 'hiccup' combines onomatopoeia with poetic aptness of description: it means 'swallow up'. *Spit* is derived from Anglo-Saxon *spaetan,* and *sputum* is from Latin *spuere,* but there can be little doubt that both of these verbs go back to the same Indo-European echoic root. *Gargle* is not directly onomatopoetic, since, like *gargoyle,* it comes from French *gargouille* 'throat'. The latter is, however, plainly related to classical words of echoic origin. *Gargarizatio* is Celsus's Latin for gargling; the Greek verb, found in Dioscorides, is *gargarizein. Quack* (formerly *quacksalver*) is another echoic word, referring to the monotonous yapping of the street vendor of patent medicines. *Mumps* is the plural of a word meaning 'grimace', allegedly representing the position of the mouth used in pronouncing the word, as in the case of *smirk* and *moué.*

The list of English names for diseases and symptoms includes many compound words: *chilblain, wryneck, frostbite, harelip, headache, smallpox.* The latter disease was so named to distinguish it from the *great pox,* or syphilis. *Pox* is a phonetic respelling of *pocks,* from Anglo-Saxon *poc* 'pustule, ulcer'. Like *measles, pox* is singular when used as the name of a disease but plural when the reference is to individual lesions; in the latter case the spelling *pocks* is preferred. Though *cowpox* is a disease of cattle as well as of man, *chickenpox* has nothing to do with chickens. The term is probably derived, a little irregularly, from Middle English *chiche* 'chick-pea', from Latin *cicer* of the same meaning.

In pathology as in anatomy, the physician may find it necessary to substitute terms coined from the classical languages for native words having too broad a range of meanings. The patient who says he is *dizzy* may be complaining of ataxia, disorientation, restlessness, somnolence, or vertigo. *Numbness* can mean anesthesia, hypesthesia, paresthesia, or muscular weakness.

Stye is a modern spelling of *styan,* from still older Anglo-Saxon *stighende* 'a rising'. Both this word and the term for a pigpen have at various periods been spelled with a final *e. Hangnail* is not quite what it seems: Anglo-Saxon *angnægl* is a compound of *ang* 'pain' and *nægl* 'nail'. *Scurvy* comes from Middle Low German *schorbuk* and owes its present form to the example of an English word meaning 'scurfy' or 'scabbed'. Modern German and French have *scorbut,* of which *scorbutus* (whence *ascorbic acid*) is a Latinization. In Dutch the word has taken the interesting form of *scheurbuik,* which in that language happens to mean 'rip-belly'.

Samuel Johnson derived *gleet* from Anglo-Saxon *glidan* 'to glide', but the *Oxford English Dictionary* traces it with more plausibility to Old French *glette* 'slime, pus'. *Jaundice* is Old French *jaunisse* 'yellowness'; the *d* is a phonetic parasite like the one that often creeps into the middle of *drowning. Colic* is a syncopated version of *colonic,* which entered the language directly from medical Latin around the thirteenth century with the sense of 'a pain in the colon'. *Corn* comes from Latin *cornu* 'horn' by way of French and is thus related to *cornea, corneum,* and *cornification.* The disease *shingles* has nothing to do with roofing materials; the term is a corruption of Latin *cingulum* 'girdle', referring to the distribution of lesions. Greek *zoster* means the same thing.

Squint, a borrowing from medieval Dutch (*schuinte* 'slope'), first appeared in English as *asquint* in about the fourteenth century. Originally *squint* meant 'strabismus', and it still has that sense in Britain. But as the word has now taken on many figurative meanings, and in American English refers to compressing the eyelids nearly shut, the older ophthalmologic denotation is lost to us. In modern Dutch, to view something *met een schuine oog* 'with a slanting eye' means to view it askance, either literally or (more often) figuratively.

Medical English preserves a few usages now considered archaic in the lay language: foreign *body, great* toe, *gall*stone, *still*birth. Many other words have been borrowed by the physician from the common speech and given restricted, technical meanings. *Plague* is a French form of Latin *plaga* 'stroke, wound.' At first *plague* referred to a purely personal affliction, and only later was it applied to epidemics, perhaps because of its use in connection with the 10 scourges called down by Moses on the Egyptians, as narrated in the Book of Exodus. *Plague* has disappeared from modern French, which preserves another derivative of the Latin word in its original sense: *plaie* 'wound'. In English, however, *plague* survives, and having been applied to the visitations of the Black Death to England and continental Europe during the sixteenth and seventeenth centuries, it has come to mean specifically the disease caused by *Yersinia* (formerly *Pasteurella*) *pestis.* The Latin term *pestis* is the source of *pestilence, pest,* and probably *pester. Pesthouse* is obsolete as a term for a hospital for the isolation of plague victims. *Pesticide,* coined in 1940 by Grant S. Peart, of course refers to rodent pests.

Migraine is another word from French whose meaning has been narrowed. Now the name of a specific disease, it meant merely a unilateral headache when it first appeared in English in the fifteenth century. It is a corruption of Greek *hemicrania,* which is currently used for any one-sided headache. *Orf* is a shortened form of Anglo-Saxon *orfcwealm,* and like many abbreviations it retains the least important part of the original (*orf* 'cattle'; *cwealm* 'death, destruction', related to modern *qualm*). Moreover, the current sense does not accord even with the part that remains of the original word, for orf is a disease of sheep that, though occasionally transmitted to humans, never afflicts cattle.

Several common English terms have special meanings to the physician that are consistently misunderstood outside the profession:

shock, heart failure, soft tissues. In technical use *strain* and *sprain* have specific and distinct meanings, and so do *stammer* and *stutter*. Many words have acquired special meanings in the jargon of psychoanalysis: *conversion, insight, projection, sublimation*. To the psychologist *guilt* is virtually synonymous with *shame*. Hence psychologic and psychiatric writings often contain statements and arguments founded on the notion that there can be wrongdoing without guilt, which is naturally disturbing to readers who are as scrupulous in their morals as in their use and interpretation of language.

Anglo-Saxon *læce* and Middle English *leech*, meaning 'physician', have frequently been tied to the name of the bloodsucking worm that was so widely used in medicine until recent times. But this etymology is highly doubtful, since the word for *physician* almost certainly comes from a different root. The Scandinavian languages still use words from this root for *physician*, for example, Swedish *läkare*.

Sick (from Anglo-Saxon *seoc*) was long the standard English adjective for *diseased* or *unwell*, but around the beginning of this century it began to yield to *ill*, a Scandinavian import that seems to have come in at the time of the Danish invasions. The change took place first in England, where *sick* had acquired the specific sense of 'vomiting or about to vomit', a sense that it still preserves there. In recent years *ill* has largely replaced *sick* in this country, too. Though the latter word is not limited to nausea without the addition of the qualifying phrase *at* (or *to*) *one's stomach*, it is regarded as a low or vulgar term for which *ill* is a more refined substitute.

Most technical words referring to modern diagnosis and therapy are of modern formation, generally from classical Latin or Greek rather than from English. *Salve* (Anglo-Saxon *sealf* 'clarified butter') has given way to the more genteel-sounding *ointment* (a corruption of Latin *unguentum*). *Draft* and *powder* have faded out because drugs are now seldom given in these forms. Once very much in vogue, these terms were often qualified with not-very-illuminating adjectives (*black draft*) or named after the originator of the drug (*Dover's powder*) or its place of origin (*Seidlitz powder*). *Witch hazel* has no connection with hags on broomsticks. The first term in the phrase is Anglo-Saxon *wice*, related to *weak* and applied to various trees with pliant branches. *Moleskin* was formerly just that; the French have borrowed the term and quaintly respelled it *molesquine*. *Lozenge*, which rhymes with *orange* though often mispronounced *lozenger*, comes from Provençal *losange*. Derived ultimately from Latin *laudare* 'to praise', this word first meant a tombstone bearing words of eulogy, then roofing slates cut in the same shape, and finally anything in that shape.

Common English names for plants often bear testimony to their medicinal properties, real or fancied: *boneset; toothwort* for toothache; *feverfew*, a delightful corruption of *febrifuge*; and *pleurisy root* and *stitchwort*, both used for a "stitch" in the side. Even the scientific name of pleurisy root (*Asclepias tuberosa*, commemorating the Greek god of medicine) proclaims its therapeutic value.

Few surgical procedures in use today have common English names. An exception is *grafting*. Old French *greffe* (from Greek *graphein* 'to write') meant 'stylus' or 'pen' and was extended figuratively to the shoot of one tree inserted in the stock of another. In English this horticultural technique was thus called *graffing* or *grafting*, and by a further extension of the metaphor the word is now used for a surgical procedure in which living tissue is moved from one site to another. The name of the surgical *sound* is a reference to the depth gauge used in navigation, which is so called from Danish *sund* 'straits' or 'shoals' (cf. *Long Island Sound*). *Splint* is a Dutch word, cognate with *spline* and *splinter*, and *stent* (a corruption of *extend*) in Middle English meant a stick used by a butcher to hold open a carcass. *Stupe* goes back at least as far as the fourteenth century and is derived from Latin *stupa* 'flannel'.

Although the medical profession seems compelled to name every new thing with a fresh coinage from Latin or Greek, a few modern concepts are expressed by good old Anglo-Saxon words: friction *rub*, *frozen* section, *heart block*, serum *sickness, slit* lamp, *wrist drop*. *Sibling* (from Anglo-Saxon *sib* 'kinsman') was listed as an obsolete word in the *Oxford English Dictionary* (*OED*), which cited no example of its use after the fifteenth century. The section of the *OED* in which *sibling* appears was issued in 1910. The Supplement Volume, published in 1933, noted the revival of the word in scientific literature late in the nineteenth century. It is intriguing to note that in the interval the English language managed nicely without a genderless word for children of the same parents.

English terms like *middle finger* and *ring finger* have the advantage of precision over the ostensibly more scientific *digitus tertius* 'third finger', whose meaning varies according to whether the thumb is taken as the first finger. There is something arresting and distinctive about Garrod's term *inborn error of metabolism.* In Romance languages the Anglo-Saxon *inborn* has to be translated by a Latinate word cognate with our *congenital,* which is not only less vivid but less specific.

No possible subject of discussion can be considered altogether taboo in the physician's consulting room, but certain words are seldom heard there. Patterns of polite or decent usage among both laymen and physicians are often erratic. In neither group is *snot* or *puke* regarded as refined language, whereas *spit, belch,* and *belly* are used by both without hesitation. Physicians may say *crotch, armpit,* or *scab* in speaking to patients but never among themselves, even though the technical term *crust* is far from being an exact equivalent of *scab.* While the fastidious nonprofessional is careful to avoid both *gut* and *guts* except in figurative expressions, the physician freely uses the singular form as a general word for the *intestine.*

Which words are considered crude, vulgar, or impolite is of course largely a matter of custom and convention. It is doubtful that many of Chaucer's contemporaries were offended by his mentioning in the Prologue to *The Wife of Bath's Tale* that "Xantippa caste pisse upon his [Socrates's] heed" or by his writing in *The Miller's Tale,* "This Nicholas anon leet fle a fart." Yet only a few generations later, speakers of English thought it proper to put an extraneous *c* in the past participle of Latin *infarcire* 'to plug up', so that we now say *infarct,* while our European colleagues use classically more correct forms, Italian *infarto* and Spanish *infartación.*

In nineteenth century America, *leg, breast,* and even *woman* were considered obscenities, not to be pronounced before female company in any context whatsoever. *Chicken* formerly meant 'the young of the domestic fowl' ("She's no spring chicken"), *-en* here being a diminutive suffix, as in *kitten* and *maiden.* Mature fowl were called by words that denoted both species and gender: *cock* and *hen.* Because these terms came to be regarded as shockingly explicit, *chicken* was substituted for them, and to this day it remains the usual term for mature fowl.

Polite society has in every era found euphemisms and circumlocutions to substitute for "street" language. Modern English makes wide use of learned words drawn from Latin: *defecation, micturition, eructation, regurgitation.* Sooner or later, euphemisms come to be so closely linked to the things named that they themselves become offensive and must be replaced in their turn. Thus Don Quixote instructs Sancho Panza that it is more genteel to say *eruct* (*erutar*) than the coarse and vulgar *burp* (*regoldar*, from Latin *regurgitare*).

The exaggerated delicacy of the last century introduced euphemisms even into medical nomenclature. The phenomenon of childbirth was cloaked in circumlocutions: *confinement*, which survives in the initialism *EDC* ('expected date of confinement'), and *lying-in*, which is only now disappearing from the names of maternity hospitals and departments. As recently as the 1920s *uterine* (or *utero-*) *gestation* was a standard euphemism for pregnancy in medical writing. The chancre of syphilis was not so named in polite medical circles but masqueraded under the name of *specific ulcer*. Similarly, gonorrhea was known as *specific urethritis*, and though this term is long gone, its opposite, *nonspecific urethritis*, is only now disappearing from use.

Though the practice of euphemism in English reached a peak during the previous century, coverup words have appeared and flourished in medical English at all periods. In 1944 *combat fatigue* was invented as a nonjudgmental term for the anxiety neuroses and stress reactions of soldiers. The *dope fiend* of a former generation is now said to be *chemically dependent* or, at worst, a *substance abuser*. *Alcoholism* has been rebaptized *ethanolism*, which is slightly equivocal since most recent terms on this pattern (*atropinism*, *iodism*) denote acute intoxication, not habituation. *Menstrual extraction* is a deliberately inaccurate term for a form of abortion.

Many of our oldest medical words prove upon analysis to be euphemisms. *Disease* is a circumlocution, naming an unpleasant subject by the negation of its opposite; so is *infirmity* ('unstrongness'). *Hospital* is cognate with *hotel* and historically meant 'guesthouse', as its derivative *hospitality* might suggest. *Hospice*, lately revived to name a facility for the care of the dying, is essentially the same word again and formerly meant simply a wayside lodging.

Stool has a long history of use in English as a polite term for feces. A close stool was a sort of toilet chair equipped with an earthenware vessel under the seat. At first the act of defecation was hinted at by referring to this article of furniture, a usage preserved in our expression *straining at stool*. Eventually the word was extended to the feces themselves. The biblical *flowers* 'menses' is borrowed from French *fleurs*, a corruption of *flueur* 'flow', from Latin *fluor*. So also *fleurs blanches* 'white flowers' is the lay French term for leukorrhea (cf. Latin *fluor albus*).

Space will not permit a thorough comparison of British and American medical usage, but a few differences may be mentioned in passing. What an American calls his *crazy bone* is an Englishman's *funny bone*. In England a lunatic is not *crazy* but *mad*, and an irate person is not *mad* but *angry*. The well-bred Englishman has a deeply rooted aversion to the word *bloody*; instead of a *bloody nose* he gets a *nosebleed*; an Englishwoman in labor does not experience *bloody show*; and no English physician with any sense of decency would ask a nurse to change a *bloody dressing*. *Stomach*, in its broad lay sense of the abdomen, is taboo in Britain, where a staid and sober patient with abdominal pain solemnly informs the doctor that his *tummy* hurts. He does not say that he *has vomited* but that he *was sick*. He does not get *goose pimples* but *goose* (or *chicken*) *flesh*.

Expatriate British physicians sometimes shock or puzzle their American colleagues by accenting the first syllable in *ephedrine* or the second in *skeletal*. They may refer to a shaking chill as a *rigor*, rhyming it with *tiger*. A British pharmacist is called a *chemist*. Britons speak of *cot deaths* rather than *crib deaths*, and *needle-drivers* rather than *needle-holders*. The American's *absorbent cotton* is the Englishman's *cotton wool* (as in cotton-wool patches of the retina), though nowadays both are probably talking about acetate rayon. What we know as *adhesive tape* is in England *sticking-plaster*; not so many years ago the usual term there was *court plaster*, an allusion to the seventeenth century custom according to which ladies of fashion appeared at court with patches of black sticking-plaster on their faces.

The British prefer older spellings of technical words from classical sources: *haemorrhage, hydrocoele, sulphonamide*. Though British spelling usually comes closer to the classical originals, it sometimes inserts an extra vowel. *Colour* and *tumour* show the influence of French, whereas our spellings of these words match the original Latin. *Fetus* and *fetor* are classically more correct than British *foetus* and *foetor*. In some cases variant forms differ not only in spelling but also in pronunciation: *malpraxis, morphia*.

In England a physician graduates with the degree of Bachelor of Medicine (M.B.), though he may pursue further study and eventually earn an M.D. In either case he is addressed as "doctor," and *Dr.* is placed before his name—unless he happens to be a surgeon. Custom demands that a surgeon be called *Mr.* whether he has a doctoral degree or not. This curious practice, still very strictly observed, dates back to the days when bloodletting, incision of abscesses, and other cutting procedures were performed by barbers rather than by members of the medical profession. A British general practitioner calls his office a *surgery*, especially if it adjoins his living quarters, even though he may never perform operative surgery there or elsewhere.

Despite the vast number of terms formed from Latin and Greek that are used in modern medical practice, many plain English words and phrases are also in good standing, some of quite recent vintage. Among these are terms relating an injury or disease to a sport or avocation in which it is apt to occur: *boxer's fracture, baseball finger, pitcher's elbow* (which is different from *tennis elbow*), *surfer's knots* (applied to at least six distinct lesions), and *guitarist's nipple.*

Numerous medical terms referring to occupational diseases have attained the status of formal terminology: *barber's itch, milker's nodes, silo filler's disease, farmer's lung, housemaid's knee, pathologist's wart,* and *writer's cramp. Weaver's bottom* is plain and proper English for bursitis at the ischial tuberosity. (But Shakespeare's Bottom the Weaver, in *A Midsummer Night's Dream*, is named after one of the implements of his craft, a *bottom* being a spindle for winding thread.) Not every occupational term indicates a condition to which practitioners of the trade named are subject. *Headwaiter's tip hand* and *obstetrician's hand* are purely imaginative, and it is not the hangman who gets a *hangman's fracture* but his client.

It would be remarkable if a language as colorful and flexible as English had not given birth to some highly picturesque terms even in the scientific disciplines. The physician often has recourse to metaphor and simile when he needs an accurate and intelligible name for an abnormal appearance, sound, odor, or other observable phenomenon. It takes no very creative intellect to invent a term like *air hunger, rusty sputum,* or *napkin-ring obstruction.* Moreover, as these are vivid, explicit, and readily understandable, they require no laborious memorization.

Abnormal configurations and movements are accurately depicted by terms like *bamboo spine, clubfoot, cogwheel rigidity, collar-*

button abscess, flame hemorrhage, greenstick fracture, hammer toe, hilar dance, mallet finger, moth-eaten lung, pill-rolling tremor, saddle nose, and *silver fork deformity.*

Sounds are called by picturesque names such as *cracked-pot resonance, gallop rhythm, machinery* and *seagull murmurs, musical rales,* and *pistol-shot pulse.* The *diamond-shaped murmur* is so termed from the shape of its record on the phonocardiogram. Even smells may acquire figurative names like the *fruity* breath of diabetic ketosis, the *mousy* odor of pharyngeal diphtheria, the *maple syrup urine* of cystinosis, *cat's urine syndrome, rancid butter syndrome,* and *oasthouse urine disease* (an *oasthouse* is a kiln for drying hops).

Dozens of descriptive figures refer to food and drink. Consider, as representative and most unappetizing samples, *oat cell carcinoma,* the *branny desquamation* of scarlatina, and the *rice-water stools* of cholera; the *mulberry molars* of congenital syphilis, the *currant-jelly stools* of intussusception, *strawberry hemangioma,* the *strawberry tongue* of scarlatina, and the *strawberry gallbladder* of cholesterosis; the *potato nodes* of sarcoidosis and the *bread-and-butter heart* of fibrinous pericarditis; the *apple-jelly lesions* of lupus vulgaris; the *Coca-Cola urine* of acute glomerulonephritis; *chocolate cysts, coffee-grounds emesis, chicken-fat clots, port-wine stain, caseous necrosis, sausage fingers,* and *milk-leg.*

Another large class of metaphors includes terms referring to animals: *staghorn calculus, spider angioma, harelip, buffalo hump, ape hand, rabbit stools, rat's tail obstruction* of a bronchus, the *parrot-beak nails* of hypertrophic osteoarthropathy, the *camel-hump wave* of the electrocardiogram, *bull neck, butterfly rash,* and *joint mice.* I might also mention the lay terms *buck teeth, pigeon breast, goose pimples,* and (on a more fanciful plane) *goose egg, Charley horse,* a *frog in the throat,* and *butterflies in the stomach.*

The *water-hammer pulse* of aortic valvular insufficiency is not named after a piece of machinery, as many think. A water hammer is a toy consisting of a large glass cylinder closed at both ends and partly filled with water. The air is exhausted before the cylinder is sealed, so that when the toy is repeatedly inverted end over end, the water slams back and forth all in a mass. One wonders how many pathologists who speak glibly of *nutmeg* and *hobnail livers* have ever seen the cut surface of whole nutmeg or a leather boot sole studded over with round-headed nails.

A few medical terms are so fanciful as to verge on the poetic. Such, for example, are *kissing ulcers, geographic tongue, proudflesh* (which goes back to the fourteenth century), *ripe cataract* (or *cervix*), and *sentinel pile*. The vernacular has provided a few vivid and colorful terms like *knock knee, wisdom teeth, black lung,* and *the bends*, which are used even by physicians. Formal terminology has no exact equivalents for the feelings described as: "My foot is asleep" and "My foot is full of pins and needles."

Adjectives

As to the Adjective: when in doubt, strike it out.

Mark Twain
Pudd'nhead Wilson

As I have already shown, modern English has discarded most of the inflectional system of Anglo-Saxon. It has also largely dispensed with certain patterns of affixation that were in common use as lately as the eighteenth century. For example, no longer does usage insist on the ending *-en* or *-n* to show that a noun like *wood* or *leather* has been turned into an adjective: *wooden, leathern*. Indeed, one of the features that make English such a succinct and economical language is its freedom in using nouns as adjectives without any change in form, as in *bone metastasis, nerve deafness, sickle cell anemia,* and *house mouse mite bite site*.

It is not, of course, strictly accurate to say that here nouns are used as adjectives. The function of a word in a given sentence, and that only, determines what part of speech it is, and once it functions as an adjective, it ceases to be a noun. What I really mean is that these adjectives do not differ in form from the corresponding nouns as *golden, chilly,* and *shrewish* differ from their nouns of origin.

Even when a formal adjective is available, an unaltered noun is often used instead: *bile pigment, sex differentiation, virus infection*. Sometimes there is a good reason for doing so, as when one says *rectus spasm* to avoid the confusion that might result from *rectal spasm* or *intention tremor* instead of *intentional tremor*, which means something else. *Medial,* in the sense of 'pertaining to the tunica media of an artery', is at least momentarily confusing because *medial* is nearly always an adjective of direction. *Multicenter study* must be given preference over *multicentric study*, which is entirely misleading. At first *multicenter* may look like a noun, but a moment's reflection will show that it is not one, since there is no such thing; compare the adjectives in *pseudoheart disease* and *interobserver variability*.

The headline or telegram style of forming noun compounds (*hepatitis carrier state, sheep cell agglutination test*) is a characteristic of all Germanic languages, in contrast to the Romance and the Slavic, which do not use it at all. German freely runs together three or four nouns to make a single word of 25 or more letters. German linguists are not all in accord as to the syntactic relations within these composite nouns. German can, for example, combine *Husten* 'cough' with *Reiz* 'tickle, irritation' to form either *Hustenreiz* or *Reizhusten*, both meaning 'an irritating cough'.

Though in a few English compounds one finds the words fused together as in German (*gallbladder, headache, pinworm*), more often they stand apart (*lung abscess, skin graft, sedimentation rate*). Neither French nor Russian can translate any of these phrases without either inserting a preposition (*ache of the head*) or turning one of the words into a formal adjective (*pulmonary abscess*). If that seems a shortcoming of these languages, it at least has the advantage of preventing a kind of confusion that is rather common in English.

To appreciate this fully we must examine two further peculiarities of modern English with respect to the adjective. One is the use of an adjective to show the object of an action expressed by a noun. Thus, *ligation of the tubes* becomes *tubal ligation*, and *resection of a segment* becomes *segmental resection*. It is peculiar that a language in which adjectives so often look like nouns (*spine films*) should insist on using a formal adjective in a role that would more logically be filled by a noun (*spinal fusion*).

A still more enigmatic use of the English adjective is seen in expressions like: "He is under observation for suspected leukemia" and "He died of a probable myocardial infarction." Speakers of most modern languages would recoil from such semantic absurdities, in each of which an adjective modifies the meaning of a whole sentence instead of just the noun to which it is appended.

Statements like the following abound in medical English: "In protracted cases of asthma, the physician must be prepared to treat possible acute congestive failure." A Spaniard or a Pole trying to decipher this sentence might well wonder what *possible acute congestive failure* is, how it differs from the ordinary kind, and whether there is an *impossible acute congestive failure* as well.

When more than one of these peculiarly English uses of the adjective come together in a sentence, the resulting construction is often ambiguous or obscure. *Hypokalemic conduction defect* and *interventricular conduction defect* may seem like parallel phrases, but on analysis they prove to have entirely different internal relations. The first means a defect, caused by hypokalemia, of conduction; the second, a defect of interventricular conduction. In other words, in the first example the first adjective modifies *conduction,* while in the second it modifies *defect.* Another such pair is *coronary artery disease* and *coronary heart disease.* When a patient is advised to avoid *oily hair preparations,* does that mean he should avoid hair preparations that are oily or preparations that are for oily hair?

Much less likely to generate confusion is the English practice of letting a formal adjective stand alone and act as a noun, as in *a pelvic [examination], the [membrana] mucosa, the lymphatic [channel]s, a coronary [occlusion], an antibiotic [drug], the [musculus] rectus,* and *the [nervus] vagus.*

In *adrenal suppression, antibiotic therapy, protozoan disease,* and *rectal glove,* words that were once adjectives and have evolved into nouns while keeping their adjectival suffixes (*-al, -an, -ic*) now function once again as adjectives but with significant differences in meaning. Consider, for example, the distinction between *rectal* when applied to *polyp* (primary adjectival sense) and when applied to *glove* (derivative sense, based on the use of the word as a noun meaning 'rectal examination').

Verbs

The verb is the most highly condensed and the most highly abstract element of discourse.

Frederick Bodmer
The Loom of Language

As in the case of adjectives, English verbs derived from nouns may bear some suffix to mark their new function (*digitalize, cannulate, cornify*), or they may not (*to curette, to biopsy, to gastroscope*). A large number of verbs in technical language have been produced by back-formation, a process in which a suffix is removed from a noun to yield what looks as if it ought to be the verb from which the noun was formed.

Physicians are especially prone to fabricate verbs in this way from Greek nouns ending in -*osis: anastomose, ankylose, cyanose, ecchymose, fibrose, metamorphose, necrose, osmose, sclerose, stenose, thrombose.* Though some of these are more acceptable than others to refined ears, they are all in common use in the spoken language of medicine. Other nouns that often generate verbs by back-formation are those ending in -*esis* (*diapedese, diaphorese, diurese, electrophorese*) and -*ion* (*counteraggress, contuse, hyperaliment, percuss, torse*).

All verbs created by back-formation are considered illegitimate, because the process implies an erroneous belief that the resulting verb actually existed before the noun on which the operation is performed. But there is certainly nothing illogical about looking for an underlying verb in a noun like *percussion* or *lysis* or *debridement*, each of which names an action. Moreover, the obvious way to get at this verb is to knock off the noun suffix. Among the back-formations that have lived down the irregularity of their birth and become perfectly respectable are *collide, diagnose, donate, edit, legislate,* and *resurrect.* The ending of *beggar* is not an agent-noun suffix, but that has not hindered the career of the irregularly formed verb *to beg.* Hence one can probably predict a long life for the equally irregular *to lase,* from *laser.*

Just as an English adjective without any distinctive suffix can sometimes be confused with its noun of origin, verbs that are formed from nouns without being altered in any way may make the hasty reader pause and backtrack. In addition, such verbs may develop widely differing connotations; contrast the sense of *to drain an abscess* with that of *to drain a cholecystectomy.* A few nouns seem to have been changed into verbs only so that they can be changed back to nouns (gerunds); thus, *imaging, parenting,* and *cloning* are far commoner in medical parlance than *to image, to parent,* and *to clone.*

At first glance one might say that the verbs *go, walk,* and *run* are irrevocably intransitive, since the actions they denote cannot logically have an object. Yet that is just what they do have in *go your way, walk the dog,* and *run an errand.* Probably no living language ever succeeded in keeping a sharp distinction between transitive and intransitive verbs. In medical English, verbs that began in one group frequently take on dual capabilities. Intransitive verbs become transitive when one speaks of *aborting* a migraine, *adhering* a graft, or *fasting* an experimental animal, and the opposite change takes place when one says that the plasma aldosterone failed *to suppress*, that a tablet *crushes* easily, or that adult lice *kill* sooner than their ova.

A transitive verb may stay transitive and yet undergo a striking shift of reference, as when one says that a catheter was instilled with heparin or that rats were injected with alloxan. It used to be that the heparin was instilled and the alloxan was injected.

The first and longest section of this chapter dealt mainly with word derivations; these later sections mainly with usage. Throughout, a recurring theme has been change: adaptation, flexibility, corruption, revision, extension and narrowing of meaning, and modification of grammatical conventions. Not all of the words and usages mentioned are in good repute. Some are too fresh to be called anything but slang, others are sinking into obsolescence. This diversity is an inescapable condition of any living language, for the kinds of change mentioned above are the very forces that keep it living. Even dead languages become subject to alteration and evolution when they are reincarnated in technical terminology, as I shall show in the next chapter.

References and Readings

American Medical Association: *Standard Nomenclature of Diseases and Operations*, 5th ed. New York, McGraw-Hill, 1961.

Blakiston's Gould Medical Dictionary, 4th ed. New York, McGraw-Hill, 1979.

Critchley M (ed.): *Butterworth's Medical Dictionary*, 2nd ed. Woburn, Massachusetts, Butterworth Publishers, Inc., 1980.

Dorland's Illustrated Medical Dictionary, 26th ed. Philadelphia, W. B. Saunders Co., 1981.

The Oxford English Dictionary. Oxford, Clarendon Press, 1933.

Shipley J: *Dictionary of Word Origins*. New York: Philosophical Library, 1945.

Stedman's Medical Dictionary, 24th ed. Baltimore, Williams & Wilkins, 1982.

CHAPTER 3

─────────◆─────────

Our Classical Heritage

Latin

Latin is a dead language, as dead as it can be;
First it killed the Romans, and now it's killing me.
Schoolboy's jeremiad

According to tradition, the city of Rome was founded by the Latians or Latins in 753 B.C. These Latins, the ancestors of the Italian race, were not the only inhabitants of Italy in that remote period, nor even the most numerous. Far more widespread were the Umbrians, who shared a common ethnic origin with the founders of Rome and whose languages, Umbrian and Oscan, were closely related to Latin. The Etruscans, originally immigrants from Asia Minor, colonized the district of Italy known as Etruria (modern Tuscany) around the tenth century before Christ and grew wealthy through their skill in metalworking. Their language, of which written records survive from as far back as 800 B.C., is still largely a riddle to scholars.

Neither the Umbrians nor the Latins had an alphabet of their own. The Umbrians eventually borrowed the alphabet of the Etruscans, but the Latins obtained theirs—essentially the one in which this book is printed—from some Greek colonists at Cumae. (According to another theory, the Greek alphabet passed through the hands of the Etruscans to the Latins.) This primeval Roman alphabet had no *g, w,* or *y* and made no distinction between *i* and *j* or between *u* and *v.* Having acquired a means of writing, the Latins lost no time in putting it into use; the oldest surviving remnants of their language were chiseled in stone before 500 B.C.

By the middle of the second century B.C., Rome had conquered Greece and Carthage and was well on her way to world dominion. She also had a rich and varied literature, which would reach its full flower during the Augustan Age (31 B.C. to 14 A.D.) in the exquisite verses of Horace, Virgil, and Ovid. As has already been mentioned, the Latin language as preserved in the works of these classical authors was not the living speech of Rome and the provinces but a refined and artificial elaboration of it. The language that broke up, during the Dark Ages, into what is called the Romance group was the common speech, or Vulgar Latin, not the polished and sometimes tortured idiom of orators, poets, and philosophers.

If Latin had survived only in the works of the classical Roman writers, it is fairly certain that it would not have become the universal medium of scholarship many centuries after the fall of the Roman Empire. But in the first and second centuries A.D., Rome was the center not only of Western civilization but also of Christianity. While the spoken language evolved and disintegrated, the written language remained nearly static, embalmed in the works of the early Fathers of the Church. Toward the end of the fourth century St. Jerome completed his Latin translation of the Bible, the so-called Vulgate edition.

Christian missionaries, beginning with St. Augustine at Canterbury in 597, carried the Latin language into Britain and first taught the Anglo-Saxons to write. It was at this early period that a number of Latin terms associated with religion (*candle, chalice, epistle, relic*) became naturalized in Old English. But it is not with ecclesiastical Latin—nor yet with the second and much greater accession of Romance words during the Norman period—that I am now concerned. During the Dark Ages, Latin was the possession of the priests and monks, who together with a few secular scholars made up the literate minority. Though these men read and relished the works of the Augustan poets, the Latin in which they daily wrote, taught, argued, and joked was a very different thing from the classical language. Since for them Latin was not a dead language, one need not be surprised if they modified its syntax and its inflectional system to suit their own taste and augmented its vocabulary with Arabic and Gothic borrowings and with derivatives and corruptions that would have aroused the wrath of Cicero or Quintilian.

With the Renaissance came a revival and diffusion of the Latin language and its literature. All of the classical writings that had survived the Dark Ages were republished, edited, analyzed, and commented on. A knowledge of Latin became not only a key to the door of learning but a means of communication among scholars across the length and breadth of the civilized world.

In medieval universities from Oxford to Buda, from Uppsala to Florence, Latin was the language of textbooks, lectures, recitations, and examinations. Inevitably this workaday academic idiom was a blend of classical, ecclesiastical, and monkish elements. It has left its mark on all modern European languages, including English. Among familiar survivals may be mentioned *alma mater, alumnus, campus, consortium, curriculum, rostrum,* and *semester. Aegrotat* 'he is sick' is a nearly defunct term for a medical excuse from attendance at lectures. *Gaudy,* once applied to the nocturnal carousings of students, comes from the medieval drinking song *Gaudeamus igitur.* A patent medicine is still called a *nostrum;* each band of traveling mountebanks referred to the panacea that they hawked from town to town as "our own [*nostrum*] secret formula."

A few Latin phrases survive in medical parlance from the days when Latin was known to virtually every educated person: *curriculum vitae, in situ, in vitro, in vivo, locum tenens.* A speaker of German writing for a reprint of a published paper may ask for a *separatum.* A large number of common English words have been taken over unchanged from Latin: *alibi, bonus, camera, caper, consensus, doctor, excelsior, genius, genus, gratis, impromptu, interest, interim, junior, medium, pauper, posse, propaganda, quorum, ratio, senator, stimulus,* and *via.* The phrases for which our abbreviations *a.m., p.m., etc., i.e.,* and *e.g.* stand are also of course Latin.

Latin also became the language of jurisprudence, and a great many modern legal terms are Latin, some of them dating back even to Roman times and the legal system first codified under the Emperor Justinian in the *Corpus Juris Civilis* (529-35 A.D.): *corpus delicti, habeas corpus, nolo contendere, prima facie, res ipsa loquitur.* Medieval Latin terms still used in mathematics and the physical sciences include *abscissa, calculus, focus, frustum, inertia, locus, momentum, pendulum, radius, specimen,* and *spectrum.*

The development of printing from movable type led to a remarkable spread of literacy. Though only the sons of the wealthy received formal educations in the liberal arts or were prepared for careers in law or medicine, nearly all boys were instructed in the rudiments of reading and writing. English elementary education from the sixteenth to the nineteenth century was largely a matter of mastering Latin grammar and perusing the works of the great Latin authors. Henry VIII and his daughter Elizabeth I were both fluent in Latin.

An immense number of new English words were framed from Latin during the post-Renaissance period. Some of these fabrications no doubt satisfied real needs, but a great many others were invented by writers who sought to produce erudite-sounding English prose and who knew that almost anyone who could read at all would be able to decipher coinages from Latin. Many of these coinages took root and became permanent parts of our language. Among these were *position, gravity,* and *solid,* which, according to available evidence, did not get into English by way of Norman French.

Many of the coinages affected by English writers of the sixteenth and seventeenth centuries were not so straightfoward as these. Among "inkhorn terms" to be found in the literature of this period are *immarescible, immorigerous, medioxumous, solertiousness, stultiloquy,* and *sufflaminate.* The modern reader, whether or not his command of Latin enables him to decipher these words, will probably brand them ludicrous monstrosities. Yet they are neither longer nor uglier than many inventions of the same vintage that still thrive in the chatter of pedants.

Like native English words, coinages from Latin have often shifted in meaning with the passing of the years. When Desdemona remarks that Othello will "return incontinent," she is not predicting that her husband will develop bladder trouble. *Incontinent* meant 'immediately' in Shakespearean English, as it does in modern French. Pope's observation, in his *Essay on Criticism,* "Fools admire [gape in wonder] but men of sense approve [put to the test]," illustrates the point that old writing in which key words have undergone a drastic change of meaning may be harder to interpret accurately than still older writing in which some words have no meaning at all for the modern reader, and so send him to the dictionary in search of enlightenment.

This seems an appropriate place to mention the interesting change that has taken place in the meanings of *art* and *science*. Classical Latin *ars* meant 'trade' or 'profession', a sense that survives in *artisan*. In the English version of Hippocrates's famous aphorism, "Art is long and life is short," the choice of wording is due to the Latin "*Ars longa, vita brevis*," where *ars* represents Greek *techne* 'trade, handicraft'. A translation more faithful to the spirit of the original would be, "The craft of healing is so complex that you will scarcely master it in a lifetime."

Scientia, by contrast, denoted an activity of the mind. Even in early modern English one finds preserved the ancient opposition between art, embracing all physical and mechanical occupations from the tilling of the soil to the erection of cathedrals, and science, comprising theology, philosophy, and literature. With the coming of the technological age this old distinction became blurred and was finally lost. The thinker—the practitioner of "science"—began to concern himself with the material world, at first only speculatively but later to put matter to work for him, to understand and control the forces of nature. Meanwhile, the sense of *art* became contracted, by the exclusion of these practical concerns, to its present narrow significance, which is almost purely esthetic.

By the nineteenth century the scientist was no longer a mere thinker or sage but an active and practical investigator of physical phenomena, while the artist had renounced his tools and his utilitarian goals to pursue and cultivate the ideals of Beauty. Thus, though the statement "Medicine is both an art and a science" conveys about the same meaning as it did 500 years ago, the two key words in the predicate have virtually exchanged meanings.

As the physical sciences gradually separated themselves from the welter of superstition that had surrounded the phenomena of nature during the Dark Ages, they began to develop and differentiate into mathematics, physics, chemistry, and biology. Naturally, the universal language of primitive science, as of letters, was Latin.

It was customary for a medieval scholar to take a Latin name upon receiving a doctoral degree. Hence many of the great names in the early history of science and medicine are just European family names with a touch of Latin gilding. The Italian Gabriello Falloppio became Fallopius; the Belgian Andreas van Wesele, Vesalius; the Dutchman Adriaan van den Spieghel, Spigelius; the Pole Nikola Koopernigk, Copernicus. Some translated their names, like the Frenchman François de la Boe, who became Sylvius.

Among the Scandinavians, Latin names were and are often passed from father to son. Anders Celsius, the inventor of the centigrade thermometer, inherited his Latin surname from his grandfather, Magnus, who chose *Celsius* to replace *Travillagaeus*, the Latin name that *he* had inherited. Other hereditary Latin names are those of Jakob Berzelius, the father of modern chemistry, and Svanté Arrhenius, the first Swede to win a Nobel Prize (1903).

The Swiss physician and chemist Theophrastus Bombastus von Hohenheim is usually known as Paracelsus, a name that he allegedly invented to show that his discoveries had led him beyond Celsus, the early Roman writer on medicine. Paracelsus devised a number of technical terms, of which a few survive, including *collodion* (originally *collodium*), *nostoc* (now the name of a bacterial genus), *synovia*, and perhaps even *zinc*. Endowed with a vivid imagination, he also gave us *gnome* and *sylph*.

Although modern scholars doubt that Celsus ever practiced medicine, his treatise *De Medicina* in eight books, dating from the first century after Christ, is the earliest and most important medical work in Latin. Hippocrates, who lived centuries before Celsus, and Galen, who lived a generation or two after him, both wrote in Greek. By a freak of history, the works of Galen and Hippocrates, as well as those of other classical Greek writers on anatomy, pharmacy, and surgery, reached medieval Europe in the form of Arabic translations and commentaries. The earliest Renaissance medical works were Latin translations in which most technical terms were given in Latinized Arabic rather than in Latin or Greek. The *Anatomia* of Mondino of Luzzi (c. 1275-1326), the most popular textbook of anatomy before Vesalius, was full of Arabic terms. In the fifteenth and sixteenth centuries, scholars like Thomas Linacre and Johannes Günther—more interested in language than in facts, in having accurate translations of Galen than in accurate dissection and observation—purged anatomic language of most Arabic terms. Hence although Arabic terms are often given by Vesalius (*De Humani Corporis Fabrica*, 1543), Latin and Greek have first place.

During the latter part of the sixteenth century, an elaborate system of Latin anatomic nomenclature was codified. Many of the terms in this system had been in use for hundreds of years, some having appeared in the works of Celsus and of pre-Christian writers. Many others were adopted or fabricated to name structures newly discovered. Much of this medieval terminology lives on in daily use. Its most striking characteristic is its metaphorical application of the names of familiar objects to bodily structures of similar shape.

Topographic and architectural features are recalled by such terms as *fornix* 'arch', *pons* 'bridge', *trabecula* 'little beam', *fossa* 'ditch', *fovea* 'pit', *sulcus* 'plowed furrow', and *cloaca* 'sewer'. There are at least four aqueducts in the human body. Every part of the house is represented, from the roof (*tectum*) to the cellars (*antrum*), from the gate (*porta*) and entry hall (*vestibulum*) to the inner court (*atrium*) and living room (*thalamus*), from bed (*torus*) and sofa (*pulvinar*) to windows (*fenestrae*) and stairs (*scalae*). The dining room supplies a dish (*patella*) and a bowl (*acetabulum*), a bottle (*ampulla*) and a cup (*calyx*), a water jug (*vas*) and a cake (*placenta*). *Infundibulum* means "funnel'; indeed, the English word is a corruption of the Latin one. The French term *bassin* for the pelvis reminds us that Latin *pelvis* means 'basin'.

The human body was a veritable zoo to the early anatomists, who found there a worm (*vermis*), a fish (*lacertus*) a snail (*cochlea*), a cock's comb (*crista galli*), a bird's claw (*calcar avis*), a goose's foot (*pes anserinus*), and a host of little mice (*musculi*), some of which were wormlike (*lumbricales*). Not only is the horse's tail (*cauda equina*) present, but bridle (*frenum*), stirrup (*stapes*), and saddle (*sella*) as well, and even the blacksmith's hammer (*malleus*) and anvil (*incus*). Other implements include a plowshare (*vomer*), a scythe (*falx*) a wine-press (*torcular*), a block and tackle (*trochlea*), a little net (*retina*), a little key (*clavicula*), and a little trough (*alveolus*). Incidentally, *stapes* and *retina* are medieval, not classical, Latin. *Habena,* from *habere* 'to have', means 'a thong, handle, or rein'. The diminutive *habenula* appears in Celsus as a term for a strip of diseased tissue debrided from the edges of a wound or ulcer. *Habenula* is unknown in this sense to modern medicine but is now the name of a part of the epithalamus.

The vegetable kingdom is represented by *uvula* 'little grape', *glans* 'nut', *ramus* 'branch', *cortex* 'bark', *lens* 'seed', *pampiniform* 'vinelike', *piriform* 'pear-shaped', and *pisiform* 'pea-shaped'. *Palma*, however, referred to the hand before it was extended to broad, flat leaves. Similarly, the use of *tibia* as a term for the shinbone preceded its application to a flute (often made from a hollow bone). In one of Phaedrus's fables there is a pun about a flute player who broke his shin.

Anatomists have frequently seen fit to name one part of the body after another when apter metaphors failed. *Os cervicis* is literally 'mouth of the neck'. *Capitellum, pedicle, ventricle, auricle,* and *lingula* are diminutives of words meaning, respectively, 'head', 'foot', 'belly', 'ear', and 'tongue'. *Geniculate* means 'like a little knee'. Not all of these diminutives are strictly rational. The lingula, for example, is considerably larger than the tongue. With these Latin metaphors may be compared English *belly of a muscle* and German *Kehlkopf* 'larynx', literally 'head of the throat'.

Many Latin anatomic terms are purely descriptive. *Quadratus* and *rotundum* mean *square* and *round*, and, incidentally, they are the originals of the English words. *Rectus* and *rectum* mean 'straight'; *vagus*, 'wandering'. *Duodenum* refers to the length of the organ, which is about 12 inches (compare German *Zwölffingerdarm* 'twelve-finger gut'). At autopsy the *jejunum* is usually found 'empty'.

Before the invention of the clock, one of the most reliable measures of brief periods of time was simply the human heartbeat. Since the pulse was often taken at the side of the head, this area was called *tempus* 'time', and our *temple* is a corruption of this word or of the derived adjective *temporalis*. For a like reason, the word for *wrist* in modern Italian is *polso* (cf. Portuguese *pulso*, Dutch *pols*, Spanish *pulsera* 'bracelet', and German *Pulswärmer* 'cuff'.)

Many other anatomic terms go all the way back to Roman times. *Abdomen* was in use in the second century B.C. and has been variously derived from *abdere* 'to hide away' and *adeps* 'fat'. It may be of interest to precisians that this word means 'stomach' in Pliny's *Historia Naturalis* (77 A.D.). *Abdomen* and *stomach* have now reversed their roles, the latter often standing for the former in English and other modern languages.

Testis means 'witness'; its use for the male gonad, which goes back at least to Horace's time, is probably derived from the primitive custom of taking an oath with a hand on the testicles. (Compare the ancient Hebrew practice noted in *Genesis* 24:3 and 47:29.) According to another explanation, Latin *testis* is a misguided translation of Greek *parastatai* 'twin supporting pillars', which got confused with the legal term *parastates* 'supporter, defender, court witness'.

Cadaver is classical Latin for a 'corpse' or 'carcass'. Its origin is the verb *cadere* 'to fall', though an early etymologist did not hesitate to make it a sort of acronym for *caro data vermibus* 'flesh given up to the worms'. The *os sacrum* 'holy bone' allegedly gets its name from the custom of offering this part of a sacrificial animal on the altar.

Mamma 'breast' is another very old word, occurring in classical Greek as well as in Latin. Both languages also used *papa* for the same meaning; compare *papilla, papule,* and *pap.* These are examples of "baby words" taken into the formal language. Other variants of *papa* include *pupil* in both of its current senses, the zoological *pupa* and French *poupée* 'doll' (whence *puppy*).

The ancient Romans were not particularly exact in their use of everyday words for parts of the body. The science of medicine was practically unknown in Rome until the second century B.C., and even then almost the only physicians there were Greeks or other foreigners. Accordingly, some Latin anatomic terms had been in use for hundreds of years before they acquired practical importance. The practitioner of medicine was compelled to impose on these terms an arbitrary narrowing of meaning, since in popular use they were vague or ambiguous. *Brachium* could mean either the whole upper extremity or just the arm. *Uterus,* like English *womb,* was roughly synonymous with *belly. Femur* referred to the entire thigh, not just its bone.

Anatomic Latin retains the classical meaning of *bucca* 'cheek', though the relics of this word in most Romance languages (Italian *bocca,* French *bouche*) mean 'mouth'. The classical adjective *buccalis* survives in our homophones *buccal* and *buckle,* the latter having at first meant the fastening of a chin-strap lying along the cheek. *Buccina* was the name of a military trumpet whose sounding demanded vigorous use of the cheek muscles; its derivative *buccinator* 'trumpeter' refers to one of these muscles in anatomic Latin.

Some terms now have narrower meanings than when they were first used by medieval anatomists, though examples of the earlier usages may persist. Thus *ligamentum* 'something that binds' has both a strict modern sense, referring to connective tissue bands that support and stabilize a joint, and an older and more general sense that survives in the hepatic and uterine ligaments.

Latin was of course the language of medieval chemistry and pharmacy as well as of anatomy. The first British *Pharmacopoeia*, issued in 1618, and the first formulary published in the North American colonies, the *Lititz* (Pennsylvania) *Pharmacopoeia* (1778), were in Latin.

Monkish Latin *officina* at first meant just a workshop or storeroom but was later restricted to a room for the preparation and storage of drugs. Hence the derived adjective *officinalis* became synonymous with *medical* or *pharmaceutical*. Many plants used as drugs have or had *officinalis* as their species names: *Althaea officinalis* 'the marsh mallow'; *Valeriana officinalis*, 'common valerian' (named from Latin *valere* 'to be healthy'); *Nasturtium officinale* 'watercress'. The medicinal leech is *Hirudo officinalis*. English *officinal* has fallen into disuse, probably because editors and typesetters have so often insisted on omitting the *n*.

The distinction between the physician and apothecary, established in the early Middle Ages, created a need for prescriptions. By the eighteenth century, prescription writing had become a complex and exacting art. A particularly accomplished practitioner might fill several pages in formulating a single concoction. Since in those days any educated person could read the doctor's Latin orders, recurring elements of the prescription were replaced by abbreviations and symbols, many of which survive today: *p.r.n., pro re nata* 'as the need arises'; *b.i.d., bis in die* 'twice a day' (we find the preposition *in* superfluous; a classical Latin writer would have omitted it, too); *stat., statim* 'immediately'; *sig., signum* 'sign, label'. *Q.*, for *quoque* or *quaque* 'every', is sometimes combined in set abbreviations with the initials of English words: *q.o.d.* 'every other day'.

Pharmaceutical Latin, which was carefully taught and practiced with great gusto to about 1950, is now virtually defunct except for a few abbreviations like those mentioned above and a few terms for vintage medicaments (*lotio alba, spiritus frumenti*). This variety of Latin was never quite the same as chemical Latin. For example, chemical formulas were not proper in a Latin prescription, and potassium and sodium were known by these names, not as *kalium* and *natrium*. Modern terms from Romance languages (*belladonna, vanilla*) were declined as though classical Latin, and virtually all terms were equipped with Latin inflectional endings (*antitoxinum, insulinum, vitamina*).

Placebo 'I shall be pleasing' has acquired its medical meaning in a roundabout way. The last sentence (verse 9) of Psalm 114 as given in the Vulgate is *"Placebo Domino in regione vivorum"* that is, "I shall be pleasing unto the Lord in the land of the living." This was adopted as the opening of the Office for the Dead in the Latin Rite. Somehow *placebo* evolved into a catchword denoting obsequiousness and servility, just as *lavabo*, from the part of Psalm 25 used in the Ordinary of the Mass, came to mean a lavatory. By the early nineteenth century *placebo* meant a medicine intended to please the patient rather than cure him.

The language of primitive pathology has not withstood the ravages of time as well as that of anatomy. This is partly because ancient and medieval notions of disease have been almost completely discarded. Some old words for diseases live on in modern parlance, however, often with new meanings. *Abscessus* 'withdrawal, separation' still aptly designates an infection that is "walled off" from surrounding tissues. It appears with that meaning in the medical writings of the Roman encyclopedist Celsus, who was contemporary with Christ. Celsus also uses *cancer* 'crab' to denote an eroding and ulcerating lesion. (*Carcinoma* is based on the Greek word for 'crab', *karkinos*.) In modern English, *cancer* means any malignant growth. *Cancrum oris* 'an erosive lesion of the mouth', *canker* (usually, pleonastically, *canker sore*; a lay term for what the physician calls, equally pleonastically, an *aphthous ulcer*), and French *chancre* are all progeny of the ancient Latin word.

Other pathologic terms found in Celsus include *caries* ('decay' in a bone; probably osteomyelitis), *carbunculus* 'hot coal', *furunculus* 'little thief', *scabies, tabes* 'wasting', *verruca, struma* (suppurative lymphadenitis), *impetigo*, and *prurigo*. The last two illustrate the tendency of postclassical Latin to create terms for skin diseases with the suffix *-igo*. Earlier the suffix could be added to any verb to make a noun: *vertigo* from *vertere* 'to turn' or *origo* from *oriri* 'to arise'. Other cutaneous *-igo's* include *vitiligo*, from *vitium* 'fault, blemish'; *intertrigo*, from *interterere* 'to rub together'; *lentigo*, from *lens* 'seed, lentil'; and *serpigo*, from *serpere* 'to creep'. The latter noun, which occurs in Shakespeare's *Measure for Measure*, is now obsolete, but the adjective *serpiginous* lives on. Incidentally, Shakespeare's *bubukle (King Henry V)*, which has puzzled many editors and commentators, seems to be a whimsical blend of *bubo* and *carbuncle*.

As early as the tenth century, *lupus* 'wolf' meant 'an erosive ulcer'. *Ranula* means 'little frog'. *Tinea* 'gnawing worm, moth' denoted a gnawed or moth-eaten appearance of the skin. *Rodent ulcer* recalls the literal meaning of our general word for rats, mice, and other *gnawing* mammals. *Fistula* at first meant 'tube', 'pipe', or 'reed'; its application to a sinus tract dates back to pre-Christian times. *Hordeolum* 'stye' is a diminutive of *hordeum* 'barleycorn'. The application of *malleus* 'hammer' in early Latin to glanders, a disease of horses sometimes acquired by smiths, grooms, and veterinarians, is based on an obscure etymology. The term survives in both genus and species of the causative organism, *Malleomyces mallei*.

Lumbago, from *lumbus* 'loin', was used in medical Latin as early as the fourth century. *Livedo* is a varient of *livor*; both mean 'a dark blue-gray color'. Similarly, *torpedo* and *torpor* mean the same thing. The former term was first given to a stinging fish or ray that induced torpor or paralysis and afterward to various underwater weapons of human fashioning.

A *tophus* is a soft concretion formed in the tissues of a person with gout. Classical Latin *tofus* meant 'any soft stone', whence the modern *tufa* for the volcanic rock around Rome in which the early Christians dug the catacombs. *Delirium* originated as an agricultural metaphor. The verb *delirare*, from *de* 'away' and *lira* 'furrow', meant to plow in a crooked line and was used figuratively to describe irresponsible or senseless behavior. The derivation of *claudication* from *claudicare* 'to limp' is curiously belied by modern references to claudication in the arm and claudication at bedrest. No doubt a false etymology tracing the word from *claudere* 'to close' is behind these usages. *Varus* and *valgus* originally meant simply 'twisted' or 'crooked'; indeed, they may ultimately be the same word. The modern distinction in their meanings is strictly a modern convention. *Varus* is the source of *prevaricate*, a fancy word meaning 'to lie', 'to walk crookedly in the discharge of one's duties'.

When Ambroise Paré developed effective techniques for the control of operative and traumatic hemorrhage and thus opened the era of modern surgery, the operator was already equipped with a formidable array of instruments, whose design had changed little since the second or third century after Christ. Modern surgery has borrowed the names for several of its instruments directly from classical Latin. The *scalpellum* (or *scalpellus*) is mentioned by Cicero as a surgical knife; the word is a diminutive of *scalprum* 'cutting tool'. The modern *vulsellum* appears in classical Latin as *vulsella* 'a pair of tweezers'. *Tenaculum* (from *tenere* 'to hold') first occurs in English medical writing in the seventeenth century, where it means a forceps with hooked jaws for picking up severed vessles in order to ligate them. *Forceps* is Augustan Latin for 'tongs' or 'pincers'.

Classical *speculum* meant 'mirror', but by the sixteenth century the word had acquired a meaning much like the modern one, 'dilator of orifices'. The cognate *specillum* in Celsus means a 'probe'; not until the Middle Ages did *proba* (from *probare* 'to try or prove') appear. From *temptare*, which also means 'to try', came *tent*, the Shakespearean synonym for *probe*. *Trepanum* is the medieval Latin term for a circular saw used to open the skull, an adaptation of Greek *trypanon* 'borer'. *Trephine* is not a corruption of this word but a deliberate variation. According to John Woodall, its seventeenth century inventor, *trephine* means *'tres fines'* or 'three ends'. *Cannula* is good classical Latin for 'little cane' or 'reed'; its use for a hollow tube in surgery is modern. The *spica* bandage was so named because its alternating oblique folds look like the blades of 'an ear of grain'. A drain or wick of thread inserted in a wound or sinus used to be called a *seton*, from medieval Latin *seto* 'thread', perhaps related to classical *seta* 'bristle'. *Sinapism*, an old-fashioned word for a mustard plaster, incorporates the Greek-Latin *sinapi* 'mustard' (cf. German *Senf*). *Luna* 'moon' was the alchemist's symbolic term for silver—hence the term *lunar caustic*, used for fused silver nitrate until well into the present century.

The system of plant and animal taxonomy published in 1735 by the Swedish naturalist Linnaeus (Karl von Linné) consisted entirely of Latin names, many of which, however, had been adapted from Greek words or roots. His system has been expanded to include all new discoveries in natural history, not least important of which have been those made with the microscope. Though the majority of taxonomic names for microorganisms are either eponymous or of Greek extraction, some few are pure Latin. For example, a genus of saprophytic cocci that tend to form cubical clusters of eight cells is called *Sarcina* from the fancied resemblance between these clusters and a soldier's pack. *Penicillium*, the name of the genus of molds that produce penicillin, means 'little brush' and is cognate with both *pencil* and *penis*.

Besides taxonomic terms, microbiologists and immunologists use a number of technical words taken from classical Latin: *bacillus* 'little rod'; *virus* 'rank substance, poison'; *serum* 'whey'. Even in the days of Pliny the Elder, the last term had an ill-defined meaning in anatomy, and during the prevalence of the humoral theory serum was viewed as one of the secondary or lesser humors. *Vaccine*, now a general word for any antigenic substance containing pathogenic microorganisms in a weakened or inert state, was first used for the infectious material of vaccinia (cowpox), from Latin *vacca* 'cow'. *Inoculation*, sometimes said to refer to the bacteriologist's loop or eye (*oculum*), is really at least as old as Shakespeare and used to refer to the grafting of plants, as did Latin *inoculatio* in pre-Christian agricultural treatises. *Inoculum* is a modern-day back-formation.

The microscope also extended the horizons of descriptive anatomy and of pathology, so that hundreds of new terms were needed. Most of these were taken bodily from Latin (*cilium* 'eyelash'; *nucleus* 'kernel'; *acinus* 'berry'; *morula* 'little mulberry'; *glomerulus* 'little ball of yarn'). The new microscopic pathology revolutionized medicine and spurred an extensive revision of terminology. *Tuberculosis* replaced both the physician's *phthisis* (Greek, 'wasting away') and the vernacular *consumption*. *Consumptive*, once synonymous with *tuberculous*, now refers to the biological or chemical "using up" of a substance, as in *consumptive hypofibrinogenemia*.

Modern scientific coinages draw more heavily on Greek than on Latin material, but until about the turn of the present century Latin was still used with considerable frequency as the language of scientific communication, particularly in northern Europe. Richard von Krafft-Ebing's monumental and controversial study of sexual deviation, *Psychopathia Sexualis*, first published in 1886, was written in German except for the more offensive details, which were given in Latin.

Many Latin medical terms, despite their classical appearance, are modern inventions. *Rubeola*, initially denoting a variety of red rashes, was coined from classical Latin *ruber* 'red' in the seventeenth century. In the early nineteenth century the term was limited to measles, but the *Oxford English Dictionary* listed this as an obsolete meaning and stated that in current parlance *rubeola* and *rubella* were synonyms. The Supplement Volume of 1933 contained no revision of this statement. German texts of the era make *rubeola* synonymous with *Röteln* ('rubella'). *Morbilli*, another Latin name for measles, began as a singular noun (*morbillus* 'little disease') but was corrupted into a plural by analogy with English *measles* and German *Masern*.

Eighteenth century Latin coinages include *torticollis*, an irregular derivative of *tortus collis* 'twisted neck', and *pertussis*, which is simply the Latin word for *cough* preceded by the intensive prefix seen in *persist* and *perfect*. *Angina* means 'quinsy' in the ancient Latin dramatist Plautus. The word comes from an Indo-European root meaning 'compression' or 'squeezing' and is cognate with *anguish, anxiety,* and *anger*. The phrase *angina pectoris* was proposed by Heberden (1768) in his classic description of the symptom. Also dating from the eighteenth century are *variola* (from *varius* 'varied, speckled') and its irregular diminutive *varicella*. In older literature both of these are sometimes found in the plural, on the same pattern as *morbilli*.

Molluscum, in the sense of a skin tumor, first appeared in the early nineteenth century. The word is actually a Neo-Latin adjective formed from classical *mollis* 'soft'. The feminine form, *mollusca*, was used as early as 1650 with reference to various soft, mushy plants and animals and was incorporated by Linnaeus into his animal taxonomy, though not in the modern sense. Other Neo-Latin medical terms that appeared during the preceding century are *talipes* (a composite of *talus* and *pes*) and *lumen* 'light', referring to the cavity of a hollow or tubular organ, probably first used by microscopists looking at cross sections of vessels. *Sanitarium* (from *sanitas* 'health') and *sana-torium* (from *sanatus* 'healed, made healthy') both came into being around 1830 and were at first synonyms. In this country the latter form was officially chosen by the National Tuberculosis Association to mean a 'tuberculosis hospital', but the two terms are frequently used interchangeably or even amalgamated in the hybrid spelling *sanitorium*.

Most twentieth century additions to the medical lexicon in which Latin figures are English words built of Latin stems and affixes. New taxonomic coinages, however, are Latin in form even when, as is usual, they are Greek in origin. New names for skin diseases are also frequently Latin phrases, in continuation of a pattern established centuries ago. *Cor bovinum, status anginosus,* and *P mitrale* are all of fairly recent vintage. Classical *praecordia*, always plural, has been replaced within the past few decades by *precordium*, probably a back-formation from *precordial*. The shift from classical *hilum* to the anatomist's *hilus* is considerably older. *Lente* is the Latin adverb meaning 'slowly'. *Ego* and *id* are, respectively, 'I' and 'it'.

Latin has exerted so vast and various an influence on the shape of medical language, and indeed of English, that one is apt to underestimate or even ignore its close cousin, classical Greek. I turn now to the language of Hippocrates and Galen.

Greek

> Cassius: *Did Cicero say anything?*
> Casca: *Ay, he spoke Greek.*
> Cassius: *To what effect?*
> Casca: *Nay . . . those that understood him smil'd at one another, and shook their heads; but for mine own part, it was Greek to me.*
>
> William Shakespeare
> *Julius Caesar*

The language in which, nearly 30 centuries ago, the blind bard Homer composed his epic poems, the *Iliad* and the *Odyssey*, sprang from the same Indo-European parent tongue as Latin. The two languages have many roots in common, and as already mentioned, the Latin alphabet is a modification of the Greek one. These are not the only points at which the two classical languages touch. When Rome conquered Greece it absorbed all the best of Hellenic learning and culture. Greek became the second language of the educated and the leisured classes. As Rome took possession of the arts and sciences of Greece, it borrowed their terminologies also, reshaping many words into Latin. This process of assimilation, which began before the Christian era, accounts for many likenesses between Latin and Greek words that are not due to the common origin of the two languages.

It is scarcely an exaggeration to say that Rome had no practitioners of medicine until after the conquest of Greece. The writings of Hippocrates were lawful booty along with all other things Greek. Indeed, much of the Greek learning, particularly in medicine and astronomy, had originally been filched from the Egyptians after the conquests of Alexander the Great. Most of the physicians who practiced in Augustan Rome were Greek slaves or freedmen, though a substantial minority were Egyptians, Syrians, or other barbarians. Since virtually all spoke Greek, the jargon of their craft was built up in that language. The Roman Celsus, writing on medicine in the first century A.D., could find Latin equivalents for only a few medical terms, and was obliged to give the rest in Greek. From his day to ours, most of those Greek terms have preserved their currency (if not their meanings), yielding neither to Latin substitutes nor to translations in modern vernaculars.

In the second century after Christ, Galen, a brilliant physician of Greek birth and training, settled in Rome and made many important discoveries in anatomy and physiology. In his extensive writings he brought together in encyclopedic fashion all the medical knowledge of his time. It is a striking evidence of the intellectual inertia of the Dark Ages, and of the slowness with which scientific medicine evolved out of its rude beginnings in the Renaissance, that Galen's collected medical works (of which about 100 still survive) were held up as the universal and unquestionable authority in medicine for no fewer than 14 centuries.

It was chiefly in Latin and Arabic translations that Galen's works were handed down through the ages, for the language and literature of ancient Greece had a very different fate from those of Rome. Whereas Latin was kept alive down through the centuries by the Christian church, no such institution existed to maintain a widespread know-ledge of Greek once the Byzantine Empire began to shrink and disintegrate. Though, for this reason, the rediscovery and diffusion of the Greek cultural and literary heritage in the Renaissance lagged behind the Roman, by the seventeenth century Greek was well established as a classical discipline. Few scholars attained proficiency in speaking it, but it was taken for granted by polite writers that every educated man knew enough Greek to decipher words fashioned from that language.

Almost from its origin, the English tongue had been receiving a slow but steady influx of words from Greek, often through Latin. *Asbestos, chaos, character, dogma, echo, emphasis, horizon, idea,* and *skeleton* are pure, untarnished Greek. A few traditional academic terms (*diploma, gymnasium, practicum, stadium, syllabus, thesis*) are of Greek rather than Latin provenance, and the names of fraternities were originally represented by Greek letters to keep their natures and purposes secret from undergraduates, who knew only Latin.

Some medical terms that look like venerable English natives are in fact corruptions of Greek words: *dropsy* from *hydrops, palsy* from *paralysis. Rickets* is generally said to be a corruption of *rachitis*, and maybe it is, but etymologists can find no proof that the scientific term existed until long after the lay word had made its appearance. It is suggested that *rickets* is a native Germanic word and that *rachitis* is a kind of learned back-formation from it.

Quinsy (from *kynanche* 'dog collar, choke halter') owes its present form partly to an intermediate Latin corruption, *quinancia* (also *squinancia*). *Pleurisy* underwent rather less change in evolving, through both Latin and French, from *pleuritis*. The Greek word for a granary or storehouse, *apotheke*, is the source of *apothecary*, which, like Latin *officina*, meant any storeroom or workshop before being narrowed down to the sense of a druggist's business premises. Though *apothec* was once good English for a pharmacy, it died out in the seventeenth century and was replaced by the roundabout *apothecary shop*. French *boutique*, a corruption of *apotheke*, means 'shop' or 'store', but in modern American usage it seems to have an unlimited range of connotations. The evolution of *apotheke* has pursued two distinct lines in Spanish, where *bodega* means 'grocery' and *botica*, 'drugstore'. *Licorice* is a corruption of Greek *glykyrrhiza* 'sweet root'. The British have further altered the word to *liquorice* (under the influence, as Wilson Follett coyly observed, of *liquor*), and the French to *réglisse*.

Though the Greek alphabet was the ancestor of ours, the two are sufficiently different that our spelling of words taken from Greek is only an approximation to the original. For example, the sounds *ps* and *th* are each represented by a single letter in Greek. The common combinations *ng* and *nx* in English words of Greek origin (*angioma, pharynx*) were spelled *gg* and *gx* by the Greeks. Since most Greek stems have entered English by way of Latin, we are indebted to the Romans for many of the conventions observed in transliterating them. The Romans Latinized the inflectional endings of most Greek words, though a few—like *amnion, hypospadias, opisthotonos* and *systole*—retain their original endings. *Dermis*, a modern variant of *derma* 'skin', seems to be a kind of back-formation from Hippocrates's *epidermis*.

The Greek alphabet had no *c* and the Roman had no *k*. Hence, *k* in Greek words generally became *c* in their Latin equivalents. Classically this *c* was hard, but during the metamorphosis of Late

Latin it was softened into a sibilant before *e, i,* or *y,* and that is the way it is pronounced in *cephalic, cirrhosis,* and *cycle.* Roots borrowed directly from Greek in the past few centuries may keep their *k: keratin, kinase, kymograph.* Greek favored some consonant pairs that the English tongue can barely manage. When one of these pairs occurs at the beginning of a word, as in *bdellium, cnidophore, ctenophore, mnemonic, pneumonia, psittacosis,* and *ptyalin,* the first consonant is suppressed in speech. Only when a vowel precedes the pair are both consonants pronounced (*gastrocnemius, amnesia, hypercapnia*)—and not always then (*antipsychotic, methoxypsoralen, pleuropneumonia*).

The Greeks had no letter corresponding to our *h.* When, in English words of Greek descent, one finds an *h* before a vowel (*hemoglobin, histology*) or after an *r* (*rhinitis, diarrhea*), it probably stands for the harsh breathing signified in Greek by a mark like a backward apostrophe ('). This harsh breathing was also heard in the consonants theta (θ), phi (ϕ), and chi (χ), generally transliterated by the digraphs *th, ph,* and *ch.* To approximate the original sounds one would have to pronounce *th* as in *penthouse, ph* as in *topheavy,* and *ch* (*kh*) as in *workhorse.* When the stem *hem-* (from *haima* 'blood') comes at the beginning of a word, the harsh breathing is kept: *hematology.* Otherwise the *h* is dropped: *hyperlipemia, hypophosphatemia.* This is in contrast to the classical practice, according to which the harsh breathing was retained: *hyphema.* Modern *leukemia* is a corruption of the more correct *leuchaemia* originally proposed by Virchow. (Other Greek coinages attributed to Virchow include *thrombosis, embolism, neuroglia, fibrinogen, ochronosis,* and the Greek-Latin hybrid *granuloma.* He also invented *Kulturkampf!*)

The preponderance of vowels and diphthongs in Greek lends the language a musical character but introduces many letters that the Anglo-Saxon ear finds superfluous. Greek *ai* and *oi* usually appear in modern American English as *e* (*hemorrhage, celiac*), though, as mentioned earlier, the variant spellings with *ae* and *oi* (*haemorrhage, coeliac*) are favored in Canada and Great Britain. The British spelling sometimes helps to distinguish two similar stems, as in the case of *ped-,* from Latin *pes* 'foot', and *paed-,* from Greek *pais* 'child'. The stems are identical in American spelling, hence the antediluvian joke about the man who took his foot trouble to a pediatrician.

British and American usage agree in substituting simple *i* for Greek *ei* (*Phthirus, chiropody*), though in *trachea* it is the *e* that survives, perhaps through the influence of *trachelos* 'neck'. We turn upsilon (*v*) into a *y* (*hyphema, chyle*) unless it is preceded by another vowel. After *a* or *e* it becomes *u* (*trauma, neuron*). When it comes after *o* it also changes to *u*, and the *o* is generally dropped (*epulis, bubo*).

Much of the Greek material in modern scientific English passed first through Latin and then through French. The influence of the latter may be seen in virtually all Greek terms ending in -*y: atony, atrophy, dysentery, epilepsy, strangury, diathermy, dosimetry, neurology, polyploidy*. The first five were genuine Greek words ending in -*ia*, which changed to -*ie* in French. The others are modern coinages that have acquired the final -*y* by analogy with the older words. *Chronaxie* (like the Latin-inspired *calorie*) has kept the French ending.

Another large group showing the influence of French comprises words and stems ending in mute -*e: aerobe* (Pasteur), *chromophobe, condyle, cytochrome, hemorrhage, heterophile, dermatome, chyle, somite, synapse*. Though the final -*e* of some authentic Greek borrowings is still pronounced (*diploë, syncope, systole*), in others this -*e* has become mute (*hydrocele, syndrome*) in imitation of modern coinages and Gallicisms. Other Greek words bearing tokens of their passage through French are *cholagogue, secretagogue, diastase*, and *technique*. Inflectional endings have vanished without a trace in either speech or writing in *aneurysm, blast, cyst, polyp, spasm*, and *symptom*.

Since Hippocrates found only the most rudimentary anatomic terminology in his native language, he was often forced into circumlocutions. He had to write "the longer bone of the forearm" when he meant the *ulna*, and he referred to the *fibula* sometimes as "the slighter bone of the leg," at other times as "the bone in line with the little toe." By Galen's day, however, a fairly rich anatomic nomenclature had sprung into being. Many of the Greek terms adopted or invented by him are still in use today.

Greek anatomic metaphors, though fewer in number than Latin ones, are every bit as colorful. *Pylorus*, for example, means 'gate-keeper'. the *tragus* of the ear is so called because in later life it develops a tuft of hair similar in appearance to the beard of a goat. The mitral valve is shaped like a bishop's miter (from Greek *mitra*).

Phalanx, a term for a close-order battle formation favored by the Greeks, was used first to name all the fingers, then a single finger, and finally just one bone of a finger. *Coccyx* means 'cuckoo', a reference to the animal's beak. *Salpinx*, used for both uterine and auditory tubes, is Greek for 'trumpet'. *Meconium* is a Latinized form of Greek *mekonion* 'inspissated poppy juice, crude opium'. *Raphe* 'seam' is related to the surgical suffix *-rrhaphy*.

Numerous anatomic names end in *-oid*, from *eidos* 'form, shape, appearance'. *Ethmoid* and *thyroid* mean, respectively, 'sievelike' and 'shieldlike'. *Coronoid* likens the part named to a crow, *sesamoid* to a sesame seed, *mastoid* to a breast, and *odontoid* to a tooth. *Disk* is classical Greek *diskos*, the stone quoit hurled in athletic contests. Other derivatives of the same root are used when one speaks of a Petri *dish*, a chart *desk*, or a speaker's *daïs*. The *azygos* vein is so styled because it is 'without a fellow' on the left side of the chest. Hippocrates called each bronchus an *aorta* (literally, 'something hung up'); Aristotle was the first to use *aorta* in its modern sense. *Trochanter*, from *trechein* 'to run', might be translated 'running apparatus'.

The combining form *urano-*, referring to the hard palate, as in *uranoplasty*, comes from Greek *ouranos* 'the sky' (cf. Uranus, god and planet). Already in Aristotle's day the term was used also for a man-made vault or ceiling and for the *roof* of the mouth. *Glottis* is a variant, known to Galen and perhaps coined by him, of *glotta* (*glossa*) 'tongue'. The anatomist calls the median cleft of the upper lip the *philtrum*, from Greek *philtron* 'love potion, charm'. Those who profess not to see the connection have been too long at their books.

The hemorrhoidal vessels are among the few structures in the body that have been named from diseases to which they are subject. The original word, *haimorrhoides* (from *haima* 'blood' and *rhein* 'to flow'), referred to bleeding piles. Afterward it was extended to the same vessels in their normal state. Similarly, the pathologic meaning of *ganglion*, 'a bland swelling on or near a tendon', was the earlier one. Galen chose it as an anatomic term for a normal thickening along the course of a nerve. Since Latin *inguen*, the source of our adjective referring to the groin, has been linked historically with Greek *aden* 'acorn, gland', it seems likely that both at first denoted swollen inguinal lymph nodes, as did Greek *boubon* (modern *bubo*). The earliest sense of *parotis* (from two Greek words meaning 'next to the ear') may have been an abscess or tumor in that area, rather than the normal parotid gland. At least, this is the meaning of the word in Celsus; Hippocrates does not use it.

The principal source of purple dye in the ancient world was the shellfish *Murex*, called in Greek *porphyra*, whence both *purpura* (Latin for 'purple') and *porphyria*. Other disease names containing allusions to animals are *bulimia* (literally, 'the appetite of a bull'); *ichthyosis* ('fishiness'); *alopecia*, from *alopex* 'fox'; *lagophthalmos* 'hare's eye'; *elephantiasis*, probably first denoting leprosy; and *hippus* ('horse'), a reference to an unusually active pupil that alternately contricts and dilates. *Kerion*, like its Latin synonym *favus*, means 'honeycomb'. *Lichen* 'tree moss' has given its name to one kind of skin affliction; *sycon* 'fig' to another (*sycosis*).

Rhagas (usually used in the plural, *rhagades*) means simply 'a rent or tear'. *Plege* means the same as its Latin twin *plaga* 'blow, stroke, wound', mentioned in the last chapter. In *paraplegia, diplegia*, and related words, it implies 'paralysis', a sense closely parelleling the special meaning of *stroke* in lay medical English. *Asphyxia* is literally 'stoppage of the pulse', and in Galen it has only that meaning. Its use for suffocation is only about two centuries old. Both *anthrax* 'hot coal' and *anthracosis* meant 'a boil' in ancient Greek; compare Latin *carbunculus*. *Podagra*, a term now entirely supplanted in medical parlance by *gout*, means 'a snare for the foot'. The latter part of this word appears also in *chiragra* ('gout in the hands') and in a rare early Latin-Greek hybrid, *mentagra*, known to Pliny and meaning 'an eruption of the chin'.

Greek *typhos* 'smoke' was used by Hippocrates for stupor or coma in a febrile patient. The word was resurrected in the eighteenth century as the name of a disease that causes a clouding of the mind. *Erysipelas* was known to Hippocrates. Its derivation from *erysis* 'redness' and *pella* 'skin' seems probable enough, but the *Oxford English Dictionary* is skeptical of this etymology. *Diabetes* (named by Aretaeus of Cappadocia in the second century after Christ) comes from *diabainein* 'to pass through', and *exanthem* from *exanthein* 'to blossom forth'. *Nausea* (Greek *nausia*), from the same root as *nautical* and *navigation*, at first meant strictly 'seasickness'. *Carphologia*, Galen's word for restless picking at the bedclothes by a semiconscious patient (first described by Hippocrates), is literally 'a gathering of twigs'.

Laudanum, the old word for tincture of opium, though sometimes traced to Latin *laudandum* 'praiseworthy', is a corruption of Greek *ladanon* 'gum, resin'. According to Herodotus, *ladanon* is in turn derived from an Arabic word referring to a gum-producing Oriental shrub. His claim that the gum was customarily gathered from the beards of goats that had been nibbling on the shrub need not be taken too seriously. *Paregoric*, now meaning another opiate preparation, at one time referred to any analgesic or sedative and comes from a Greek word meaning 'soothing or consoling'. *Calamine* is derived from the Greek *kadmia*, an ancient term for zinc ore. *Arsenic* gets its name from Greek *arsenikon* 'masculine', applied for obscure reasons to the naturally occurring trisulfide, also known as *orpiment*. In *arsenic* one finds the older form of the root meaning 'male'; the later form is seen in *arrhenoblastoma*.

The Greek word for *bow*, 'toxon' (cf. *toxophily* 'archery'), is the progenitor of *toxic* and *toxin*. Formerly referring to archery in general, *toxikos* acquired a narrower application to poisonous substances in which arrows were dipped. *Tetanus (tetanos)* 'muscular spasm' meant lockjaw in particular as early as Hippocrates's time. *Tetany* is a much more modern word from the same source, invented in French as *tétanie*. Ancient Greek *klinikos*, signifying a physician who visits his patients while they are confined by illness, and *klinike*, the art or method of such a physician, are formed from *kline* 'bed'. As early as the fifth century the Numidian medical writer Caelius Aurelianus used *chronic* (from *chronos* 'time') in its modern sense and contrasted it with *acute* (Latin *acutus* 'sharp'), which had appeared in the works of Celsus.

A number of medical terms of Greek ancestry that were once in common use have virtually dropped out of the language. For *apoplexy*, *clyster* (also spelled *glister*), and *lyssa* have been substituted *stroke, enema,* and *rabies*. *Imposthume*, a corruption of *apostema*, has given way to *abscess*, and *fleam*, a corruption of *phlebotomus*, has been replaced by *lancet*. Though *catarrh* (*katarrhoos* 'a flowing down') has now yielded to *postnasal drip*, one still speaks of the catarrhal stages of measles and whooping cough.

Plethora, meaning 'overfullness', at first implied the excess of some "humor," but by the nineteenth century it had been restricted to the supposed excess of erythrocytes. At present it has fallen out of medical use entirely and means simply 'too much of anything'— money, debts, worries, even words. *Hectic,* once referring to a habitual or constitutional disorder, has likewise been abandoned by the physician and appropriated by the citizenry at large.

With some notable exceptions, the examples cited in this chapter have been Greek and Latin words, not English words assembled from Greek and Latin parts. Modern coinages from classical languages will be considered in detail in Chapter 5.

References and Readings

Andrews EA: *A Copious and Critical Latin-English Lexicon.* New York, Harper & Brothers, 1854.

Buck CD: *Comparative Grammar of Greek and Latin.* Chicago, University of Chicago Press, 1933.

Celsus AC: *De Medicina.* Cambridge, Harvard University Press, 1960.

Dauzat A: *Dictionnaire Étymologique.* Paris, Larousse, 1938.

Grandsaignes d'Hauterive R: *Dictionnaire des Racines des Langues Européennes.* Paris, Larousse, 1948.

Leider M., Rosenblum M: *A Dictionary of Dermatologic Words, Terms, and Phrases.* West Haven, Connecticut, Dome Laboratories, 1976.

Liddell HG, Scott R: *A Greek-English Lexicon.* New York, Harper & Brothers, 1859.

Martin F: *Les Mots Grecs.* Paris, Hachette, 1937.

McCulloch JA: *A Medical Greek and Latin Workbook.* Springfield, Illinois, Charles C. Thomas, 1962.

Muldoon HC: *Lessons in Pharmaceutical Latin and Prescription Writing and Interpretation,* 4th ed. New York, John Wiley & Sons, 1946.

Palmer LR: *The Latin Language.* New York, Barnes & Noble, 1955.

Pliny (Caius Plinius Secundus): *Natural History.* Cambridge, Harvard University Press, 1979.

Pope A: *Poetical Works.* London: Macmillan & Co., 1897.

CHAPTER 4

A Museum in Words

Language has been called man's most effective tool for the preservation and transmission of culture. In earlier chapters I have shown that our everyday speech teems with monuments of events long past and rings with the echoes of languages no longer spoken. I have also noted how copiously it has been augmented with borrowings from living languages and with relics of dead ones. As we are soon to discover, proper names of persons and places have contributed another large share to our hoard of words. Indeed, language is such a rich depository of curios and artifacts from ancient times and remote places—and of mementos of persons celebrated in history, myth, and folklore—that no violent stretch of the imagination is needed to see it as a kind of ubiquitous and self-perpetuating museum.

Scientific terminology, like the vernacular, is a fascinating storehouse of the antique and the exotic. The periodic table of the elements might have been conceived as a paradigm of the diversity of sources from which technical language is drawn. *Gold, silver,* and *lead* are of Anglo-Saxon descent, though their symbols (*Au, Ag, Pb*) are taken from their Latin international names, *aurum, argentum,* and *plumbum. Barium, bromine,* and *phosphorus* are built from Greek

stems; *zirconium* and *boron*, from Persian; and *antimony* from
Arabic. German is the source of *bismuth*; Celtic, of *iron*; and
Swedish, of *tungsten*.

More than half of the elements have been named after real or
mythical persons or places. Roman mythology has inspired *mercury*
and *titanium*; Greek, *palladium* and *promethium*; Norse, *thorium*
and *vanadium*. *Cobalt* and *nickel* are named from superstitions
popular in eighteenth century Europe. *Cadmium, curium,* and
gadolinium are eponyms, while *berkelium, californium,* and *ameri-
cium* are among more than 20 elements named after places.

In this chapter I shall review some of the treasures and some of
the oddities preserved in the museum of medical language.

Historical Curiosities

*There is in constancy and stability a general and lasting
advantage, which will always overbalance the slow improvements of gradual correction.*

Samuel Johnson
A Dictionary of the English Language

As a science advances, its special language evolves with it, not
only through expansion but also through revision. Modern discoveries
correct ancient errors, and old theories yield to new. A name given to
something once poorly understood may prove a misnomer when fuller
knowledge is reached. Though the obvious course would then seem to
be to discard the erroneous name and find another, it is remarkable
how often we seem to think it easier to keep the word to which we
have grown accustomed and impose a different meaning on it. The
inconvenience of this practice is less of an objection to it than the
violence that it often does to common sense and the risk that it carries
of perpetuating the former error, or at least of misleading the
uninitiated.

Cervical *erosion*, retinal *exudates*, and *clockwise* rotation of the
heart survive even though these terms are no longer in accord with
current understanding of the things named. It is no longer believed
that *Haemophilus influenzae* causes influenza or that *Neisseria
catarrhalis* is responsible for nasal catarrh, but the names live on.
Artery, which means 'air passage', is still used as a term for what have
long been known to be blood vessels. And one still says *pancreas*,

though it is no longer believed that the gland is 'all flesh'. (Modern Dutch *alveesklier* does not even trouble to hide the old error in a dead language.) Hippocrates (*On the Sacred Disease*) wrote that the misuse of *phrenes* 'mind' (cf. *schizophrenia*) as a term for the diaphragm arose from the fact that strong emotion was noted to cause a gripping or tightening in the midriff. Though the Father of Medicine assured his readers 24 centuries ago that the diaphragm had no cognitive function, physicians have not yet given up *phrenic* as a synonym for *diaphragmatic*. We likewise cling to *hysteria*, though we do not now believe that the womb (Greek *hyster*) is the seat of mental afflictions.

As is generally known, ancient and medieval medicine was largely based on a system of simple, mechanistic concepts of health and disease, which were embodied in the so-called humoral theory. Though the last vestiges of this theory were scrapped generations ago, much of its jargon lives on in our midst. *Temper, temperament, humorous, in a good* (or *bad*) *humor, sanguine, bilious, liverish, phlegmatic,* and *choleric* are all more or less current in vernacular English. *Distemper*, once virtually synonymous with *disease*, is now the exclusive property of the veterinarian. Meanwhile, the physician speaks of the aqueous and vitreous humors of the eye, humoral immunity, humoral products of tumors, and neurohumoral agents.

Cholera was so called because the vomiting and diarrhea characteristic of the disease were thought to be a discharge of malignant bilious humor (Greek *chole* 'bile'). The pituitary gland was believed by ancient anatomists to produce nasopharyngeal mucus (Latin *pituita* 'phlegm'), another of the humors. The Greek name for phlegm was *rheuma*, from the verb meaning 'to flow'. *Rheum* is now obsolete as an English word for nasal discharge, but the stem survives in *rheumatic fever, rheumatoid arthritis,* and *rheumatism*. From the name of a third humor, black bile, comes the psychiatric term *melancholia*.

Dyscrasia, an old Greek word with a nebulous reference to unwholesome air, drags out a pitiful existence as a modern term of equally nebulous sense. The impressively resonant term *parenchyma* proves on translation to be pure nonsense: 'something poured in'. Coined in the third century B.C. by Erasistratus, the term referred to his fallacious idea that the inner substance of solid viscera (liver, spleen, kidney) was infused and coagulated blood. *Gout* is a Gallicized form of Latin *gutta* 'drop'; deposits of urate crystals were thought to be drops of some noxious humor. *Hypochondria* refers to the ancient belief that the liver and spleen, situated 'under the (costal) cartilages', were at fault in persons of gloomy and introspective disposition.

Not much survives of the astrologic side of ancient medicine except the lay term *lunatic* and the Italian loan-word *influenza*, which refers to the supposed influence of the stars in inducing disease. Terms of alchemical origin that are only now becoming obsolete are *lunar caustic*, a term for silver nitrate based on the identification of the moon with silver, and *saturnism*, referring to poisoning with lead, identified with Saturn. The arthropathy of lead poisoning is still known as *saturnine gout*.

Borrowings from Nonclassical Languages

I have often wished, that as in our constitution there are several persons whose business it is to watch over our laws, our liberties, and our commerce, certain men might be set apart as super-intendants of our language, to hinder any words of a foreign coin from passing among us; and in particular to prohibit any French phrases from becoming current in this kingdom, when those of our own stamp are altogether as valuable.

Joseph Addison
Spectator, No. 165

Dead languages are not the only ones from which medical terminology has levied contributions. Just as the English common speech is continually borrowing words from other living languages with whose speakers we have political, commercial, or literary ties, the language of science is as cosmopolitan as science itself.

Among the oldest foreign words still current in medical English are several terms related to chemistry and pharmacy that have been inherited from the Arabian alchemists: *alcohol, camphor, caramel, elixir, senna, sugar, syrup,* and perhaps also *amalgam, soda,* and *tartar* (potassium bitartrate). The suffix *-al* for naming aldehydes is taken from the first syllable of *alcohol*, and the suffix *-ol* for alcohols from the last. (The few similar terms with a suffix derived from Latin *oleum* 'oil' are properly spelled with a final *-e*: *indole, pyrrole*.)

Aniline, from Sanskrit *nila* 'dark blue', is a direct offshoot of Arabic and Persian *nil* 'the indigo plant'. Arabic *al qaliy* 'ashes' has produced both *alkali* and *kalium*—whence the symbol *K* for potassium. *Natron*, the source of *natrium* and so of the symbol *Na* for sodium, was probably adapted by Arabic from a Greek word, which in turn is perhaps related to *nitron*; both may have come originally from Hebrew. Though *chemistry* entered modern European languages from Arabic, its origin was probably a Greek word cognate with *chyme*.

Arabic *qahwah*, by way of Turkish *kahveh* and French *café*, has given us *coffee* and *caffeine*. *Bezoar*, ultimately Persian, was once an Arabic pharmacal term meaning 'antidote'. Its present sense stems from the ancient belief that concretions found in the stomachs of animals have the power of neutralizing poisons. When Arabic *luban jawi* 'frankincense of Java' was borrowed in the fifteenth century by Italian, it underwent a change called aphesis, losing its first syllable, which was too much like the Italian definite article *lo* to survive as part of the word. The result was *benzoi*, later altered to *benzoin*, a form found in most European languages by the seventeenth century. *Benzoic, benzine, benzol,* and *benzene* followed. English is indebted to Arabic also for *antimony, bejel, cubeb, safranin, saphenous, senna,* and *sumbul*. The Latin anatomic terms *dura mater* 'tough mother' and *pia mater* 'gentle mother' have engendered much confusion and speculation. These are medieval translations of Arabic *umm al-jafiyah* and *umm raqiqah*, respectively—too literal translations, since here Arabic *umm* 'mother' refers to relations other than human.

As one would expect, the languages of western Europe have been the principal contributors to medical terminology in modern times. Several German words have joined the international vocabulary of histology and pathology through the influence of Virchow and his school: *gitter* 'lattice'; *mast* 'stuffed'; *Stab* 'staff'; *wasserhelle* 'water-clear' cells; *Anlage* 'plan, foundation'; and *Polkissen* 'polar cushion'. *Gestalt* 'form, shape' owes to von Ehrenfels its introduction as a technical term in psychology. Billroth and his disciples have given us *Magenstrasse*; Neufeld, the *Quellung* reaction.

The *K* of *EKG* refers to the German term *Elektrokardiogramm* first used by the Dutch physiologist Einthoven. The *K* of *ketone* (*Keton*, a variation on *acetone*) is the work of the German chemist Gmelin, who also invented *ester*, from *Essig* (German for 'vinegar', a corruption of Latin *acetum*) and *Äther*. Vitamin K was so named by the Danish biochemist Dam, who isolated it, after the fuller German term *Koagulationsvitamin.* Mandelic acid was named from German *Mandel* 'almond'.

Sitzbath is a partial translation of *Sitzbad; ground substance,* a too literal one of *Grundsubstanz. Eye grounds* is perhaps derived from *Augenhintergrund. Mittelschmerz* has a long history as a term for ovulatory pain. More recent loans include the *Blutwelle* of pulmonary embolism and the *Spinnbarkeit* of cervical mucus. The O and H antigens of *Salmonella typhi* are so designated because colonies of flagellated microorganisms (originally, *Proteus vulgaris*) spread over an agar medium in a thin film (*Hauch*), whereas nonflagellated colonies are compact and discrete (*ohne Hauch* 'without film'). *Kernicterus* and *mastocyte* are blends of German and Greek. Another, *Antikörper,* was the model for English *antibody.*

Borrowings from French easily outnumber those from any other foreign language even if one excludes words like *chancre, douche, goiter, grippe, lavage, malaise,* and *morgue,* which have long been naturalized in English. There is scarcely a branch of medicine that does not have at least two or three French borrowings in its special vocabulary. Thus, the anatomist uses *sac* and *fourchette*; the surgeon, *bougie, curette, débridement, en bloc, rongeur, tamponade*; the internist, *ballottement, bruit, grand mal, petit mal, rale*; the radiologist, *cassette, niche en plateau, coeur en sabot*; the clinical pathologist, *burette, titer, rouleaux*; the physiatrist, *massage, effleur-age, pétrissage*; the obstetrician, *fontanel, souffle, couvade, cerclage*; the psychiatrist, *déjà vu, folie à deux*; the electrocardiographer, *torsade de pointes*; the geneticist, *cri du chat*; the neurosurgeon, *contrecoup.* The pharmacist dispenses *perles* and *pastilles.* In short, wherever one looks within the realm of medicine, one finds a sprinkling of French terms.

Not all medical terms of French provenance betray their origins as plainly as these. *Frambesia* (in Europe, *framboesia*) is Neo-Latin formed from French *framboise* 'raspberry'. The suffix *-ase,* used in naming enzymes, first appeared in *diastase,* an eighteenth century Gallicization of Greek *diastasis* 'separation'. The sugar suffix *-ose* began with French *glucose,* adapted in 1838 by the French Academy of Sciences from Greek *gleukos* 'sweet wine' (not from *glykys* 'sweet'). *Cellulose* followed in 1839; *levulose* and *dextrose* are contractions of *laevo-glucose* and *dextro-glucose*. *Bagassosis* incorporates the French word for sugar cane husks, *bagasse*. Other hybrids of French and Greek are *culdoscopy* and *culdocentesis*, each beginning with an unorthodox combining form of *cul de sac*.

The dermatologist's *id reaction*, though not as French as *café au lait* spots or *perlèche*, passed through that language on its way from Greek to English. The classical Greek patronymic suffix *-ides* (*Asklepiades* 'son of Asklepios') was borrowed for the creation of several nineteenth century French dermatologic terms such as *syphilide* and *tuberculide*. On entering English the suffix lost another letter and, appended to a variety of stems, acquired the general meaning of 'a skin condition caused by': *dermatophytid*. *Id* is now a full-fledged word for an allergic dermatitis occurring at a site remote from that exposed to the allergen.

Italian has contributed several lilting and musical words to the international language of medicine: *petechia; scarlatina; malaria* 'bad air', *pellagra* 'rough skin'. *Belladonna* 'lovely lady' supposedly refers to the use of the herb as a mydriatic to enhance feminine charms. A disease believed due to the influence of the stars was called *influenza*.

Cascara, espundia, marijuana, and *pinta* are of Spanish lineage. *Chiclero ulcer* is named from the Spanish word for a chicle farmer. *Dengue* is also Spanish but was probably adapted from a Swahili word. Other medical terms from African languages are *buchu* and *kino* (names of outmoded pharmaceuticals), *tsetse* fly (it is so called in Bechuana), *kwashiorkor* (which means 'displaced child' in the language of Ghana), and *ouabain* (a Gallicized version of the Somali word for the strophanthus plant). *Ainhum* is a Portuguese adaptation of the Yoruba (Nigerian) word *ayun* 'to saw or cut'. *Albino*, whence *albinism*, is also Portuguese.

Indic languages have supplied *kala-azar* (Assamese for *black disease*), *runche* (which means 'the crying one' in Nepal), and *beriberi* (from Sinhalese *bæri* 'weakness'; the repetition adds emphasis: *great* weakness). The Hindustani word for a native washerman appears in *dhobie itch*. From Japanese have been borrowed *tsutsugamushi* 'dangerous bug' and *sodoku*, modified from Canton Chinese *shué* 'rat' and *tûk* 'poison'. Japanese *urushi* 'lacquer' is the basis of the term *urushiol* for irritant substances from plants of the *Rhus* genus. *Agar-agar* is the Malay word for the seaweed from which the bacteriologist's agar is made; *catechu* and *sago* are also Malay.

Curare, guanine, ipecac, and *quinine* are derived from South American Indian words, as are *jaborandi,* the name of the plant source of pilocarpine, and perhaps *alastrim,* though this has also been traced to Portuguese *alastrar* 'to scatter'. Coumarin gets its name from *cumaru,* the word used by the Arawak Indians of Guiana for the tonka bean. *Papaya* (whence *papain*) is an altered form of a Carib term for fruits of the genus *Carica. Guaiacum* and its derivatives, from Spanish *guayaco,* are descended more remotely from a native Haitian word.

References to Literature and Mythology

I beg leave to ask the candid reader, how he can prove to me that all the heroes and heroines that have made him hope, fear, admire, hate, love, shed tears, and laugh till his sides were ready to burst, in novels and poems, are not in possession of as perfect credentials of their existence as the fattest of us? Common physical palpability is only a proof of mortality.

James Leigh Hunt
Men, Women and Books

It has been well said that the *caput medusae* is found invariably in textbooks of physical diagnosis but very seldom in patients. The condition, not less spectacular than rare, takes its name from the Medusa of Greek myth, whose head bore a tangle of snakes instead of hair.

Until the early part of the present century, a nodding acquaintance with the principal figures of Greek and Roman mythology was *de rigueur* for anyone with the least pretension to education and culture. That is why one finds, among the words in everyday use, such relics of ancient superstition as *January, jovial, martial, Saturday, siren, tantalize,* and *volcano.*

Medical terminology contains numerous references to classical myths. The otic *labyrinth* recalls the subterranean maze on the island of Crete, to the center of which Theseus penetrated to slay the Minotaur. Venus the love goddess is commemorated in *mons veneris* and *venereal disease.* The *tendo Achillis* refers to the only vulnerable spot of the Greek hero in the *Iliad. Atlas*, who bore the world on his shoulders, has given his name to the first cervical vertebra.

The dermatitis seen around the necks of workers exposed to flying sparks is called the *collar of Vulcan* after the Olympian blacksmith. *Lethargy* is related to the waters of Lethe, reputed in Greek myth to induce forgetfulness. *Morphine* is named for Morpheus, god of sleep, and *atropine* for Atropos, one of the three Fates, who was said to cut off one's thread of life at the moment appointed for him to die.

Narcissism recalls the handsome youth who fell in love with his reflection in the water. The term *Faun's beard* for a tuft of hair associated with spina bifida occulta refers to the woodland deities of Latin mythology. From the lecherous tribe of Satyrs, the Greek equivalent of Fauni, comes *satyriasis*. Galen used *satyriasis* for an enlargement of the temporal bones, fancied to resemble a satyr's horns. *Priapism* is named after Priapus, a fertility god. The myth of Oedipus is almost as widely known as the complex named for it. Proteus, who could change his appearance at will, has given us the adjective *protean*, referring to a disease of variable symptoms and signs, and the bacterial genus name *Proteus*.

Arachne, Hygieia, Hymen, Iris, and the Sphinx were mythical figures whose names are cognate with the Greek words or derivatives *arachnidism, hygiene, hymen, iris,* and *sphincter. Hermaphroditism* is named after the son of Hermes and Aphrodite, whose body fused with that of a nymph so that it possessed physical features of both sexes. Siren and the Cyclops are also commemorated in teratology. The name of Hebe, goddess of youth, appears in *hebephrenic* and *ephebiatrics*.

Ammonia was first extracted from *sal ammoniac*, a salt collected near the Libyan city of Ammonia, which was named for the shrine of Jupiter Ammon built there. This deity, identical with the Egyptian Amun or Amon, was often represented with a ram's head and large curved horns, hence the term *Ammon's horn* for the hippocampus. *Hippocampus*, a mythical sea monster, gave its name first to the seahorse and then to a part of the brain thought to resemble it.

Both the Aesculapian staff and the wand of Mercury often mistaken for it have their origins in mythology. The former, with one snake, is properly a symbol of medicine and healing. The latter, known as the *caduceus*, has two snakes and a pair of wings. Though it has no historical connection with medicine, it has been adopted by the United States Army as the symbol of the medical corps.

Works of literature become classics when they touch the most sensitive and universal chords of human nature, capturing the imagination and engaging the sympathies of readers of every capacity and temperament. It is not surprising that some of the figures of modern literature have become as familiar and real to us as historical personages and that they are referred to in our daily speech and writing. Everyone who understands English is expected to know that a Jekyll-Hyde personality is a changeable one, that a Scrooge is a miser, and that a Frankenstein's monster is an experiment or enterprise gone awry (if not amok). True classics have international currency. The adjectives *quixotic* (from Cervantes's Spanish classic) and *gargantuan* (from Rabelais's French one) are as familiar and meaningful to us as our home-grown *lilliputian*.

Nouns and adjectives borrowed by the language of medicine from modern literary classics are seldom either apt or useful. Most of them seem to have been introduced by medical writers who, pretending to an intimate acquaintance with literature, have succeeded only in revealing the superficiality and inexactness of their knowledge. A patient who repeatedly seeks medical attention for nonexistent illnesses without motives of gain is said to exemplify *Münchausen's syndrome*, a reference to the eighteenth century German cavalry officer Karl Friedrich Hieronymus, Baron von Munchhausen. A collection of fantastic hunting and travel stories attributed spuriously to the Baron was published in England in 1785 by Rudolph Erich Raspe, who respelled his hero's name *Munchausen*. Nowhere is there any record of an encounter between the Baron and a physician.

The *pickwickian syndrome* takes its name from Charles Dickens's *Pickwick Papers*. The reference is not to the title character but to Mr. Wardle's servant Joe, usually called simply "the fat boy," who falls asleep whenever he stops moving, even when he is on his feet. The connection between Mr. Pickwick and the disorder that bears his name (pulmonary alveolar hypoventilation associated with corpulence) is thus exceedingly tenuous. Equally farfetched is the name *Ondine's curse* or *Ondine syndrome*, which is taken from medieval German and Scandinavian folklore. The legend of the water nymph Undine has furnished material for many fictional and dramatic works, including a 1939 play by Jean Giraudoux, whence the French spelling with initial *O*. Giraudoux was faithful to his source, a nineteenth century novella by Friedrich de la Motte-Fouqué, until the end of the play, where he altered the way in which the nymph's mortal husband died. There is not much similarity between the curse of lethargy and paralysis (imposed not by Ondine but by her father) and primary alveolar hypoventilation.

Among other terms drawn from literature and legend may be mentioned the *Humpty-Dumpty syndrome* (the tendency to blame on a catastrophic accident all subsequent physical, mental, and social disabilities) and the *Alice in Wonderland syndrome* (*metamorphopsia*, in which the size, shape, and position of objects are incorrectly perceived). Sairy Gamp, the embodiment of all that a nurse should not be, is another of Dickens's characters, appearing in *Martin Chuzzlewit*.

Biblical narratives are the sources of the fanciful *Adam's apple* and the often misapplied *onanism*. *Mannitol* and its kin are named after *manna*, a vegetable exudation that in turn takes its name from the biblical *manna* (Exodus 16:13-36). Several popular names for hospitals are drawn from Bible sources. On *Mount Sinai* God gave Moses the tables of the law (Exodus 19); Solomon built his temple with the wood of the *cedars of Lebanon* (I Kings 5:6). The name of St. Luke the Evangelist has been adopted by many hospitals because he was called by St. Paul "the beloved physician" (Colossians 4:14). The parable of the *good Samaritan* appears in Luke 10:30-37, and the health-restoring pool of *Bethesda* is described in John 5:2-4. *Lazaret* and *lazar-house* are obsolete terms for a hospital for lepers or plague victims, derived from *lazar* 'a leper'. This word is based on the parable of the rich man and Lazarus in Luke 16:19-31, not on the name of the better-known Lazarus whom Jesus raised from the dead (John 11:1-44), and who is commemorated in the modern term *Lazarus syndrome*. In Dutch, *lazarus* is slang for 'drunk' or 'crazy'.

Geographic Terms

We find that medicinal plants are named in various ways. . . . Some retain the names of the regions from which they were first imported. Thus, Median apples are called after Media, where they were first found. Punic apples, or pomegranates, are brought from Punicia, which we call Carthage. Ligusticum, commonly known as lovage, is imported from

Liguria in Italy. Rhubarb gets its name from the River Rha in
Barbary—at least, so says Ammianus. To these we may add
santonica, fenugreek, persicaria and a host of others.

François Rabelais
Gargantua and Pantagruel

The attachment of place-names to common things is a practice of
great antiquity. Since the finest paper obtainable was once that made
at Pergamon in Asia Minor (the birthplace of Galen), this paper came
to be known simply as *pergamon*, of which *parchment* is a corruption.
Place-names are the bases of many other English common nouns,
including *bayonet* (from Bayonne, France), *canary* (Canary Islands),
coach (Kocs, Hungary), *copper* (Cyprus), *gauze* (Gaza), *peach*
(Persia), and *sherry* (Xeres, Spain). Some of our nouns have been
adapted from place-adjectives: *cordovan* (from Cordoba, Spain),
majolica (Majorcan), *spaniel* (Spanish), *suede* (Swedish), *turquoise*
(Turkish), and *wiener* (Viennese). Others refer to nations or races:
cravat (Croatian), *slave* (Slav), and *vandal* (Vandals, ancient
Teutonic tribe).

Though most of the geographic allusions in medical terminology
are straightforward, like *Aleppo boil* and *Zanzibar swelling*, in some
cases the original form of the place-name is obscured or lost. For
example, *vernix*, a medieval Latin word used unchanged in obstetrics,
and as the corruption *varnish* in the vernacular, evolved from
Berenike, the ancient name of Benghazi (Libya), where varnish was
first made. The disease caused by *Coxiella burnetti* was called *Q* (for
'query') *fever* before its cause was discovered. Afterward this term
stuck because it was thought by many to refer to the state of
Queensland in Australia.

In the nineteenth chapter of Genesis is recounted the destruction
of the Cities of the Plain by fire and brimstone. One of these, Sodom,
has given its name to *sodomy*. The *risus sardonicus* of tetany and
strychnine poisoning was supposedly first seen in persons poisoned
with a plant that grew on Sardinia. The Latin phrase, which is the
germ of English *sardonic*, means 'Sardinian grin'. *Jalap*, a cathartic
now out of fashion, was named after the Mexican city of Jalapa
(Aztec *Xalapan*). Though *balsam of Peru* now comes almost
exclusively from El Salvador, pharmacologists can be excused for
clinging to the shorter term. Tolú, a city in Colombia, has given its
name to *balsam of Tolu* and its derivatives *toluene* and related
compounds.

Gum arabic is the source of *arabinose*, both chemically and etymologically. *Indole* bears a similar relation to *indigo*, a dyestuff from India. *Bengal rose, Congo red, Coomassie* (Kumasi, Ghana) *blue*, and *Sudan III* are other medically important coloring agents with geographic names. *Seltzer*, an old term for effervescent mineral water, which is perpetuated in the trade names of various modern patent medicines, is a corruption of *Selterser* 'from Selters', referring to the Prussian village where the water was obtained. *Epsom salts* are named after an English town in Surrey whose mineral waters owe their medicinal effect chiefly to a high concentration of magnesium sulfate. *Magnesium*, incidentally, is indebted for its name to the ancient city of Magnesia in Thessaly.

From Verona, Italy, came *Veronal*, the trade name of barbital, which still drags out a haphazard existence as an occasional poison in murder mysteries. The *nitroprusside* radical gets part of its name from Prussia, by way of *prussic acid* (also beloved by writers of sensational literature) and earlier *Prussian blue*, a primitive name for ferric ferrocyanide. *Bedlam* is a corruption of *St. Mary of Bethlehem*, the name of an asylum for lunatics established in London early in the fifteenth century. The term became generic for a mental institution (or, as in Bunyan's *Pilgrim's Progress*, for an inmate of such an institution) before passing into metaphor.

Because the epicanthal folds of children with certain genetic abnormalities gave their faces an Asiatic configuration (in the view of some Western observers), they were dubbed *mongoloid*. The lay term for conjoined twins is *Siamese*, after Chang and Eng, who were born in Siam in 1811 and were for many years a major attraction in P. T. Barnum's sideshows. *Thalassemia*, from classical Greek *thalassa* 'the sea', is another name for *Mediterranean anemia*, a congenital hemolytic disorder affecting particularly the races inhabiting the Mediterranean littoral. *Shepherd's Bush hemoglobin* is named for a suburb of London.

Bougie, French for 'candle', got its surgical meaning from the early practice of making dilators out of waxed linen. The French word has a geographic origin, being derived from the town of Bougie (Arabic *Bijiyah*) in Algeria, which carried on a trade in wax. Typhus was once known as the *Hungarian disease*, and pellagra as *Italian* (or *Lombardy*) *leprosy*. When trench fever was first recognized during World War I, some called it *Polish influenza (influenza polonica)*. Until comparatively recent times, cholera was always distinguished as

Asiatic. The sixteenth century term *morbus Gallicus* 'French disease' for syphilis naturally found little favor in France, where the affliction was commonly fathered on the Spanish.

Ethnic or national designations such as these are generally thought too opprobrious nowadays to obtain international currency. German *Englische Krankheit,* Dutch *Engelse ziekte,* and Danish *engelsk syge* become *rickets* in English; the literal translation, 'English disease', is never seen. During World War I, *German measles* was rechristened *liberty measles* in the United States, but the new term survived no longer than *liberty cabbage,* which was substituted for *sauerkraut* in the same era. German measles of course has nothing to do with Germany. The adjective was attached with the somewhat whimsical sense of *variant* or *illusory.* At times rubella has also been called *French measles.* These unscientific terms drive laymen and even physicians to amusing shifts in speaking of rubeola, which may be called *regular, hard,* or even *American measles.*

Taxonomic terms often include geographic references, usually at the species level: *Dracunculus medinensis* (of Medina); *Brucella melitensis* (Maltese); *Clonorchis sinensis* (Chinese); *Schistosoma japonicum* (Japanese); *Trypanosoma gambiense* and *rhodesiense.* Numerous species of *Salmonella* are named after cities where outbreaks of salmonellosis have occurred: *S. dar-es-salaam, S. eastbourne, S. hartford, S. montevideo, S. newport, S. saint paul.*

Several American place-names have found their way into the medical lexicon. *Haverhill fever, Boston exanthem, San Joaquin Valley fever* (coccidioidomycosis), and *Rocky Mountain spotted fever* are among the more familiar. *Tularemia* and *Francisella tularensis* are named after Tulare County, California. *Coxsackievirus* was first isolated in 1950 from a patient in Coxsackie, New York. Other American cities are commemorated in *Milwaukee brace, Chicago disease* (North American blastomycosis), and *St. Louis encephalitis.*

Eponyms

Some medicinal herbs bear the name of him who first discovered them, cultivated them, or investigated and published their virtues; thus mercuriale, from Mercury; panacea, from Panace, the daughter of Aesculapius; armois, from Artemis, also called

Diana; eupatoria, from King Eupator; euphorbium, from Euphorbius, physician to King Juba; clymenos, from Clymenus; alcibiadon, from Alcibiades; and gentian, from Gentius, King of Sclavonia.

François Rabelais
Gargantua and Pantagruel

Except for Linnaean taxonomy and perhaps geography, no system of nomenclature ever devised contains as many names of things derived from names of persons as does the language of medicine. *Addison's disease* and *Zenker's diverticulum* are usually called eponyms, though the traditional sense of *eponym* is 'a person for whom something is named'. Webster records and compounds the modern confusion by giving, as an alternative definition of *eponym*, 'a name (as of a drug or a disease) based on or derived from an eponym'.

Terms incorporating personal names have become so abundant in medical parlance that physicians who have not been thus immortalized (perhaps no longer the majority) are beginning to resist the creation of more eponyms. Though *Hansen's disease* and *Down's syndrome* continue to gain favor as less offensive alternatives to *leprosy* and *mongolism*, respectively, the general trend is to let eponyms fall into disuse. *Eustachian, fallopian, müllerian,* and *wolffian* are no longer part of official anatomic nomenclature. Still, it will probably be decades before they drop out of daily use.

A principal objection to the use of personal names is the difficulty of spelling them correctly. Although the developer of Burow's solution was German, Americans seem irresistibly tempted to make him an English Burrows or Burroughs. The final *s* of *Chagas, Coombs, Graves, Homans, Krebs, Meigs, Perthes, Sims,* and *Wilms* is often erroneously separated by an apostrophe, while an extraneous *s* is often engrafted on *Ayre, Down, Towne,* and *Water,* a cluster of names offering limitless possibilities to the mnemonic addict.

As for pronunciation, American physicians seem more interested in consistency than in correctness. *Lutembacher* and *Gaucher,* usually pronounced more or less as though they were German, are actually French. By contrast, French pronunciations are often imposed on *eustachian,* formed from the name of an Italian anatomist, and *Behçet,* which is Turkish. *Gelpi retractor,* usually mispronounced with hard *g*, is sometimes further transformed into *guppy retractor*, no doubt because of its delicate piscine contour. So, too, the rechristening of the Gigli bone saw as *jiggly saw* is not without a certain aptness.

The layman often fails to recognize an eponym as such and tries to render what he has heard with a common noun: *charcoal* (for Charcot) *joints, change-strokes* (for Cheyne-Stokes) *breathing, roaring shock* (for Rorschach) *test,* and *silk stocking* (for Sengstaken) *tube.* Consider also *leg of Perthes* (for Legg-Perthes disease) and *cushionoid* (for cushingoid). Physicians have occasionally been led into such errors, too. The *corpora Arantii* of the cardiac valves are not 'orange bodies' (as if medieval Latin *aurantia*, the issue of an irregular union between Latin *aurum* 'gold' and Arabic *naranj* 'orange') but 'the bodies of Arantius' (Italian anatomist Giulio Aranzi). The *Sippy diet* is not called that because much of it can be sipped, but because it was devised by Dr. Bertram Sippy.

The reverse error—finding a proper name where there is none— is by no means limited to the laity. Terms borrowed from German have often been thought eponymous because of the German practice of capitalizing the first letter of every noun. *Grenz* rays are not named after a pioneer radiologist. *Grenz* is German for 'margin' or 'border' and refers to the wavelength of the rays, which lies on the border between ultraviolet and x-ray. *Wickel,* the name of a physio-therapeutic technique in which the patient is tightly rolled in a wet sheet, is German for 'wrapping'. The German for 'iodine', *Jod,* has sometimes been taken for an eponym when *Jod-Basedowsche Krankheit* 'iodine-induced Basedow's disease' has been turned into English *Jod-Basedow's disease.*

Brown mixture is named for its color, not its inventor. The *coudé catheter* was not designed by Dr. Coudé; the word is French for 'bent'. *Emerson's* (for *emesis*) *basin* is a hardy perennial among nonprofessional hospital personnel, and even nurses are often guilty of *Collagen's disease, Caisson's disease,* and *Plantar's* (or *planter's*?) *wart.* A British medical writer whose name, printed at the head of one of his articles, was followed by "A. B. Cantab.," indicating that he held a Bachelor of Arts degree from Cambridge, learned to his astonishment that bibliographers had given a nonexistent Dr. Cantab credit as coauthor. The nineteenth century parasitologist Hlava suffered an even worse fate when credit for his work on amebiasis was transferred to "O. Uplavici." Actually "O Uplavici" was the title of Hlava's paper; it means 'On Dysentery' in Czech.

A compound eponym may refer to more than one person (*Hand-Schüller-Christian, Laurence-Moon-Biedl*), or it may be a double name borne by one person: *Brown-Séquard* and *Hoppe-Seyler*, with hyphen; *Ramsay Hunt* and *Graham Steell*, without. In *Fitz–Hugh—Curtis syndrome* the longer hyphen joins the names of two persons, the former of which is a hyphenated name. In contrast, the *Swyer-James/McLeod syndrome* was described by Swyer and James in one paper and by McLeod in another.

When the same name is attached to two or more diseases, distinguishing phrases must be added: *Paget's disease of the nipple, Paget's disease of bone; von Recklinghausen's disease of bone, von Recklinghausen's disease of skin.* The *Goltz-Gorlin syndrome* is focal dermal hypoplasia, whereas the *Gorlin-Goltz syndrome* includes basal cell nevi and other ectodermal dysplasias and anomalies.

Often a common noun qualified by a proper one is omitted, and the personal name is left to stand alone. A *Kelly hemostat* is usually just a *Kelly*, and few physicians take the time to say or write *Foley catheter* or *Babinski sign*. Sometimes a proper noun is abbreviated beyond recognition. Only the first syllable of the name of George Papanicolaou, the pioneer in cervical cytology, is preserved in *Pap smear*. Initialisms that conceal eponyms include *NPH insulin* ('neutral protamine, Hagedorn'), *BCG vaccine* ('bacillus of Calmette and Guérin'), and *BAL* ('British antilewisite', which contains the name of the chemist W. Lee Lewis).

We often use compound or derivative words containing proper names without marking them as such with capital letters: *bartholinectomy, chagoma, descemetocele, galenical, graafian, marfanoid, pagetic, parkinsonism, politzerize, roentgenogram, skenitis, voltage.* Species names in taxonomy are also spelled with small initial letters even when derived from proper nouns: *Rickettsia parkeri, Schistosoma mansoni, Trypanosoma cruzi, Shigella boydii.*

Genus names, on the other hand, are spelled with a capital letter whether eponymous or not. The suffixes *-ia* (less often *-a*) and *-ella* (less often *-iella*) are used to turn proper names into genus names: *Rauwolfia, Leishmania, Gaffkya, Brucella, Pasteurella, Klebsiella.* A genus of tropical plant once used as an anthelminthic was called *Quassia* by Linnaeus after Graman Quassi, a native of Surinam who discovered its medicinal properties. The last *e* of *Herellea* is part of the name *d'Hérelle*, but the *n* in *Miyagawanella*, which commemorates Yoneji Miyagawa, has been inserted for euphony. In contrast,

Shigella omits the final vowel of the name of Kiyoshi Shiga. *Nicotiana*, from *Nicot*, and *Sabouraudites*, from *Sabouraud*, vary from the usual pattern of genus names.

The name of a disease may depend on the doctor's nationality. In English-speaking countries, thyrotoxicosis with exophthalmia is known as *Graves' disease*, after the Irish physician who described it in 1835. But speakers of German commonly name it after Basedow, and in Italy it is known as *Flaiani's disease*.

Not every medical eponym refers to the discoverer or inventor of the thing named. Taxonomic terms have sometimes been chosen to honor famous public figures. *Cinchona*, the genus name of the plant source of quinine, has no connection with *quina*, the Indian name for 'Peruvian bark' and the word from which *quinine* is derived. Linnaeus chose the name *Cinchona* to commemorate the Spanish Countess of Chinchon, who was cured of a fever with the bark during a sojourn in South America. *Serratia* is named after Serafino Serrati, who (according to the Italians) invented the steamship. *Listeria* honors Lord Lister, who died long before the genus was discovered. The brand name *Listerine*, however, was coined in his lifetime, and he spent vast sums of money in unsuccessful efforts to suppress the term, which seemed to link him with a product that had no connection with him or his work. The Family APGAR Questionnaire contains an acronym (*adaptability, partnership, growth, affection, resolve*) deliberately formed to match the name of Virginia Apgar, whose scoring system for the health status of neonates is used throughout the world.

Sadism and *masochism* are named after two novelists, the French Count (usually called Marquis) de Sade and the Austrian Leopold von Sacher-Masoch, in whose works these perversions were described. *Christmas disease* was first identified in a patient whose surname was Christmas. *Musset's sign*, a rhythmic nodding of the head seen in aortic valvular regurgitation, is named for the French poet and novelist Alfred de Musset, who was so afflicted. *Daltonism*, an old term for 'colorblindness', refers to the English physicist John Dalton, whose inability to distinguish colors occasionally led to his wearing clothing whose hues scandalized his fellow Quakers.

Pott's fracture is named after the English surgeon Percivall Pott, who devised a method of treating this severe form of ankle fracture after suffering such an injury himself. *Carrión's disease* takes its name from the young South American bacteriologist who elucidated its nature by inoculating himself with it—an experiment that proved fatal. The *hunterian chancre* recalls another self-inoculation, by the English anatomist John Hunter. *Rickettsia prowazekii*, the organism that causes epidemic typhus, claimed the lives of both Ricketts and von Prowazek.

HeLa cells, malignant human cells grown in tissue culture, are all descended from a cervical carcinoma from which Henrietta Lacks, commemorated in the name, died in 1951. *Jeryl Lynn mumps vaccine* is prepared from a strain of virus originally isolated from a patient of that name. An antibiotic first identified in 1945 in wound drainage from Margaret Tracey was called *bacitracin* in her honor. *Legionnaire's disease* and its causative organism, *Legionella pneumophila*, have both been named so recently that the connection with the American Legion is familiar to all.

The *caesarean section* has traditionally been traced to Julius Caesar, who was allegedly delivered by this means. *Chorea* was formerly *chorea Sancti Viti* 'St. Vitus' dance', after the third century Roman martyr who miraculously cured the son of the Emperor Diocletian of a convulsive disorder, and in recompense was accused of sorcery and tortured to death. Both erysipelas and ergotism been called *St. Anthony's fire* after Vitus's contemporary, St. Anthony of Egypt. The seventeenth century Danish anatomist after whom *Stensen's duct* is named made his famous discovery while still in his twenties. He later renounced medicine and died a Roman Catholic bishop. Periumbilical metastases in gastric carcinoma are called *Sister Joseph's sign* after the director of St. Mary's Hospital in Rochester, Minnesota, who first drew this finding to the attention of Dr. William Mayo.

Modern medicine has not completely lost sight of the colossal figures who presided over its origins. A herbal medicine or simple is still called a *galenical*, because Galen preferred vegetable drugs to mineral ones. The *great vein of Galen* in the cerebral circulation will probably keep that unofficial name for a long time to come. *Hippocratic clubbing* and the *hippocratic facies* are not named merely to honor the Father of Medicine. Both digital swelling in empyema and the face of the moribund patient were accurately described by Hippocrates in his *Prognostics*. *Hippocrates' sleeve*, however, is a fanciful term for a conical linen bag used as a filter in the preparation of drugs. It was also used to make a spiced wine, which was therefore called *Hippocras* or *Ypocras*.

The most telling objection to the continued manufacture of medical eponyms is not the difficulty of pronouncing *Chvostek* or *Guillain-Barré* or of deciding whether to say and write *Tourette, la Tourette, de la Tourette,* or *Gilles de la Tourette syndrome.* A more troublesome feature of eponymy is that it produces lexically empty terms—words that supply no clue to their reference or bearing. Quite apart from the needless trouble that this causes the learner, it runs directly counter to the spirit of scientific terminology, which strives for order, consistency, and at least some measure of ready intelligibility.

An eponym is rather more liable to undergo semantic mutation than a term coined from meaningful language material. Many diseases are no longer defined by the criteria laid down by the persons whose names they still bear. Someone has determined that only half of Hodgkin's original cases had Hodgkin's disease. Given two eponyms, one has no way of knowing whether they refer to related concepts, are synonymous, or have no logical association whatever. These semantic disadvantages of eponymy are compounded by medical writers who constantly burden our technical lexicon with newly created ones.

References and Readings

Comroe JH Jr: Frankenstein, Pickwick and Ondine. *Am Rev Resp Dis* 1975;111:689-692.

Dalessio DJ: Hyperventilation, the vapors, effort syndrome, neurasthenia: anxiety by any other name is just as disturbing. *J Am Med Assoc* 1978;239:1401-1402.

Hippocrates: *Works.* Cambridge, Harvard University Press, 1972.

Jablonski S: *Illustrated Dictionary of Eponymic Syndromes and Diseases.* Philadelphia, W. B. Saunders Co., 1969.

Modern Coinages, Abbreviations, and Trade Names

Modern Coinages

When things newly discovered demand terms newly framed to express them clearly, there is no objection to the coinage of words, provided that the process is carried out with judgment and taste.... Words of recent fabrication always find ready acceptance when they are built out of Greek material.

Horace
The Art of Poetry

The role of Latin as the lingua franca of Western scholars in the post-Renaissance world was a major reason why the terminologies of the emerging natural sciences consisted chiefly of Latin and Latinized Greek words. But there was a second and no less cogent reason: Latin was a dead language. No longer anyone's mother tongue, it was hardly more subject to alteration or corruption through use than the alphabet or the multiplication table.

Latin afforded a vast fund of words to which specific technical meanings might be arbitrarily assigned without danger of conflict or confusion with vernacular or idiomatic usages. The early anatomists

85

found it more practical to build up a nomenclature consisting of words such as *femur, ilium, acetabulum,* and *gluteus* than to assign one of these meanings exclusively to a vernacular word like *hip,* which in everyday use could mean any of them, or all of them together. Moreover, Latin and Greek were gold mines of root words and affixes from which the scientist could fashion new terms that, if not altogether self-explanatory, were at least readily understood and remembered by any educated person.

These principles apply just as truly today as they did 400 years ago. Whether one likes it or not, our language retains a cumbersome and foreign-seeming terminology consisting of borrowings and adaptations from dead languages—deader than ever now that they no longer figure as integral parts of a secondary education. The difficulty of changing to a new terminology based on the vernacular may be judged from the extreme slowness with which authoritative revisions in nomenclature are learned, accepted, and adopted by the medical profession. Although *eustachian tube* and *fallopian tube* were both officially laid to rest a generation ago, they still flourish in daily speech and even in textbooks. The genus names *Staphylococcus* and *Streptococcus* live on despite the efforts of Bergey and others since 1948 to substitute *Micrococcus.*

The history of technical coinages is a fascinating subject of study. The interaction of terms used by Hippocrates with others made up yesterday, the often ingenious and sometimes violent adaptation of classical material to new concepts, the evolution and corruption of roots and affixes, the devious patterns of analogy and opposition that evolve among fabricated words, the vagaries of their pronunciation— all should be of more than passing interest to the physician, who says and writes these terms every day of his professional career.

Almost no new technical term is created out of thin air. It was once believed that *gas,* a word proposed in the seventeenth century by the Belgian monk and physician Jan van Helmont, was a pure invention. Later a passage was found in his writings that traced *gas* to Greek *chaos* 'formless void'. *Gas* is nevertheless unusual in containing but a single meaningful element (morpheme or formative); most technical neologisms contain at least two. Other exceptions to this rule are *sol, gel, gene,* and *heme* (British *haem*).

New words are built up from existing lexical elements—that is, from groups of letters (sounds) already having conventional meanings—by two processes, affixation and compounding. *Affixation* refers to the attachment of a prefix (*non-*, *peri-*) or suffix (*-osis, -ation*) to a word or stem. *Compounding* is the joining of two or more words or stems, as in *pyosalpinx* and *erythrocyte*. The distinction between affixation and compounding is not so clear-cut as linguists would like it to be. In both processes one sees the operation of one of the most universal and abiding laws of language: phrases often repeated become condensed into single words, with phonetic simplification and with relaxation of the grammatical rules that normally govern relations within a phrase.

In Indo-European languages (including Greek, Latin, and English), where inflectional changes consistently occur at the very end of a word, the difference between prefix and suffix goes far beyond a merely accidental difference of position. Whereas a prefix ordinarily modifies the *meaning* of the word to which it is attached, a suffix usually changes the grammatical category or *function* of the word. Thus, the prefixes *a-, in-, non-,* and *un-* generally negate or reverse the idea contained in the base word: *asystole, insoluble, nonsteroid, unsaturated*. In each case, the base word, by remaining the final element, retains its grammatical function; that is, it does not change from one part of speech to another.

Suffixes, on the other hand, by operating at the end of a word, alter its grammatical nature. I am not concerned here with inflectional suffixes, such as those used to make nouns plural, but rather with derivational suffixes, which extend the usefulness of a base word by changing it to another part of speech. Thus, *-al, -ic, -ish,* and *-ous* turn the base word to an adjective; *-ation, -ism, -osis,* to a noun; and *-ate, -ify, -ize,* to a verb. It should be noted that a few noun suffixes change meaning rather than function: *-ess, -ette, -ine, -trix*.

Most of the prefixes used in technical terminology are prepositions borrowed more or less intact from classical languages. The Greek *a-* (*alpha privativum*) 'without' appears in hundreds of technical terms. When the word to which it is attached begins with a vowel or *h*, this prefix resumes its original form, *an-*, as in *anisocytosis, anencephalic,* and *anhydrous*. This *an-* is not to be confused with *ana-*, an unrelated preposition meaning 'up to', seen in *anabolic* and *anasarca*.

In *atrophy* and *apnea* the prefixed *a-* is usually pronounced as in *cat*; in *aphasia* and *anemia*, as in *canoe*; and in *achlorhydria* and *asystole*, as in *cake*. The initial *a-* is a source of no little confusion in spoken French, where, for example, *la symétrie* 'symmetry' and *l'asymétrie* 'asymmetry' are pronounced exactly the same. In English, the prefixed *a-* is sometimes taken by the layman for the indefinite article and dropped at will: *'stigmatism, 'rrhythmia.*

Although the Greek preposition *anti* 'against' and the Latin *ante* 'before' are usually pronounced alike in English, they are seldom confused. Strongly contrasted in meaning as prefixes, they are ultimately the same preposition. So in English a table may be said to be *before* or *against* a wall. Before a vowel or *h, anti-* becomes *ant-* (*antacid, anthelminthic*), but *ante-* does not. *Antibrachium*, anatomic Latin for 'forearm' is a medieval variation on the more logical *antebrachium*. (But cf. *anticipation.*)

Latin *pro* corresponds roughly to the same word in Greek, but the closest Latin equivalent to Greek *pro* is *prae*, which in modern usage is spelled *pre*. This word originally meant 'in front of' but later took on the additional meaning 'earlier than'. In a number of medical terms of recent vintage, *pre-* plays an adjectival role with the sense of "nascent" or "preclinical": *prediabetes, preleukemia, preeclampsia. Pro-* conveys a related but distinct idea in *prothrombin, proinsulin, promyelocyte.* In *progeria* it means 'early' or 'precocious'. A *prodrug* has been defined as 'a compound that is therapeutically inactive until biotransformed into its parent compound' (a striking instance of mangled metaphor: how can a thing be "transformed into its parent"?).

Greek *eso-* and *exo-* meaning 'inside' and 'outside', are found in several pairs of terms like *eso-/exophoria* and *eso-/exotropia.* Apparently, though, *eso-* played no part in the origin of *esophagus* (British *oesophagus*), whose etymology is obscure. *Intussusception* and its derivatives are the only English words formed with the Latin adverb *intus* 'within'.

Occasionally, the prefix *in-* leads to ambiguity, since its force may be intensive (*infection, inflammation*), negative (*innocuous, insoluble*), or locative (*injection, inoculation*). In the last sense it closely resembles the Germanic *in-* seen in *inborn* and *indwelling.* Latin words that have come into English through French change initial *in-* to *en-* (*entire*), though some also preserve the classical form of the prefix as a varient (*enquire, inquire*). In the majority of modern words from Latin beginning with *in-*, the prefix has a negative value, just like that of English *un-* and Greek *a-*. Hence the ambiguity of *inflammable*, which was officially been replaced by *flammable* in the labeling of containers. (The pathologist, however, still diagnoses *inflammation.*) Before certain consonants, negative *in-* changes by assimilation: *illiterate, impervious, irreversible.* The negative *in-* is never prefixed to a word already beginning with *in-*: *noninflammatory, unintelligible.*

The negative and reversive prefix *dis-* (*disagree, disorientation*) cannot claim direct descent from Latin *dis-*, which meant 'dual, twofold' (*disrupt* 'break in two'). Rather, modern *dis-* evolved from Latin *de-* (still active, as in *defibrinate, decarboxylase*) under the influence of Greek *dys-*. Remnants of confusion survive in a few doublets: *descant, discant; despatch, dispatch.* Modern word makers seem to prefer the Greek form: *dysfunction, dysrhythmia.*

In classical Greek, *dys-* conveyed the general meaning 'bad, unfavorable, difficult' and took on a more specific coloring from the word to which it was attached. This lability of meaning continues to the present day, for in modern medical terminology *dys-* may mean 'painful' (*dyspareunia*), 'difficult' (*dyspnea*), 'abnormal' (*dysgenesis*), or even 'lack of' (*dyssynergia*). In *dysuria* its meaning vacillates, in common usage, between 'difficult' and 'painful'.

Peroral and *pervaginal* are superfluous adjectives formed irregularly from the Latin phrases *per os* and *per vaginam.* No doubt modeled on similar usages are medical expressions in which *per* acts as an English preposition: *per vein, per tube, per Foley.* In a few terms, the prefix *per-* is not the Latin preposition meaning 'through' but the Latin intensifying prefix: *pertussis* 'a terrible cough'; *peroxide* 'having an extra amount of oxygen'. *Extravert*, coined by C. G. Jung, early became *extrovert* by analogy with *introvert* and words containing a connecting *o*, despite the nearer analogy of *extradition* and *extraocular.* *Extrasystole* is not a learned word containing the prefix *extra-* but just a fusion of the English phrase *extra systole.*

Suffixes, as noted earlier, serve mainly to extend the functional capabilities of words by changing them from one part of speech to another. Suffixes that make adjectives from nouns are among the most prolific. Greek *-ikos* has thousands of offspring in general and technical language, most of them formed from Greek noun stems (*cyclic, demonic, Doric, lyric, panic, ascitic, diabetic, emetic, hepatic, prostatic*) but a few from Latin (*acetic, pubic*) or other languages (*scorbutic, alcoholic*). When the base word ends in *-a*, the suffix may lose its *i*: *cardiac, ·hemophiliac, maniac*; but contrast *anemic, eosinophilic, manic.*

The use of the corresponding suffix *-icus* in Latin was more restricted than that of -*ikos*. The usual means of converting a Latin noun into an adjective was by adding -*alis* to its stem. This suffix is found in modern terms of Latin origin (*anginal, dental, pedal*) and also frequently attached to Greek stems (*coccal, dermal, laryngeal*). When *l* comes at or near the end of the stem, -*aris* is substituted for -*alis* by dissimilation (*alveolar, bulbar, muscular, vulvar*). (*Osmolal* was created in defiance of this rule to provide an arbitrary distinction from *osmolar*.) Occasionally, this alternative suffix is found when *l* is at or near the beginning of the stem: *lumbar, columnar, plantar, linear*. Since nearly all Latin diminutive suffixes contain *l*, adjectives formed from Latin diminutives generally end in -*ar*: *lamellar, radicular, areolar, tonsillar*.

The suffix -*ilis* and its English forms -*ile* and -*il* are found almost exclusively with Latin *i*-stem nouns and verbs: *febrile, fragile, penile, volatile, civil, fossil*. The English adjectival suffix -*ary* may represent either Latin -*aris* (*biliary, miliary*) or -*arius* (*coronary, urinary*). Most nouns ending in -*ary* are formed from the related Latin agent suffix -*arius* (-*arium*): *depilatory, pessary, ovary*.

Latin -*osus* is usually rendered by -*ous* in English (*calculous, adenomatous, nervous*) but occasionally by -*ose* (*racemose, rugose, varicose*). In chemistry -*ic* (from -*ikos*) and -*ous* have been adopted as suffixes for positive ions, the former signifying the ion of higher valence (*ferric, ferrous; nitric, nitrous*). Adjectival suffixes are often used in technical parlance to set up such arbitrary distinctions: contrast *mammary* and *mammal, bilious* and biliary, tertian and *tertiary*.

In classical Greek, -*itis* was just another adjectival suffix, with which, for example, *arthron* 'joint' could be turned into *arthritis* 'pertaining to a joint'. To Hippocrates the phrase *arthritis nosos* meant ' a disease of joints'. In time the noun was dropped and the adjective was used by itself with the same meaning as the full expression. By convention the suffix -*itis* now has a sharply restricted meaning, 'inflammation of'. It should be noted that -*itis* is a feminine ending, agreeing with *nosos* 'disease'. For this reason, medical nouns ending in -*itis* are feminine, and any qualifying Latin adjectives must also be feminine: *linitis plastica, retinitis pigmentosa*.

The related masculine adjectival ending, -*ites*, does not appear as such in modern medical terminology; *ascites* and *tympanites* are formed on a different principle. However, -*ites* may be considered the origin of the widely used suffix *-ite*, as in *anthracite, dynamite, somite, dendrite, Levite, pre-Raphaelite, suburbanite, Brooklynite*, and even the fictitious *cellulite* (but not *nitrite* or *sulfite*).

The ending *-itic* is used to form adjectives from nouns ending in *-itis*, even if the base noun has been corrupted (*pleurisy, pleuritic*). It also appears in a few terms, such as *pruritic* and *syphilitic*, where it does not properly belong. *Diphtheritic* was derived from the original name of the disease, *diphtheritis*, coined (as *diphthérite*) by Bretonneau in 1826. In 1855 he renamed the disease *diphthérie* as a concession to the many who objected that the earlier term was not formed on classical or even contemporary models (Greek *diphthera* means 'membrane'). Though English, French, Spanish, and German now favor shorter and more correct forms for the noun, Italian *difterite* and Dutch *diphteritis* perpetuate Bretonneau's lapse, as does our adjective *diphtheritic* and its congeners in most other Western languages.

The chemical and pharmaceutical suffix *-ine* has a long and intricate history. In its primitive form it was used in Greek and Latin to make adjectives from nouns, particularly from place-names: Greek *Byzantinos*; Latin *marinus, femininus*, and even *Latinus*. Variants of this suffix, formed with other vowels, appear in *Romanus, mediterraneus*, and *tribunus*. Among modern anatomic terms containing adjectives formed on the old models are *pes anserinus, cauda equina*, and *tensor veli palatini*. Such English nouns as *intestine* and *saline* were once adjectives of the same family.

In modern English, *-ine*, derived from Latin *-inus* by way of French, appears in diminutives (*figurine; cholerine*, an obsolete term for mild cholera), feminines (*heroine*), and attributives. In the early days of modern science, this suffix was used widely and indiscriminately to create names for substances newly discovered, prepared, or extracted. Presently its use in general chemistry is confined to names for elements of the class known as halogens (*chlorine, bromine, fluorine, iodine*) and for certain simple compounds (*aniline, amine, phosphine, pyridine*). In biochemistry and pharmacology the ending *-ine* appears in the names of numerous substances differing greatly in origin and composition. Except for the names of alkaloids (*atropine, morphine*), amino acids (*tyrosine, leucine*), and intermediary metabolites (*cytosine, guanine*), most of these terms have lost the final *-e* in modern practice, which, however, is far from uniform: *adrenalin* (but *epinephrine*), *albumin, antivenin, digitoxin, elastin, gelatin, hemoglobin, insulin* (but *thyroxine*), *lanolin, lecithin, penicillin* (but *tetracycline*), *riboflavin, trypsin, tuberculin.* It is interesting to note that most of the terms that have lost the final *-e* formerly belonged to a large class of neuter nouns in pharmaceutical Latin ending in *-inum,* whereas most of those that retain the *e* belonged to the feminine class ending in *-ina.* Incidentally, adjectives that end in *-crine* (*endocrine, holocrine*) get their final syllable from Greek *krinein* 'to separate'. Many of these formerly ended in *-crinic* or *-crinal* but were cut down by the potent example of the many other words ending in the adjectival *-ine.* Similarly, the final syllable of *chromaffin, paraffin,* and related words comes from Latin *affinis* 'akin'.

The pronunciation of *-ine* in scientific terms varies as erratically as in lay language. (Note the difference of vowel lengths in *Alpine* and *Florentine* and of accent in *figurine* and *heroine.*) In medicine, *-ine* now usually rhymes with *dean,* with certain peculiar exceptions. It is usually clipped short, with the neutral vowel sound that has favored the shorter spelling *-in* in other cases, in *thyroxine, epinephrine,* and *ephedrine,* while it often rhymes with *wine* in *iodine, strychnine,* and *quinine.* Contrast the sounds of the *i*'s in the closely related *quinidine* and in the British pronunciation QUEE-nyne. Words ending in *-ine* are frequently accented on the last syllable (chlor-EEN, vac-CEEN, ah-MEEN), probably by analogy with French borrowings such as *machine* and *ravine.*

Although at first *betaine, cocaine, codeine,* and *caffeine* had three syllables apiece, in each case the *i* of the suffix later fused with the preceding vowel by a process called syneresis to form a diphthong, so that *betaine* and *cocaine* (as well as all other 'caines') now rhyme with *rain; codeine* and *caffeine,* with   *keen.* The *Oxford English Dictionary* castigates Selmi for having "blunderingly" derived the term *ptomaine* (Italian *ptomaina*) from Greek *ptoma* 'corpse' and observes that the more correct form *ptomatine* would have obviated the "illiterate" pronunciation of *ptomaine* with two syllables. *Protein* was regularly given three syllables in English until the 1940s. Biochemists habitually pronounce *cysteine* to rhyme with *wine* so as to avoid confusion with *cystine.* Although in *benzoin* the vowel group *oi* is usually made a diphthong (as in *oil*), the vowels are kept distinct in *allantoin* and *heroin.*

The suffix *-ine* is immensely popular with pharmacologists and drug manufacturers. A survey of several hundred brand names chosen at random shows that 40 percent end with the sound of *n*, the short vowel sound (spelled *-in* or *-yn*) predominating 3:1 over the longer sound (spelled *-ine*, occasionally *-ene* or *een*). Among generic names for drugs, a staggering 65 percent have a final *n* sound, but here the *-ine* pronunciation leads *-in* 2:1.

Another prolific suffix, yielding derivatives of various types, is *-ate*, taken from the ending *-atum* of Latin past participles. Unlike the other suffixes I have been discussing, which are derivational, *-atum* is an inflectional ending like English *-ed* and *-en* in *incised* and *broken*. Thus, from the first-conjugation verb *excavare* 'to dig out', Latin forms *excavatum* 'dug out', as in *pectus excavatum*. English adjectives developed on this pattern include *circinate, decerebrate,* and *particulate*.

The common practice of using such participles as nouns has given us such technical terms as *exudate* (*exsudatum* 'something sweated out') and *distillate* (*distillatum* 'something that has dripped down'). Often, as in the latter case, a verb originally intransitive has been altered, at least conceptually, to a transitive one. Though it was formerly the distillate itself that was said to distil, it is now the chemist (or moonshiner). Similarly, *flagellate* now means not 'whipped' but 'equipped with a whip' (Latin *flagellum*).

On the analogy of genuine Latin participles like *exudate* and *aspirate*, the English suffix *-ate* has been freely appended to verb stems from Greek (*homogenate, dialysate*) and English (*filtrate, leachate*) and to Latin verbs that do not belong to the first conjugation (*eluate, triturate*). In *expressate* the suffix has been linked not to the third-conjugation Latin verb stem *exprim-* but to the corresponding English verb, which was itself formed from the participle *expressum*. *Isolate* (verb and noun) contains an Italian variant of the Latin stem seen in *insulate*, which latter is presently used only as a verb. Numerous technical verbs have also been formed with the suffix *-ate*: *coagulate, desiccate, desquamate, eviscerate, vaccinate*. These belong to a large class of English words formed at various periods directly from Latin stems and including *concentrate, masticate,* and *separate*.

The chemist's *-ate* arose from invented participles like *sulphatum, phosphatum*, and *arsenatum*, which, when joined to a noun denoting a metal, meant that the latter had been "sulfured," "phosphorused," and so on. *Calcium sulphatum* thus signified 'calcium treated with, and made to combine chemically with, sulfur' (actually with sulfuric acid). Later this use of a participle was deemed scientifically unsound, since one might with equal propriety say that the sulfuric acid had been "calciumed." Therefore, anions, while still called -*ate* in English, were placed in a newly created class of dog-Latin nouns ending in -*as* (genitive, -*atis*). *Calcium sulphatum* then became *calcii sulphas* 'sulfate of calcium'. (Similarly, the ending -*ite* became represented in chemical Latin by -*is*, -*itis*.) Nowadays, -*ate* also figures in terms for organic anions such as *lactate* and *morrhuate* (Latin *morua* 'codfish') and in pharmaceutical shorthand terms like *edetate* and *hyclate*.

Suffixes that turn verb stems to nouns are nearly as prolific as adjectival suffixes. Some of these taken from Greek have become narrowly specialized in technical nomenclature. The suffix -*sis* appears in dozens of familiar medical nouns formed from Greek verbs: *crisis, emesis, lysis, mydriasis, proptosis, sepsis, stasis.* Classical words ending in -*iasis* were all formed on verbs containing a thematic -*i*-: *lithiasis* from *lithian* 'to become stony'; *elephantiasis* from *elephantian* 'to become like an elephant'; *phthiriasis* from *phthirian* 'to be infested with lice'. Early in the modern era this -*iasis*, having acquired a specialized meaning—'infestation'—was extended to verbs without -*i*- stems, then to Latin words, and finally to nouns and taxonomic terms. It can now be attached to any noun regardless of stem vowel: *candidiasis, filariasis, myiasis, paragonimiasis, trichomoniasis.*

Classical words ending in -*osis* were all abstract nouns derived from verbs having *o* as their thematic vowel, as in *amaurosis,* from *amaurein* 'to darken'. Later -*osis* was tacked onto adjectives (*cyanosis,* from *kyan* 'blue'), nouns (*thrombosis,* from *thrombos* 'lump'), and Latin words (*pediculosis,* from *pediculus* 'little foot', a reference to the shape of the body louse). Meanwhile the sense of this suffix had also become specialized. It denotes an abnormal state or condition in *keratosis, mucoviscidosis, psychoneurosis*; and excess of a normal substance, tissue, or cell in *hemochromatosis, gliosis, lymphocytosis*; a state induced by a noxious foreign substance in *asbestosis, bagassosis, byssinosis;* and an infection in *toxoplasmosis, listeriosis, rickettsiosis.* Confusion between the Greek noun suffix -*osis* (*sclerosis*) and the Latin adjective suffix -*osus* (*sclerosus*) leads to many spelling errors.

A Greek noun suffix that is scarcely less fertile in technical terms than *-sis* is *-ma*, found in such words as *asthma, bregma, coloboma, derma, ecthyma, edema, magma, plasma, trauma, xanthelasma,* and *zygoma*. In modern English usage many terms formed with this suffix have either lost the final *-a* (*anoderm, exanthem, gram, protoplasm*) or, under French influence, weakened it to a mute *-e* (*chyme, theme, scheme*). *Gram* and compounds ending in *-gram* are derived from Greek *gramma* 'writing', a noun formed from the verb *graphein* 'to write'. The distinction, still fairly well preserved, between *-graph* forms (*electrocardiograph, radiograph*) as verbs and the matching *-gram* forms as nouns is based on this etymology.

The union of the suffix *-ma* with the thematic *o* of *karkinomai* 'to nibble like a crab', *kondylomai* 'to become knobby', and *sarcoun* 'to become fleshy' yielded the nouns *carcinoma, condyloma,* and *sarcoma* (the first two used by Hippocrates) and set the stage for the adoption of *-oma* as a generic ending for the names of neoplastic tumors and other abnormal masses. Modern derivatives are extremely numerous and include examples in which the stem word indicates the site of the tumor (*hepatoma, hypernephroma*), its physical features (*granuloma*; *psammoma*, from Greek *psammos* 'sand'), its histologic type (*epithelioma, adenoma*), its biochemical composition (*atheroma, cholesteatoma*), its product or secretion (*insulinoma, gastrinoma*), the causative microorganism (*ameboma, mycetoma*), and even the eponym attached to the tissue of origin (*schwannoma*) or to the underlying disease (*chagoma*). In the genus name *Amblyomma* one finds not a misspelling or corruption of this suffix but an entirely distinct lexical form, Greek *omma* 'vision' related to *ophthalmic, optic,* and *ocular*.

Leider and Rosenblum first pointed out to modern physicians and lexicographers that the *o* of *-oma* was, in classical Greek words, a thematic vowel—that is, part of the stem rather than of the suffix. The *o* of the familiar suffix *-oid* also represents a thematic or connecting vowel. When added to the combining form *kephalo-*, the classical Greek suffix *-eides* (from *eidos* 'form') changed it to an adjective, *kephaloeides* (another good Hippocratic word) 'like a head, cephaloid'. In arriving at our modern English form of this suffix, we have not only substituted *i* for the diphthong *ei* and annexed the *o* of the preceding stem, but also turned these two vowels into a new diphthong, as in *void*. The ancient Greeks sometimes went even further than that, cutting the fusion of stern vowel and suffix down to *-odes*, as in (*cystosarcoma*) *phyllodes* (from *phyllon* 'leaf').

Another Greek noun suffix of importance in medicine is *-smos*, usually seen in the form *-ismos* because it is attached to *i*-stem verbs. With this suffix, *exorkizein* 'to cast out a devil' is converted to *exorkismos* 'the act of casting out a devil'. The suffix occurs in many medical terms both ancient and modern, including *bruxism* (formed, a little irregularly, from classical *brychismos*), *metabolism*, and *organism*. English *-ism* is a living suffix in the general language, where it is used to name doctrines (*Buddhism, Protestantism*); theories (*behaviorism, rationalism*); personal traits, habits, and attitudes (*altruism, absenteeism, negativism*); statements or expressions (*spoonerism, truism*); and many other abstractions.

In the language of medicine, *-ism* may be used to derive disease names from proper nouns (*parkinsonism, daltonism*) or from words designating those afflicted with the diseases (*albinism, dwarfism, gargoylism, cretinism*) or to indicate intoxications (*atropinism, cinchonism*), abnormal excesses (*hirsutism, ptyalism*), or indeed any abnormal state (*meningism, prostatism*). The suffix is coupled with a prefix in *dysraphism, hypertelorism,* and *hyperaldosteronism* and appears in its Latin form in *hemiballismus* and *strabismus*.

Among nouns formed with this suffix but not containing the thematic *i* may be mentioned *aneurysm, spasm,* and *tenesmus*. Perhaps by mistaken identification with *tenesmus* 'painful straining to void or defecate' and *trismus* 'painful spasm of the jaw muscles', the meaning of *laryngismus* long ago shifted from the classical sense of 'the act of shouting' to 'spasm of the vocal cords'. It was evidently on this model that Sims, in the 1860s, fashioned the term *vaginismus*. *Esophagismus* now obsolete, belongs in the same class.

The most versatile of Greek nouns suffixes is *-ia*, which in the classical language served to form abstract nouns from adjectives (*sophia* 'wisdom', *from sophos* 'wise'), from verbs (*mania* 'madness', from *mainomai* 'to rage'), or from other nouns (*hegemonia* 'sovereignty' from *hegemon* 'leader'). Most medical terms with this ending denote diseases or abnormal states and depend on prefixes for their specific meanings: *hyperemia, achlorhydria, dyskinesia*. The suffix may also be attached to a base unit containing two nouns (*stranguria*), a noun with an adjective (*xerophthalmia*), or a verb with an adverb (*neoplasia*). In a few old terms (*hysteria, ophthalmia, pneumonia*) and at least one modern one (*paronychia*), the suffix implies disease or abnormality with no help from qualifying terms or prefixes. (Cf. also *nausia* 'seasickness' from *naus* 'ship'.) As mentioned earlier, words that have come into English through French have often had the final *-ia* weakened to *-ie*, represented in modern spelling by *-y*: *atrophy, dysentery, tetany.*

An abstract term ending in *-ia* (*-y*) can sometimes be matched with a more concrete one containing the same base words but a different suffix: *neoplasia, neoplasm; exophthalmia, exophthalmos; ureteromegaly, megaureter.* Or a term ending in *-ia* may carry a more general connotation than a corresponding term that is already abstract: *telangiectasis,* a telangiectatic lesion in a given patient; *telangiectasia,* the condition considered in general. So also the Greek words *algos, odyne,* and *pathos,* all denoting pain or suffering and hence pure abstractions (except to the sufferer), appear in medical terms only as further abstractions: *-algia, -odynia,* and *-pathia.*

I have shown that a prefix and a suffix can work together as a pair, forming a large group of sandwich words with various included stems. Thus, the pair *hyper——osis* denotes an excess; *a(n)——ia,* a deficiency; *peri——ium,* an investing membrane; and *de——ase,* an enzyme reversing a chemical reaction. In some cases, there is no suffix at all, or, as a linguist would say, the pair contains a suffix zero. For example, when *meso-* is prefixed to the name of an organ to denote its supporting membrane, the ending of the base noun remains unchanged: *mesoduodenum, mesoappendix, mesocolon.* In this connection I might also mention certain modern anatomic nouns that have come into being irregularly as back-formations from adjectives: *interstitium, perianus, precordium, retroperitoneum, synovium.*

As I implied earlier, affixes cannot always be clearly distinguished from base words. It is customary to define an affix as an indivisible meaningful unit (morpheme or formant) that cannot stand alone. The distinction is valid for most Anglo-Saxon words, where the dependent status of affixes (*mis-, un-, -dom, -ness*) contrasts sharply with the independence of the elements that go to form compounds like *breakdown, headache,* and *lockjaw.* But in words built of Greek and Latin material there is no such difference.

It is a matter of common observation that a classical noun generally undergoes a certain slight change of structure on forming a derivative or compound, and often before adding a plural ending.

Thus, spasm(os), spast–ic; hepar, hepat–oma; corpus, corpor–a. The noun stems *spast-*, *hepat-*, and *corpor-* can no more stand alone than the affixes *non-*, *peri-*, *-ic*, and *-oma*. Classical verb and adjective stems also typically differ from freestanding forms.

Though one may think of *-emia, -uria, -philia,* and *-ectomy* as suffixes, only the final *-ia* (*-y*) in these terms is a suffix in the strict sense, since the other elements represent nouns, verbs, and modifiers in classical Greek. One might even deny that any part of *philia* 'love' or *penia* 'poverty' can be called an affix, since these were freestanding nouns in the classical language, in contrast to such modern collocations as *-emia, -odontia,* and *-uria.*

Occasionally, one of these modern compound suffixes achieves independent status: contrast *blepharoplasty* and *scar plasty; colostomy* and *ostomy care.* But these examples notwithstanding, it can generally be stated that if dependence were the only test of an affix, then most words formed from classical sources would have to be called conglomerations of prefixes and suffixes, attached not to base words but to each other.

The venerable botanic metaphors *stem* and *root* often get confounded in linguistics. A root is a primitive lexical element that carries a fairly broad range of meanings and may appear in a large number of related words functioning as various parts of speech. In historical and comparative linguistics, a root is not confined to one language but may be traced through whole dynasties of languages, appearing (often with substantial variations) in written records thousands of years apart in age.

A Greek term and a Latin one that have been derived from the same Indo-European root generally bear a close family resemblance: *cardia* and *cor* 'heart'; *keras* and *cera* 'wax'; *neura* and *nervus* 'sinew, nerve'; *oon* and *ovum* 'egg'; *onyx* and *unguis* 'nail'; *pous* and *pes* 'foot'. The Greek root *TOM*, referring to cutting, appears in *anatomic, appendectomy, atomizer, Phlebotomus, thoracotomy, tomogram,* and hundreds of other words.

A root vowel is typically labile: compare *empiric* and *pore; organ* and *energy; osteitis* and *astragalus; septic* and *saprophyte; splenic* and *splanchnic; tonus, tetany,* and *taenia.* This phenomenon of root vowel gradation, or ablaut, is less common in Latin (*column, culmination, excellent*) than in Greek, much more so in Germanic languages (*band, bend, bind, bindle, bond, bound, bundle*). The frequent association of vowel shift with variation in meaning is nicely

illustrated in a parallel Latin-English example: *cadere* 'to fall';
caedere 'to fell'. Here the vowel gradation marks a shift from passive
to active voice. Other common variations in the structure of a root are
addition of a consonant (*colon, scoliosis; syncope, scaphoid*) and
jumbling or metathesis (*polymorphic, plethora; sternum, stroma;
sclerosis, skeleton*).

A stem is by definition the part of any word that remains when its
inflectional ending has been removed. Since, in a scantily inflected
language like ours, this definition is usually without application, *base*
or *base word* is perhaps a more useful term than *stem*. Even in Greek
and Latin, finding a stem is not so simple as one might wish. The
freestanding, nominative form of a classical noun—the form that is
used almost exclusively in English (*hepar, cor, femur, gaster,
pectus*)—instead of containing the stem as it might be expected to do,
often lacks a syllable or at least a letter or two belonging to the stem.
In effect, this nominative form is a mutilated or phonetically eroded
form of that stem. In other forms (cases) of the noun, the inflectional
endings may merge with or displace the final vowel of the stem
(thematic vowel). Similar changes take place in verbs.

Thus, the thematic vowels of the Latin stems *ama-* and *horto-* are
not seen in the inflectional forms *amo* 'I love', *amentur* 'may they be
loved', *hortus* 'garden', or *horti* 'gardens'. When there is no thematic
vowel, the final consonant of a noun stem may be altered in the
nominative (*gigant-*, nominative *gigas*; *hepat-*, *hepar*) or even
dropped (*cord-*, *cor*; *galact-*, *gala*). Internal vowel mutation may
occur along with this consonant shift (*pector-*, *pectus*) or without it
(*femor-*, *femur*). Vowel insertion is also common: *gastro-*, *gaster*.

A compound word such as *gallstone, breakdown, venipuncture,*
or *pyosalpinx* can be considered a fused phrase. But whereas fusions
of Anglo-Saxon material typically contain unmodified base words
(*gall, stone, break, down*), classical ones almost always use the stem
form (*veni-, pyo-*) for any component that is not in the end position.
Thus, while *thrix* 'hair' and *pharynx* appear in person in *Leptothrix*
and *hypopharynx*, they are represented by their stems in *Tricho-
monas* and *pharyngitis*. Exceptions to this practice in compounds of
classical vintage (such as Latin *nomenclatura* and Greek *Phosphorus* instead of the expected *nominiclatura* and *Photophorus*) are
rare. Modern terms, on the other hand, often build on to the end of an
unmodified base word (*herpesvirus, pilomatrixoma, psychedelic,
sinusitis*). Equally often, they contain incorrect or irregular stem

forms, as in *amniotic, luetic, myositis, obstetrical,* and *scabietic* for the more regular *amniac, luic, myitis, obstetricial,* and *scabid*.

The form of a word that is customarily used before another element in a compound is called its *combining form*. Before a vowel this is usually just the stem, minus any thematic vowel: *arthr–algia, chol–angitis, hemat–uria, leuc–onychia*. Before a consonant the combining form usually consists of the stem followed by *o*, which may replace a thematic vowel. This use of *o* to make combining forms is a practice of great antiquity. In classical Greek the *o* was employed regularly after adjective stems, regardless of thematic vowel. The pattern of such words is seen in *Akropolis*, a fusion of the phrase *akra polis* 'highest city' in which the adjective changes its feminine ending *-a* to *-o* on becoming a combining form. Very early the process was extended to nouns (*cardio-, osteo-*) and verbs (*crypto-, schizo-*).

The Latin language, much more conservative than Greek in forming compounds, favored *i* as a connecting vowel (*uniformis, multiplex, testimonium*). When—long before the Christian era— Rome entered into cultural relations with Greece, the *o* began to appear in Latin compounds. Nowadays it is found more often than not in combining forms of Latin words: *granulo-, oculo-, oro-, proprio-, recto-, temporo-, veno-*. The combining form *plano-* (seen in *planoconcave* and *planoconvex*) has achieved independent status as an adjective: *plano lens*.

The Latin connecting *i* has not altogether disappeared. It customarily follows certain Latin stems (*colorimetry, scintigraphy, sensorimotor, tumorigenic*). It has also fused with the beginning of a few Latin stems and appears as a coupling device even when these are preceded by Greek elements (*chondrification, epileptiform, spermicidal*). According to the original issue of the *Oxford English Dictionary*, *artifact* is the correct form and *artefact* is a variant. The Supplement Volume published in 1933 reversed these and identified *artefact* as the original term. There is really no question of a connecting vowel here, however, since *artefact* is a coalescent phrase, *arte factum* 'made by art'. Similarly, *venesection* is a composite of *venae sectio* 'cutting of a vein'. *Verumontanum* is another run-on phrase, *veru montanum* 'mountain range'.

The manner of making combining forms is by no means consistent, and never has been. The connecting *o* is often inserted, seemingly without need, before a vowel: *neuroendocrine, psycho- analysis*. The combining form of a Greek noun whose thematic vowel is *e* (*chole-, chyle-, pyle-*) or of a Latin one in *u* (*acu-, arcu-, cornu-, genu-, manu-*) usually keeps this vowel instead of substituting an *o*. But contrast *quadruped* and *quadrilateral, telemetry* and *telogen*. Note also the unorthodox spellings of *anuscope, funduscopic,* and *virucidal. Neurilemma* was originally spelled with only one *m*, since its second element is Greek *eilema* 'covering'. The change of spelling was made by medical writers who believed the last part of the word was Greek *lemma* 'hull' and who apparently were not troubled by the un-Hellenic connecting *i*.

There is at present a trend toward making combining forms with *a*, particularly when this vowel appears at or near the end of the supposed stem: *agoraphobia, collagen, dermatome, erythemagenic, fecalith, mutagenic, plasmacyte, portacaval, prostaglandin*. In some of these cases, there are not only unorthodox junctures but shortened versions of stems, as seen also in *bactibilia, herpangina, iritis,* and *orchiopexy*. (Cf. classical Latin *homicidium* for *hominicidium*.) Indeed, many combining forms with long and distinguished histories contain whittled-down stems: *dermo-* for *dermato-, hemo-* for *hemato-, chromo-* for *chromato-, teno-* for *tenonto-*. *Pneumo-* does double duty as the abbreviated version of *pneumato-*, referring to air or breath (*pneuma*), and *pneumono-*, referring to the lung (*pneumon*): contrast *pneumothorax* and *pneumoconiosis*. For some stems both full and shortened forms are in use: *chromosomal, psychosomatic; ectodermal, dermatitis; pseudomonal, Pseudomonadaceae*. Trimming down chemical names is a practice of long standing: *sulfo-, arsen-, phospho-, oxy-*.

Some terms of recent invention have been telescoped by deliberate omission of awkward syllables. Haplology is the dropping of a repeating syllable or consonant, as in classical Latin *nutrix* 'nurse' for *nutritrix* and modern English *idolatry* for *idololatry*. Medical examples of haplology include *cephalgia* for *cephalalgia, esophagram* for *esophagogram, Pulmotor* for *pulmomotor* (or *pulmonomotor*), and *urinalysis* for *urinanalysis*. (The spelling *uranalysis* was once equally correct.)

Not only has *dilation* been accepted as a legitimate variant of *dilatation*, but it has even been accorded a meaning different from that of the original word. The purist's objection to *dilation* is that since the syllable *lat* comes from Latin *latum* 'wide', a second *at* is needed to represent the verbal noun suffix *-atio*. The purist has lost this battle, and he will eventually lose another over *adaption*, a modern corruption of *adaptation*. Compare *indention* for *indentation* and *updation*, a gobbledygook noun derived from *update*.

Examples of syncopated forms in which vowels have been dropped are *nuclide* for *nucleide* and *presbycusis* for *presbyacusis*. The classicist not unnaturally objects to the standard prefix *hecto-* 'hundred', irregularly derived from Greek *hekaton* 'hundred' and seemingly invading the territory of Greek *hektos* 'sixth'. *Thoracentesis* and *appendectomy* are abbreviated forms of *thoracocentesis* and *appendicectomy*, which latter have not altogether died out in British usage. In *urothelial* the significant affix *epi-* (of *epithelial*) has disappeared. Occasionally an entire stem vanishes without a trace in the formation of a long compound word, as does *cyte* in *leukopenia* (*leukocytopenia*) and *thrombasthenia* (*thrombocytasthenia*). The classical practice of doubling the initial *r* of a Greek stem when it follows another in a compound (*arrhythmia*) has been abandoned in modern terms (*biorhythm*).

Thus far, I have said little about the meanings of classical stems in technical terms. The meaning attached to a stem by the modern user may owe more to convention or association than to classical precedent. Thus, *anastomosis* means 'an opening' in Galen, though the modern sense is 'a closing together'. Moreover, a stem may come to have two or more divergent senses. The Greek stem *path*, for example, forms two distinct classes of English words. In *pathology, adenopathy, idiopathic,* and *psychopath* it preserves its original meaning (*pathos* 'suffering'), but in *naturopathy, homeopathic,* and *osteopath* is refers to 'treatment'. The stem *gen* (from *gennan* 'to beget') has likewise spawned divergent lines of offspring: in *pathogenic, diabetogenic,* and *goitrogenic* it means 'causing', whereas in *cryptogenic, psychogenic,* and *cardiogenic* it means 'caused by' or 'originating in'. In a few words (*allergenic, mutagenic*) it can have either meaning.

The closely allied suffix *-genous* adds another set of variant meanings: in *hematogenous* and *exogenous* it refers to route or direction, while in *myelogenous* and *nephrogenous* it indicates the place where something is generated or begotten. Of all these adjectival variants, only the first meaning noted for *-genic* has corresponding nouns in *-genesis* (*pathogenesis*) and *-gen* (*carcinogen*). In connection with the latter, I may mention also a large group of biochemical precursors: *fibrinogen, pepsinogen; prothrombinogen. Antigen* is theoretically a syncopation of *antibodygen*, which, if it ever existed at all, must have been strangled at birth.

Occasionally, the process of coinage by compounding produces a term of dual significance, as in *dermatome* and *sclerotome*. Besides these artificial homonyms, medical language contains some authentic classical ones that may cause confusion either when used alone or when embedded in compounds. Latin *os* may mean either 'mouth' or 'bone'; in compounds the stem consonants (*or-*, *oss-*) show the distinction. *Tarsus* may mean either the 'ankle' or 'a plate of connective tissue reinforcing the eyelid', and *calx* may mean either 'heel' or 'stone, lime, chalk'. *Natal* may be derived from *natus* 'newborn' or *nates* 'buttocks'; *mental*, from *mens* 'mind' or *mentum* 'chin'.

Greek *io-* may refer to the color violet (*iodopsin*), to iodine or its compounds (*iopanoic*), to ions (*iometer*), or to poison (*iophobia*). The Romanization of Greek words abolished the distinction between long and short *e* (*η* and *ε*) and long and short *o* (*ω* and *o*). Hence *osmo-* can refer either to 'smell' (*ŏsme*) or to 'pressure' (*ŏsmos*); *cer-* to 'wax' (*kēros*) or 'horn' (*kĕras*)'; *metr-* to 'mother' (*mēter*), 'womb' (*mētra*), or 'measurement' (*mĕtron*). The modern coinage *osteoporosis*, from *pŏros* 'pore', might well be traced by one knowing more about Greek than medicine to classical *pōrosis* 'hardness'. Modern American spelling further confounds *koilos* 'hollow', as in *celiac*, with *kele* 'tumor', as in *hydrocele*.

Confusion may also arise between similar stems in the two languages: compare Greek *corone* 'crow' and Latin *corona* 'crown'; *manos* 'thin' and *manus* 'hand'; *pais* 'child' and *pes* 'foot'; *pyr* 'fire' and *pyrum* (more properly, *pirum*) 'pear'.

For more than a century now, most new medical, chemical, and taxonomic words have been made with Greek material. One of the reasons for this is that often the corresponding Latin term had already been used. Thus, *tyrosine* was derived (irregularly) from Greek *tyros* 'cheese' because Latin *caseus* had already yielded *casein*. In some cases, inventors of words preferred Greek because it offered some distinctive or euphonious form, as in *opsonin* (Wright and Douglas) from *opson* 'cooked meat' and *hormone* (Starling) from *hormon* 'setting in motion'. But until comparatively recent times a far more pervasive and powerful motive governed the word maker's choice between Greek and Latin.

It is a quirk of medical English that while our anatomic nouns tend to be of Anglo-Saxon lineage, the corresponding adjectives are very often Latin, and the pathologic and surgical terms are Greek: *breast-mammary-mastectomy; kidney-renal-nephrosis; bladder-vesical-cystitis.* This is hardly a rule, since exceptions to the pattern far outnumber perfect examples. But the pattern is there, inviting explanation. The suggestion that the Anglo-Saxons and the Romans were the best anatomists, while the Greeks excelled in pathology and surgery, lacks historical foundation. The Anglo-Saxon terms survive because of the strong tendency of technical terminology to cling to nouns from the vernacular. The Latin adjectives have come down from medieval anatomic and medical writings. The Greek terms were not coined from that language to honor Hippocrates and Galen but chiefly to perpetuate a petty and senseless linguistic prejudice against mixing words of different language stocks.

The combination of Greek and Latin material in the same word was once regarded as a serious breach of linguistic decorum, such hybrids being stigmatized as bastard words. According to this view, some of the medical terms most often used—*audiogram, diverticulosis, granuloma, hypertension, neutrophil, polyvalent, radiology, retinitis*—are vulgar amalgamations, to be eschewed by cultivated speakers and writers. The suffixes *-itis*, *-ectomy*, and *-osis* came into medical language in a few Greek words of ancient vintage and stayed. Since Latin could supply no corresponding suffixes, it was thought necessary, in making new words with *-itis*, *-osis*, *-emia*, *-ectomy*, *-otomy*, *-pexy*, *-rrhaphy*, and the rest, to combine these with Greek stems instead of the more familiar Latin ones. In consequence a whole language full of largely superfluous roots and stems was dumped into the already tangled muddle of medical language. One inevitable result was the coinage of unneeded synonyms: *cribriform* with *ethmoid, ensiform* with *xiphoid, dermal* with *cutaneous.*

A prejudice against intermixing two language stocks in the formation of new words seems laughable in speakers of English, which is probably more of a patchwork than any other language ever used. The determination of linguists, lexicographers, grammarians, and other self-appointed custodians of the public speech to keep language stocks segregated is one of those petty crotchets that have brought exponents of the liberal disciplines into disrepute in modern times. One cannot help being reminded of the objections of Kaiser Wilhelm II and Adolf Hitler to German words coined from Greek.

Long before these nationalist fanatics decreed that a telephone must be called a *Fernsprecher* by all good Aryans, the Teutonic languages other than English had been far more sparing than we in their use of Greek and Latin borrowings. Instead of *pericardium*, the German says *Herzbeutel* 'heart bag'; our *tenosynovitis* is his *Sehnenscheidenentzündung* 'sinew sheath enkindling'; our *albumin* is his *Eiweisskörper* 'eggwhite bodies'. German names for common chemical elements are rugged and homely Teutonic compounds: *Sauerstoff* 'acid-forming substance' translates Greek *oxygen*, as *Wasserstoff* does *hydrogen*. Nitrogen is *Stickstoff* 'choking substance'. Dutch and the Scandinavian languages also prefer to render Greek and Latin technical terms into the vernacular. But I have strayed from my subject.

Greek and Latin, as mentioned earlier, are both Indo-European languages and are therefore derived from the same long-lost parent tongue. Granted that by the beginning of recorded history the two languages had already diverged enough to be mutually unintelligible, classical philologists debated whether Latin should be considered a dialect of Greek.

No living language can remain pure for long unless its speakers live in total isolation. Some Homeric terms once regarded as purest Hellenic are now believed to be Hittite loans. Some Augustan Latin words were borrowings from the Celts and the Etruscans. Small wonder that Latin and Greek, quite irrespective of their common origin, have shared and exchanged words at all periods. In Cicero's day such pilfered Greek words as *aenigma, butyrum* 'butter' *calix* 'chalice, cup', and *dogma* were indispensable parts of an educated Roman's vocabulary. Conversely, New Testament Greek contains many words taken over from imperial Latin (*denarion, koustodia, legeon, praitorion*). In the declining days of the empire, when Greek and Latin were both official languages, cross contamination occurred to a much greater extent. Hence the modern effort to segregate the two language stocks smacks of ignorance and narrow-mindedness, not of scholarship and reason.

Words and word fragments in active use have no nationality. As soon as a Greek word is rewritten in Roman letters, it becomes a sort of hybrid. When, having performed this transliteration, one changes a Greek inflectional ending -*os* or -*e* to Latin -*us* or -*a*, one has, in effect, a Latin word, just as one has an English one when the flections -*ed* and -*ing* are added to a verb, regardless of its source. Once the stage is reached of putting the Latin adjectival suffix -al on a Greek stem (*coccal, parenteral*) or Greek -ic on a Latin one (*acidic, pulmonic*), it is already too late to worry about nationalities and hybrids. A word used by speakers of English is an English word, and its national origins (supposing that these could really be ascertained) are of purely academic interest.

For centuries the assimilation of classical elements into English has been so extensive that Greek has been as hard to keep away from Latin as the sons of Israel from the daughters of Canaan. Pedantic prejudice has failed to prevent the conjunction of Greek and Latin in anatomic terms like *pterygomandibular* and *pancreaticoduodenal* or in biochemical ones like *acetylcholine* and *pyruvic*. Similarly, purebred Greek *colpitis* and *phlebogram* have fallen by the wayside, while their hybrid synonyms *vaginitis* and *venogram* flourish.

Fortunately, the bias against blends of Greek and Latin began to disappear in English-speaking countries when classical studies began to drop out of the high school curriculum. Nowadays there is little objection to combining Greek with Latin or, for that matter, with Arabic (*alkalosis*), Persian (*phytobezoar*), German (*kernicterus*), French (*goitrogenic*), or English (*beeturia*). But old prejudices die hard. A commission on the nomenclature of inorganic chemistry lately recommended keeping Latin and Greek material apart in chemical names. Taxonomic coinages seldom mix the two languages. And an American ophthalmologist of Greek extraction has proposed to rectify the terminology of his specialty by getting rid of well-known Latin stems presently yoked to Greek ones and substituting others from *modern* Greek!

The subject of chemical nomenclature presents several features of interest that I shall consider in concluding this discussion of word coinage. Older names of organic compounds and radicals are usually based on classical words for the animal or vegetable sources from which they were first extracted. *Methyl* is a back-formation from *methylene* (Greek *methy* 'wine' and *hyle* 'wood'). However, all other terms ending in -*yl* were formed on the analogy of *benzoyl*, the first radical named with this termination: *ethyl* (from Greek *aither* 'pure or rarefied air'), *amyl* (a misnomer, from Latin *amylum* 'starch'), *vinyl* (from Latin *vinum* 'wine'), *allyl* (from Latin *allium* 'garlic'), *butyl* (through *butyric*, from *butyrum* 'butter'). *Lactic acid* is named from Latin *lac* 'milk'; *acetic*, from *acetum* 'vinegar'; *succinic* and *oxalic* (both christened by Lavoisier), from *succinum* 'amber' and *oxalis* 'wood sorrel'; *sorbic*, from *sorbum* 'service berry'; *fumaric*, from the medicinal herb *fumitory* (*Fumaria officinalis*). *Hippuric acid* was first recovered from the urine (*ouron*) of a horse (*hippos*); *ornithine*, from that of a fowl (*ornis*); *taurocholic acid*, from ox-bile; and *formic acid* from ants (*formicae*). *Caproic acid* (Latin *caper 'goat'*) is named for its scent, not its source. *Palmitic* is derived, not from *palmes, palmitis* 'young shoot of a vine', as the Latinist might suppose, but simply from *palma*. The name was proposed by Frémy in 1840 for derivatives of palm because the more logical *palmic* was already in use for castor oil and its derivatives. (In medieval Latin the castor oil plant was called *palma Christi*.) *Tannic* is based on medieval Latin *tannum*, a word of Celtic origin referring to oak bark used for tanning leather.

Whereas chemical nomenclature displays an exemplary consistency in its use of prefixes and suffixes, it goes to the opposite extreme in the freedom with which it derives one stem from another by arbitrary phonetic mutation. *Manganese* was at first simply a corruption of *magnesium* (more accurately, of *magnesia*). *Yttrium* and *ytterbium*, rare earth metals, are both named after Ytterby, Sweden. *Aspartic* is an arbitrary variation on *asparagine* (from *asparagus*), *tropine* on *atropine, malonic* and *maleic* on *malic* (Latin *malum*, "apple"), *amine* on *ammonia* (and *imine* on *amine*), *-ite* on *-ate*. As mentioned earlier, a chemical combining form often drops a considerable part of the stem, as in *prop-* from *propionic* (Greek *pion* 'fat') and *ar-* from *aromatic.*

In this section, I have surveyed the processes whereby technical terms have been and are being formed from classical language material, showing how modern practice sometimes follows classical precedent and just as often departs from it. If any practical lesson is to be drawn from this presentation, it is that the connections between classical elements in modern terms and their Greek and Latin origins are tenuous, devious, and sometimes dubious. The form of borrowed material is subject to modification by modern notions of spelling and pronunciation, and its meaning depends largely on analogy and association. For all that, our modern systems of anatomic, taxonomic, chemical, and pathologic nomenclature are remarkably flexible, serviceable, and durable.

One who has convinced himself that a new term *must* be fabricated would do well to employ stems and affixes already in use instead of digging unknown ones out of the lexicon, and should follow modern usage with respect to meaning, spelling, and pronunciation rather than try to resurrect the rules of dead languages. Quintilian, wisest of Roman rhetoricians, put it this way nearly 2,000 years ago: "It is safest to preserve words already in current use: inventing new ones is not without its dangers. If they find acceptance, they bring but scant praise to our discourse; if rejected, they only invite ridicule."

Abbreviations

It is one thing to abbreviate by contracting, another by cutting off.
Francis Bacon
Essays

There seems to be a universal tendency for people of all races and languages to abridge their utterances, when possible, by shortening or omitting words and, if they number writing among their accomplishments, to abbreviate that, too.

Some shortenings in speech are prompted by a natural striving for economy of expression, as when we say, "He has been doing that procedure for longer than I," and deliberately omit the rest of the sentence, "have been doing that procedure," which is so obvious as to be superfluous. The words *yes* and *no* save us the trouble and tedium of turning every question that we answer into a statement and so repeating it to the questioner.

We often add to the vividness and pungency of words by subtracting syllables from them that seem unnecessary. Thus have been fashioned *auto* from *automobile, cab* from *cabriolet, mob* from *mobile vulgus*, and *piano* from *pianoforte*. These are all examples of clipped forms that have been legitimized by long use. Others that are still regarded as slang are *ammo* (*ammunition*), *info* (*information*), *lube* (*lubrication*), and *natch* (*naturally*).

Abbreviations are found in the writings of all nations and periods. Variously prompted by haste, laziness, or the wish to conserve writing materials, written abbreviations range from representations of spoken ones (as when one writes *bike* instead of *bicycle*, just as one would substitute the short form in speech) to much more sparsely skeletal remnants like *cm, MD*, and *USA*. In turn, letter abbreviations like these usually find their way into speech: "He was questioned by the MPs at the PX because he didn't have his ID."

The physician, in his sometimes frantic and usually futile efforts to conserve time, has recourse to many abbreviations in speech and writing. He may omit the beginning of a word (*scope* for *endoscope*); the middle (*appy* for *appendectomy*, itself an abridgment of *appendicectomy*); or the end (*neuro* for *neurology* or *neurologic*). Spoken clippings like these belong to the argot of medicine and will be discussed in the next chapter. My concern at the moment is with more or less standard written abbreviations.

The modern physician may be interested to learn that Hippocrates and Galen used quite a variety of standard abbreviations as a kind of shorthand to list the salient features of instructive cases. In their system, Δ stood for *diarrhea* or *diaphoresis*; *M* for *mania* or *metra* 'uterus'; *N* for *necrosis*; O for *odunai* 'pains'; θ for *thanatos* 'death'; *T* for *tokos* 'childbirth, delivery'; and so on.

Particularly common in modern medical writing is the *initialism*, which consists of the first letters of the words that compose a phrase; *CBC* 'complete blood count'; *ENT* 'ear nose, and throat'; *BUN* 'blood urea nitrogen'. Not only are these generally understood within the profession, but they are almost invariably substituted, even in print, for the full expressions. Some initialisms include *and*: *T and A* 'tonsillectomy and adenoidectomy'; *D and C* 'dilatation and curettage'.

An abbreviation made up of the first two or three letters of a word, pronounced separately (*CA* 'cancer'; *OB* 'obstetrics'; *GYN* 'gynecology'; *AB* 'abortion') is one common variant of the initialism. Another contains a letter for each syllable or morpheme in the base word: *DC* or *D/C* 'discharge' or 'discontinue'; *IV* 'intravenous(ly)'. Hybrids are common: *IVP* 'intravenous pyelogram'; *TUR* 'transurethral resection'; *PCN* 'penicillin'; *HB* or *HGB* 'hemoglobin'.

Initialisms are especially popular for the names of diseases and of diagnostic and therapeutic procedures: *ASHD* 'arteriosclerotic heart disease'; *CPK* 'creatine phosphokinase'; *IPPB* 'intermittent positive pressure breathing'; *BSO* 'bilateral salpingo-oophorectomy'. Any of these might be printed in a learned journal, but there is another class of abbreviations that is seldom seen except in handwritten clinical records. *WDWNWM-NAD* would be readily translated by most physicians trained in the United States as 'a well-developed, well-nourished white male in no acute distress'. *UCD* 'usual childhood diseases'; *PERLA* 'pupils are equal, react to light, and accommodate'; and *PMI* 'point of maximum intensity' are all used and understood throughout the country. These expressions belong to a system of informal clinical shorthand sometimes called *internlingua*.

Every specialty and every paramedical field has its own set of abbreviations. *MOD* 'medical officer of the day' and *MHB* 'maximum hospital benefit' have been carried into civilian practice by thousands of physicians trained in military and veterans' hospitals. *TPR* 'temperature, pulse, respirations' is the nurse's expression for what the physicial calls *vital signs*. The laboratory technician performing a urinalysis might record the number of white blood cells per high-power field as *TNTC* 'too numerous to count' or the specific gravity as *QNS* 'quantity not sufficient' (to float a hydrometer).

Medical abbreviations that have found their way into the vernacular are *OD* 'overdose', *DOA* 'dead on arrival', and *DTs* 'delirium tremens', the latter abbreviation retaining the final *s* of the Latin participle and thus becoming a spurious plural. Such borrowings may serve the laity as euphemisms: *BM* 'bowel movement'; *VD* 'venereal disease'.

The pharmaceutical ℞ is probably an abbreviation for Latin *recipe* 'take', perhaps influenced by ♃ , the alchemist's sign for his patron deity Jupiter, or ☥, an Egyptian symbol known as the eye of Horus. ℞ has become a symbol of medical treatment in general and has spawned a whole alphabet of abbreviations in its image, including *Fx* 'fracture'; *Dx* 'diagnosis'; *Sx* 'symptoms' or 'surgery'; and *Hx* 'history'. *Cx* 'cervix' is a cousin with a better title to the final *x*.

Abbreviations of Latin pharmaceutical terms may become contaminated with English elements, as in *q.o.d.* 'quaque other day' and *gtts.*, in which the English plural ending *s* is engrafted on Latin *gutta*. Shorthand expressions are sometimes invented with tongue in cheek, as when T_7 is used as the name of a laboratory determination based on measurement of T_3 resin uptake and circulating T_4. Some are frankly jocular, like *TLC* ('tender, loving care') and *3-H enema* ('high, hot, and hell of a lot').

An *acronym* is an initialism that can be, and customarily is, pronounced like a word—for example, *NATO* 'North Atlantic Treaty Organization' and *SCUBA* 'self-contained underwater breathing apparatus'. If physicians pronounced *BUN* as "bun" (which they never on any account do), it would be an acronym. Even initialisms that are apparently unpronounceable can be turned into acronyms by insertion of extraneous vowel sounds, as in the case of *CABG* ('coronary artery bypass graft'), pronounced "cabbage." Whereas speakers of English nearly always accent an initialism on the last letter, regardless of the placement of stress in the full phrase, they usually accent an acronym on the first syllable. Why this is so is one of the insoluble mysteries of language.

When the *ECHO* ('enteric cytopathogenic human orphan') virus was first isolated, it was believed not to cause any disease; hence the fanciful epithet *orphan*. *IMViC* (with small *i* inserted for euphony) is a well-known acronym for 'indole, methyl red, Voges-Proskauer, and citrate', representing the battery of tests used to detect fecal contamination of water. *REM* sleep is 'that phase of sleep character-ized by rapid eye movement' (not to be confused with the radiologist's lower case *rem* 'roentgen equivalents in man').

Only a few pure acronyms have been accorded the privilege of being spelled with lowercase letters. Others besides *rem* are *dopa* ('dihydroxyphenylalanine') and *laser* ('light amplification by stimu-lated emission of radiation'). But when an acronym is incorporated into another word, it is never capitalized. *RNA* ('ribonucleic acid') serves as a stem in *picornavirus* and *oncornavirus*, while the older acronym *DORN* (for 'deoxyribonucleic acid') appears in *strepto-dornase*. A *vipoma* is a tumor that secretes *VIP* ('vasoactive intestinal peptide'). A special kind of acronym is formed from the first syllables of the words in a phrase. This practice is commoner in German (*Gestapo, geheime Staatspolizei*) than in English. Medical examples are *arbovirus* (for 'arthropod-borne virus') and *aldehyde*, a legitimized shorthand version of 'alcohol dehydrogenatum'.

Among the more colorful acronyms to be found in modern medical use are *PEEP* ('positive end-expiratory pressure'), *CASH* ('chronic addiction serum hepatitis'), *ALAS* ('aminolevulinic acid synthetase'), *GEE* ('glycine ethyl ester'), *OH-DOC* ('hydroxy-deoxycorticosterone'), *PANS* ('puromycin aminonucleoside'), *VAMP* ('vincristine, amethopterin, 6-mercaptopurine, prednisone'), *EGG* ('electrogastrogram'), *SCAT* ('sheep cell agglutination test'), *IRMA* ('intraretinal microvascular abnormality'), and *SOAP* ('symp-toms, observations, assessment, plan').

Many of the mnemonics traditionally used by students and practitioners of medicine are acronyms. *INSULAR*, for example, contains clues to the diagnostic features of multiple sclerosis: intention tremor, nystagmus, scanning speech, urinary difficulties, and loss of abdominal reflexes. The nonbacterial neonatal infections, toxoplasmosis, rubella, cytomegalovirus, and herpes, are represented by *TORCH*, in which the *O*, originally inserted for euphony, later came to stand for 'other'. The *CREST syndrome* consists of calcinosis, Raynaud's phenomenon, esophageal dysfunction, sclerodactyly, and telangiectasia. *Leopard syndrome*, coined by Gorlin, Anderson, and Blaw in 1969, comes as close to perfection as such a term can, being both an apt metaphor and an acronymic mnemonic for lentigines, ECG changes, ocular hypertelorism, pulmonary stenosis, abnormalities of genitalia, retardation, and deafness.

A widely used form of shortened speech and writing other than abbreviation of words is the arbitrarily chosen *letter* or *number symbol*. Arabic numerals are often employed in a scale running from 1 to 4 (or 1-plus to 4-plus), according to which anything from prostatic enlargements to glycosuria can be roughly graded. Other uses of Arabic numerals include the typing of bacterial and viral strains and the gauges of catheters, dilators, and suture materials. Roman numerals serve in grading hypertensive changes in the retina and in distinguishing the clotting factors and the phenotypes of hyperlipidemia. They are used as numerals in their own right in prescriptions and drug orders.

Arbitrary letter symbols are also common. Roman letters designate vitamins, blood types, and groups of hemolytic streptococci. Most letter symbols are drawn from the first part of the alphabet; among exceptions may be mentioned the P, Q, R, S, and T waves of the electrocardiogram, X and Y chromosomes, and x-rays. Greek letters distinguish ring positions of cyclic compounds, secretory cells of the pancreatic islets, rhythms of the elctroencephalogram, adrenergic receptors, and serum components such as lipoproteins and globulins that are separated by electrophoresis.

Not all letter and number symbols are chosen arbitrarily. *L-forms, Z-plasty,* and *T* and *Y antibodies* are named for their resemblance to the shapes of the letters. The terms *deltoid, lambdoid, sigmoid, hyoid,* and *chiasm* refer to the shapes of the Greek letters Δ, Λ, ς, τ, and χ, respectively. Among the ancient Greeks, a cripple was sometimes nicknamed Lambda (λ). In German, *genu varum* 'bowleg' is called *O-Beine* ('O legs'); *genu valgum* 'knock knee', *X-Beine.* Here may be mentioned also the *O sign*, a whimsical reference to the gaping mouth of a stuporous or comatose patient, and the even more ominous *Q sign* (O sign with protruding tongue). A term may even refer to the shape of a numeral (*figure-of-eight bandage*) or of a punctuation mark (*Vibrio comma*). Phonetic abbreviations along the lines of *IOU* and *EZ* are not unknown in medicine: XS 'excess'; B9 'benign'.

A few symbols that are neither letters nor numerals have found their way into medical shorthand. The popular symbols for male and female are adapted from ancient astrological marks, the former representing the arrow of Mars and the latter the mirror of Venus. Physicians often adorn handwritten records with arrows, rebuses, pictograms, and a variety of symbols borrowed from pharmacy, chemistry, and mathematics.

Convenient though they are, abbreviations have no meaning until they have been explained; that is, unlike compound coinages from familiar stems and affixes, they offer the uninitiated no clue to their significance. Moreover, even abbreviations in common use can be dangerously ambiguous. Does *C* after a temperature stand for 'centigrade' or 'Celsius'? Does *CAT* (*scan*) mean 'computer-assisted tomography' or 'computed axial tomography'? These questions are academic. But when a physician's admitting note reports that the patient "had PE 3 weeks ago," the fact may be reassuring or ominous depending on whether the abbreviation stands for 'physical examination' or 'pulmonary embolism'. A drug abuser who admits taking *THC* may mean either 'terpin hydrate with codeine' or 'tetrahydrocannabinol'.

The intended meaning is often apparent from the context. It seems unlikely that the three common meanings of *MS* ('morphine sulfate', 'multiple sclerosis', 'mitral stenosis') or the three meanings of *BS* ('blood sugar', 'breath sounds', 'bowel sounds') could often be confounded in practice. Nevertheless, most hospitals have found it advisable to limit and standardize the abbreviations that physicians may use in writing orders. The United States Pharmacopeia (USP) restricts the abbreviation *sulf.* to *sulfate* and directs that *sulfide* and *sulfite* must be written in full. The USP formerly came into conflict with metric usage by requiring *gram* to be abbreviated *Gm.*, so as to avoid confusion with *grain*, once officially *gr.* but now officially dead.

A great many abbreviations in common use have lost all connection with their origins. *Streptolysin O* is so distinguished because it is inactivated by oxygen, but to a physician interested in his patient's *ASO* ('antistreptolysin O') *titer*, that fact is of no particular concern or use. *TB* was originally an abbreviation for 'tubercle bacillus' but was quickly picked up by the laity as a euphemism for *tuberculosis*. In a similar way *GC*, in modern professional parlance, has come to stand not for *gonococcus* but for the disease it causes. Although, in the exact sciences, *mL* ('milliliter') long ago replaced *cc* ('cubic centimeter'), many physicians preserve the latter term, partly because for practical purposes in medicine the two volumes are identical.

When an abbreviation has become common and familiar, it may be retained even after the full term has gone out of use. *SGOT*, which stands for 'serum glutamic-oxaloacetic transaminase', is still used although the enzyme is now called *aspartate aminotransferase*. Similarly, *SGPT* ('serum glutamic-pyruvic transaminase') now refers to *alanine aminotransferase*.

The whole purpose of abbreviation is defeated when an initialism or acronym acquires a life of its own, its users forgetting what the letters stand for. What is the point, it may well be asked, of abbreviating *protamine zinc insulin* to *PZI* and then saying, "PZI insulin"? Why turn *military antishock trousers* into *MAST* if one must say "MAST trousers" for the expression to be understood?

The tendency of speakers and writers to shorten what they say and write is a natural and generally salutary one, which only occasionally results in gibberish. To curb this tendency would be neither reasonable nor possible. Indeed, it is hard to decide whether the fabric of language is more distorted and its operation more hampered by ill-advised compression and ellipsis or by aimless augmentation and inflation. In language as in finance, inflation is so common and inescapable that no form of economy should be very strongly discouraged.

Trade Names

The American advertiser is also a very diligent manufacturer of wholly new terms, and many of his coinages . . . have come into general acceptance as common nouns.

H. L. Mencken
The American Language

Trade names make up a significant part of the terminology of medicine, as they do of vernacular English. Some, like *Bird* and *Bennett*, are simply manufacturers' names that have come to stand for certain products or appliances, as do the terms *Cadillac* and *Leica*.

Others are inventions, which run the gamut between coinages from Greek (*Elastoplast*) and variations on English words (*Stockinet*). *Trampoline, zipper, deep freeze,* and even *aspirin* began as registered trade names.

Just as the public has taken up prominent trade names like these and applied them generically to all similar products, the medical profession often absorbs a trade name into its vocabulary and, eventually forgetting its origin, drops the capital letter. *Vaseline* is Chesebrough's trade name for petrolatum, introduced in 1872. Supposedly the term is a compound of German *Wasser* 'water', Greek *elaion* 'oil', and the suffix *-ine*. *Band-Aid* is the property of Johnson & Johnson, and *Hyfrecator* is the Burdick Company's registered trademark for its *high f*requency desic*cator*. *Tabloid* was registered in 1884 by Burroughs, Wellcome as a trademark for compressed medicinal tablets. The application of the word to a small newspaper, dating from the turn of the century, is a derivative (though not illegal) use.

Perhaps the majority of trade names that physicians use are patented drug names. The naming of new drugs poses a continuing challenge to pharmaceutical manufacturers and to the medical profession, for each drug name must be different enough from all others to minimize the risk of confusion in speech and writing. The ideal name is also short, easy to spell and pronounce, and associated in some way with the composition or action of the drug.

The systematization of generic (nonproprietary) drug names in recent years has been a noteworthy achievement. Though terms like *edetate* and *pamoate* draw chuckles from professional chemists, they are at least easier for physicians to remember and write than *ethylenediaminetetraacetate* or *1, 1'-methylenbis (2-hydroxy-3-naphthoate)*. The United States Adopted Names (USAN) Council was formed in 1964 to find appropriate generic names for all new drugs developed in the United States. Sponsored jointly by the American Medical Association, the American Pharmaceutical Association, and the United States Pharmacopeial Convention, Inc., the council works with pharmaceutical manufacturers in the selection of meaningful and distinctive names for new drugs and cooperates with other national and international agencies toward a maximum degree of standardization in generic naming of drugs.

The brand names chosen for drugs, though subject to approval by the Federal Food and Drug Administration, are of course invented by the manufacturers. So difficult has it become to select new drug names that will satisfy all the other requirements—and that will also look good on a label and sound melodious to the ear—that drug manufacturers have resorted to mechanical fabrication of names. Hundreds of prefixes, suffixes, and stems are fed into a computer and matched at random. In a printout of several thousand specimens, only a handful may be worthy of consideration. Some must be rejected because they are too much like existing names, others because they are misleading, ludicrous, unpronounceable, or simply ugly.

Brand names of drugs range from the ingenious to the bizarre. Some are based, straightforwardly enough, on therapeutic action: *Diuril*, a diuretic; *Apresoline*, an antihypertensive; *Lomotil*, a drug to reduce intestinal motility. The physician is usually on safe ground if he concludes that a drug whose name ends in *-ase* is an enzyme or that a *-mycin* or a *-myxin* is an antibiotic. The syllables *cort, cill, bel,* and *barb* almost invariably point, respectively, to an adrenal cortical hormone, a penicillin, a belladonna alkaloid, and a barbiturate.

Cocaine (from *coca*, the plant source, and *-ine*, the alkaloid suffix) was the first local anesthetic used in modern surgery. When a synthetic drug was developed that had less serious side effects, it was called *procaine* (from Latin *pro* 'for' and *-caine*, a fragment arbitrarily chopped off *cocaine*) and first marketed as *Novocain* (from Latin *novus* 'new'). Since then most newly developed local anesthetics have been called *-caines* whether or not they are chemically related to the parent drug.

Sometimes a brand name is a phonetic spelling of the generic name or part of it (*Sudafed* 'pseudoephedrine'; *Ascodeen* 'aspirin with codeine'), or even of letters (*Kay-Ciel* 'KCl, potassium chloride'). Others are simplifications of cumbersome terms (*Carfusin* 'carbol fuchsin') or eponyms (*Vlem-Dome* 'Vleminckx solution' and *Dome-Boro*, yet another misspelling of *Burow's* solution). Many are built up of other trade names (*Combid* 'Compazine and Darbid'; *Ser-Ap-Es* 'Serpasil, Apresoline, and Esidrix').

A few are acronymic: *Capla* '*c*entrally *a*cting *p*ressure-*l*owering *a*gent'; *Ansolysen*, a ganglionic blocking agent, from *a*utonomic *n*ervous *s*ystem and Greek *lysis* 'loosening'. The coumarin derivative *warfarin*, first marketed as a rodenticide, was not so called because man's efforts to control the rat population are a never-ending warfare but after the *W*isconsin *A*lumni *R*esearch *F*oundation and the last four letters of the chemical name. *Premarin* is built up from *pregn*ant *mare*s' ur*ine*, which indicates the source of the drug. The Johnson & Johnson Company has traced the trade name *K Y Jelly* to an early twentieth century research laboratory employee named Sawtell. Once, when asked what the letters *K Y* meant, Sawtell evasively replied that they stood for Greek or Persian words that would have no meaning to the public. A company official suggests that Sawtell simply coined the expression out of thin air as a novel and easily remembered name.

Among oddities may be mentioned *Amen, Miltown, Marplan,* and *Letter,* which do not sound like drug names at all and for that reason are probably much easier to remember. A levorotatory isomer of *Darvon* (dextro-propoxyphene) bears the mirror-image name *Novrad.* Many brand names contain references to the manufacturer's name: *Robitussin* and *Robinul,* made by A. H. Robins; *Wyanoids* and *Wycillin,* by Wyeth; *Talwin,* by Winthrop. Smith, Kline & French markets a line of drugs beginning with a phonetic spelling of *S, K: Eskabarb, Eskalith.*

Manufacturers sometimes alter drug names in curious ways, as when *Pyralgin* became *Pyrilgin,* and *Petrolagar* was metathesized to *Petrogalar.* Generic names are subject to similar changes. Thus, *metapyrone* became *metyrapone,* and the drug called *furosemide* in the United States is called *frusemide* in the United Kingdom. Equally remarkable is the practice of drug manufacturers of retaining a brand name despite a change in formula. For example, *Phenaphen* was so named because it contained *phen*acetin, *a*spirin, and *pheno*barbital. The product now marketed under this name contains acetaminophen but none of the original ingredients. *Neosynephrine* is phenylephrine; *Neosynephrine II* is an entirely unrelated substance, xylometrazoline.

References and Readings

Cole F: *The Doctor's Shorthand.* Philadelphia, W. B. Saunders Co., 1970.

Current Medical Abbreviations. Bowie, Maryland, Charles Press Publishers, Inc., 1976.

Jerome JB, Sagan P. The USAN nomenclature system. *J Am Med Assoc* 1975;232:294–299.

Leider M, Rosenblum M: *A Dictionary of Dermatologic Words, Terms, and Phrases*. West Haven, Connecticut, Dome Laboratories, 1976.

CHAPTER 6

Slang, Jargon,
and Gibberish

Medicalese I

*One of the constant butts of ridicule, both in the old comedies
and novels, is the professional jargon of the medical tribe. Yet it
cannot be denied that this jargon, however affected it may seem,
is the natural language of apothecaries and physicians, the
mother-tongue of pharmacy! It is that by which their knowledge
first comes to them, that with which they have the most obstinate
associations, that in which they can express themselves the most
readily and with the best effect upon their hearers; and though
there may be some assumption of superiority in all this, yet it is
only by an effort of circumlocution that they could condescend to
explain themselves in ordinary language.*

William Hazlitt
'On Pedantry,' in
The Round Table

Now as in Hazlitt's day, pedants and busybodies often ridicule
and condemn the informal language in which physicians converse
among themselves about medicine and that they use in keeping
clinical records as tangled, obscure, bombastic, and silly. Nowadays

the jargon of the profession is stigmatized as 'medspeak' or 'medicant,' and seminars and courses are conducted by nonphysicians to teach physicians how to talk and keep records in plain English.

Most of the criticisms of medical argot fall into one of two broad categories. Typical of the first was the frenetic spiel of a medical-records-librarian-turned-grammar-pundit who railed against *digitalize* as a graceless, pretentious, and unnecessary way of saying "give digitalis." At length a physician put her out of her misery by informing her that to digitalize a patient does not mean simply to administer digitalis but to administer it in such a way as to elicit a particular pharmacologic response. *Digitalize* is actually a compact and highly efficient means of expressing an intricate concept.

Every professional or trade jargon seems obscure and bizarre to outsiders. Medicalese is no more unintelligible or awkward to physicians than the jargons of arc welding, banking, or baseball to those who use them daily.

The second kind of criticism pokes fun at some apparently absurd or incoherent passage lifted from a hastily scribbled hospital record, such as, "Pt. has been straining to void for 4-5 yr." I say *apparently* absurd or incoherent because every physician clearly understands this sentence on first reading, and few would even think of the humorous alternative meaning unless it were drawn to their attention.

Why should informal speech and writing be held to the standards of formal speech and writing, or professional jargon be expected to conform to the canons of general language? A system of communication that transmits messages clearly and effectively among those who use it serves its function adequately. Why should it be altered to suit the tastes of librarians and schoolteachers or of physicians with muddled and authoritarian notions about the "correctness" or "fitness" of language?

Any effort to clean up medical jargon should start with those uncommon expressions that truly distort meaning, such as *60-decibel hearing loss* instead of *60-decibel hearing threshold*, or *reversal of A/G* ('albumin-globulin') *ratio* instead of *shift* or *abnormality of A/G ratio*. But it is not my purpose here to sort out the faults of medical jargon, only to survey the subject. Informal, unconventional, and unorthodox it may be, but scarcely meaningless or unwieldy to those who use it daily.

Linguists and lexicographers have tried, with little success, to distinguish argot, slang, cant, and jargon, assigning a special definition to each. According to the only widely accepted distinction, *slang* refers to informal usages in the general language, while an *argot, cant,* or *jargon* is a special idiom understood and used almost exclusively by members of a trade, profession, or "subculture."

Slang is easier to recognize than to define. Perhaps its most essential trait is its novelty, its departure from well-trodden paths of form, meaning, and propriety. Among other characteristics may be mentioned its use of humor, often wry and based on ingenuity or incongruity; its tendency to be blunt and pejorative, despite occasional flashes of euphemism; its extravagance; and its evanescence. Not one slang coinage in ten thousand becomes a lasting part of the language. Those that do survive may change radically in meaning.

Technical argot, like slang, is a dynamic and rapidly evolving medium, with regional peculiarities and shifting conventions. Medicalese includes a broad range of terms and usages, from the crassly vulgar to the slightly quaint. Though medical argot is born in speech, as are all other forms of language, it soon gets into writing—first in medical records and then, despite the vigilance of editors, in published matter. The succinctness, directness, and vigor of many of these new and unconventional words and phrases lend them so strong an appeal that, in defiance of purists and pedants, they become legitimized by long usage. *Leukocytosis with a left shift, a high index of suspicion, soft irradiation, pastpointing, thyroid storm, sticky rales, medical curettage, sick sinus syndrome,* and *lupoderma* are all irregular in formation or eccentric in tone, or both, but they have won general acceptance because they are apt and vivid.

Nearly every piece of argot is either a metaphor (*bug* 'pathogenic microorganism'), a neologism (*crock* 'hypochondriac'), or a variation on a legitimate word (*sed rate* 'sedimentation rate'; *orthopod* 'orthopedist'), usage (*urgency* 'an urgent medical problem', on the analogy of *emergency*; *emergent* 'of the nature of an emergency', on the analogy of *urgent*), or meaning (*visualize* 'make visible', in radiography; *seize* 'have a seizure').

To a great extent medicalese consists of common English words used in special ways. The preposition *on*, for example, has acquired the meaning 'under treatment with', no doubt by analogy with its sense in general slang (*on dope, on the sauce*). This usage has been extended to modes of treatment other than drugs, and even to diagnostic procedures, so that a patient may be said to be put, placed, started, or tried on nasal oxygen, on postural drainage, or on strained urines. "She was placed on hot packs" means that hot packs were placed on her. *On* also means 'about' or 'in the case of', as: "We did a count on her," or "We may have to go in on him yet tonight." Still another sense of this word is seen in: "On auscultation a pericardial friction rub was heard" and "On section the liver was hyperemic."

Physicians also use *for* in many ways that may appear unidiomatic to lay observers: *secretagogues for* ('stimulating release of') *insulin; antiserum specific for* ('specifically against') *pancreatic glucagon; dysphagia for* ('caused by swallowing') *solids; negative for* ('when tested for') *protein; positive family history for* ('of') *diabetes; at increased risk for* ('of developing') *hypertension.*

To have appears in a variety of medical idioms, perhaps most of them parallel to expressions in the general language. A patient can have a symptom (chills), a sign (crepitant rales), a disease (pneumonia), a diagnostic procedure (sputum smear), a laboratory finding (gram-positive diplococci), a drug (penicillin), a therapeutic procedure (tracheal aspiration), a surgical operation (segmental resection), and an uneventful recovery. He may even be said to have something that he does not have: "The patient had absent breath sounds at the left base posteriorly."

To *have* all these things, the patient must first *get* them. In discussing a given disease, physicians often use the formula, "They get . . . ," referring to symptoms and complications that may affect persons with the disease. *Get* can also mean 'to order or perform a test' ("I got a bilirubin"), 'to be treated with' ("He was getting chlorpromazine"), or 'to become' ("He was getting jaundiced"). *To run* figures in several specialized idioms, where it may mean 'to perform a test' ("We ran serial blood cultures") or 'to display an abnormal sign' ("He was running four-plus albumins"). *To pass* means 'to expel some material or substance from a natural or other orifice', as blood in the urine, stones in the bile, or mucus in the stool. *To spill* ("She's spilling sugar and acetone") refers to substances abnormally excreted in the urine.

Besides meaning that an unconscious patient is 'coming to', the verb *respond* may apply to a disease that improves with treatment:

"Anginal pain responded to nitroglycerine", "penicillin-responsive fever." Both patients and diseases may be said to *present*: "The patient presented with sudden complete loss of vision in the right eye"; "Multiple sclerosis may present as acute urinary retention."

A *study* is any diagnostic procedure ("radiographic studies of the colon"; "liver function studies"), but *work* usually implies clinical laboratory tests, as in *blood work*. Many a *work-up* 'thorough diagnostic evaluation' consists largely of this kind of *work*. Physicians *read* x-rays, electrocardiograms, thermometers, and even skin tests. *To monitor* is 'to maintain surveillance over a natural or abnormal state or process by frequent or continuous collection of data'. *To see* a patient is 'to interview, examine, or treat him'; *to follow* him is 'to continue to see him at intervals'. *To scrub on a case*, or simply *to scrub*, means 'to take an active part in a surgical operation'. *To round* means 'to make hospital rounds', as in "the rounding group."

An intravenous infusion of fluid has long been known as a *drip* because of the drip-chamber method of noting flow rate. Gastric and colonic infusions were so called even earlier. Rapid injection of a drug directly into the circulation is called a *push*; it may also be termed an *IV bolus*. Bottles of intravenous solution connected in tandem are said to be *piggybacked*. A mixture of drugs prepared just before administration may be called a *cocktail*.

Many usages peculiar to medicine do not strike the physician as argot because he fails to notice how far they diverge from lay English. The surest test of what is argot and what is not may be the reaction of an outsider. As examples of conventional words with unconventional meanings in medicalese, consider the following: acute hepatic *insult*, a *generous* biopsy, to *discourage* keloid formation, diabetes *intractable to* oral *agents*, peptic ulcer *refractory to* conservative management, an *episode* of hypoglycemia, *documented* pancreatitis, a pulmonary *cripple, classical* migraine, lymphocytes are *elevated*, the patient is *sensitive* to penicillin, the infecting organism is *sensitive* to penicillin, an increase in unconjugated *values*, aspirin was *incriminated, heroic* doses, *elderly* primigravida, and blood *picture* (source or imitation of German *Blutbild*?)

Secondary to now invariably means not merely 'following after' but 'caused by'. *Void*, a euphemism unfamiliar to most lay persons, loses its literal sense in *postvoiding residual*. On first meeting an expression like *rule out chronic pancreatitis*, the nonphysician will probably suppose that the diagnosis has already been excluded. *Diagnostic impression: gastroenteritis vs. food poisoning* may suggest an internal warfare between the two diseases (a veritable *bellum intestinum*).

Even a technical term having a strict dictionary definition may be used in a much broader sense in daily speech and sometimes even in formal writing: *acute* digitalization, *acute* release of thyroid hormone, *chronic* anticonvulsant therapy, *noninflammatory* synovial fluid, she looks *toxic*. A suspension of antigenic dust or pollen is frequently called a *vaccine* or even a *serum*. Terms borrowed by medicine from other scientific disciplines seldom retain their meanings intact. *Titration of dosage* is an instantly intelligible metaphor. But *aliquot*, for any measured quantity, and *increment*, for any small quantity, are not so much metaphors as mistakes.

When *noninvasive* first entered the language of medicine, it referred to tumors. Later it was used for diagnostic procedures in cardiology that do not require the introduction of instruments or foreign materials into the vascular system. Given this context, the antonym *invasive* might be thought to carry a slightly derogatory sense. Such, however, is not the case: the recently certified specialist proudly announces to prospective employers that he is fully trained as an *invasive* cardiologist.

The creation of new jargon is typically spontaneous, an almost haphazard response to a suddenly felt want. Families of terms may come into existence almost overnight. For example, in announcing a cardiopulmonary emergency on a hospital public address system it is customary to use a code expression so as to avoid upsetting patients and visitors: "Code Ninety-Nine, Six East." Hence any effort at cardiopulmonary resuscitation in the hospital has come to be known as a *code*, and from this new piece of jargon derivatives continue to be formed: *to call a code* 'to announce the need for cardiopulmonary resuscitation'; *a successful code* 'a resuscitation effort that saved the patient'; *code cart* 'a wheeled cabinet containing drugs and supplies for resuscitation'; *code drug* 'a drug that belongs on the code cart'; *no-code patient* 'a patient whose doctor or family has countermanded resuscitation efforts in the event of cardiac arrest'.

If many of the usages in medicalese seem to hover between argot and conventional language, others quite plainly represent a deliberate retreat from formal terminology, as when a severed blood vessel is called a *bleeder, spurter,* or *gusher;* a contaminated instrument is referred to as *dirty;* a blood culture is said to be *cooking;* or *Mycobacterium tuberculosis* is called the *red bug* or *red snapper* (allusions to its appearance in a smear stained by the acid-fast method).

Some informal locutions are particularly vigorous: *slap a PPD on him, he blew out an aneurysm, she's been flipping PVCs* (or *emboli*), *he's going to clank* ('have a grand mal seizure'), *he spiked a fever, they reamed out her left carotid three years ago, wastebasket diagnosis, shotgun therapy.* Some are even brutal: *It's time to yank his gizzard, he needs a dose of cold steel* ('surgery'), *I have to water the vegetables* ('administer intravenous fluids to comatose patients'), *we'll have to crack her squash* (or *gourd*) ('perform craniotomy'). In French medical argot, incidentally, the latter expression (*fendre la calebasse*) refers to an abdominal operation. Though *duck* is American hospital slang for 'a urinal', French *canard* 'duck' means 'a vaginal speculum'. The French physician, who refers to blood as *sauce* and to a nurse as *Mme Piquefesse* 'Mrs. Piercebottom', says that a patient in the lithotomy position has *monté le chameau* 'mounted the camel'.

Words and phrases may be debarred from formal terminology simply because they sound slightly jocular. Among these may be mentioned informal adjectives ending in *-y* (*schizzy, shocky*), alliterations (*pink puffer, blue bloater*), and rhymes (*jelly belly* 'pseudo-myxoma peritonei'). Nouns used as verbs usually start by shocking the staid (*to guaiac, to Swan-Ganz*) and end by becoming standard (*to bandage, to bronchoscope*). A similar development is typical of verbs formed with *-ize: hemoptysize, heparinize,* and *digitalize.*

Syncopated, abbreviated, and elliptical terms are usually too pert and breezy for medical editors and compilers of dictionaries. Often the beginning or end of a word is omitted in speech: (*electro*)*lytes,* (*electrocardio*)*gram, multip*(*ara*), *osteo*(*myelitis*), *staph*(*ylococcus*), *strep*(*tococcus*). Though aortic *regurge* ('regurgitation') and *rehab* ('rehabilitation') are still considered a bit crude, *consult* ('consultation') and *assist* ('assistance at surgery') are now generally accepted. *Prep,* from *prepare,* in hospital parlance can mean either 'to shave the skin in preparation for surgery' or 'to empty the colon before x-ray examination'. *Hemostat,* from *hemostatic forceps,* has entirely supplanted the longer term. It sometimes crops up nowadays as a nonce word referring to the control of erythropoiesis, on the analogy of *thermostat*. To a dentist a hemostat is not an instrument but a chemical or packing material.

Equally common is the practice of omitting one or more words from a standard phrase: *white (blood cell) count, differential (white blood cell count)* or *(diagnosis), (adrenal cortical) steroid, (x-ray examination of the) upper GI (tract), (hydrogen) peroxide, post (mortem examination). Coronary*, for *coronary thrombosis*, has been abandoned by the medical profession in favor of *myocardial infarction* and is now a lay term. Often the part of a phrase that is retained seems less meaningful than what is omitted, as when a gynecologist speaks of the *portio (vaginalis of the cervix)* or a thoracic surgeon of a *pectus (excavatum). Medulla*, Latin for 'pith or marrow', classically refers to the spinal cord, but when qualified by the participle *oblongata* 'prolonged, extended', it means (by an almost whimsical stretch of the imagination) 'that part of the brain that is an extension of the cord'. Yet it is just to that part of the brain, and almost never to the cord, that the unqualified term *medulla* refers in modern medicalese. As these examples suggest, this kind of truncation is especially common with non-English phrases. It also occurs with taxonomic terms: the frequent use of *coli* for *Bacillus* (later *Escherichia*) *coli* led to the formation of the mongrel adjective *coliform*. Another irregularity of this type that has been ratified by usage is the conversion of the Latin participle *alternans* (as in *pulsus alternans*) into a noun, *electrical alternans.*

English freely forms noun phrases by juxtaposition of two or more words whose syntactic relations are erratic or elusive. Imagine a foreigner with a pocket dictionary trying to decipher *quarter horse, flea collar,* or *baby-sitter*. Examples of this kind of double Dutch in medicalese are *acute abdomen, ambulant facilities, extrapyramidal signs, febrile agglutinins, liver panel, lordotic film, mechanical diet, parturient purpura, split renal functions,* and *street virus.*

Some medical jargon, without being elliptical, seems horribly vague to the uninitiated. *Shake lotion* tells nothing about ingredients or purpose. *Cutdown* might mean almost any surgical procedure instead of just venesection with placement of a catheter. It has been objected that *accident* is too indefinite in *cerebrovascular accident (CVA)*. But Italian *accidente* and Portuguese *acidente*, besides denoting casualties due to external violence, are the lay words for 'a stroke'.

The technical language of medicine is long on names for diseases and short on terms for persons afflicted with those diseases. Except for a few convenient words like *albino, cretin,* and *pellagrin,* epithets for patients are usually nouns such as *hypertensive, diabetic,* and *cirrhotic* that retain the suffixes of the adjectives from which they were formed. Even these terms, which some have condemned as harsh and degrading, are in remarkably short supply. One cannot say that a patient is a *tuberculotic* or a *hypertriglyceridemic.* One can say *a hemophiliac* but not *an eosinophiliac; a somnambulist* but not *a prostatist; an amputee* but not a *gastrojejunostomee.* Hence terms for patients are often inventions whose awkwardness or irregularity dooms them to remain in the realm of argot. Among these are agent nouns ending in -*er* (*sickler; stone-former; GI bleeder; couch-diver* 'one who is eager for psychotherapy') and such variants as *stroker* and *Raynauder.* Perhaps the most common expedient is to say that a patient *is,* for example, a *lymphosarcoma of the stomach,* a *diabetes insipidus,* or a *pancreatectomy.* Usually only the proper name is retained if the word for the disease is an eponym: "He's *a Ménière's*" (or, if the disease is of long standing, "*an old Ménière's*").

Physicians are adept at measuring things by the most convenient yardstick. Because a *two-diopter choke* (of the optic disc), *three-pillow orthopnea,* and *four fingerbreadths of hepatic enlargement* have no metric equivalents, they may be thought a bit informal for printed reports. The same may be said of a *thrombosed hemorrhoid at five o'clock.*

The comic element so typical of general slang finds expression in the argot of medicine principally in wisecracks and nonce words, witty but evanescent. One may in moments of levity call a proctologist a *rear admiral* or refer to cavitary tuberculosis as *conspicuous consumption,* but even this puerile level of humor is lacking in the workaday expressions that belong to the more lasting and widespread part of medicalese.

The argot of medicine is drawn from many sources. In his student days the physician learns the ancient tag, *freshman's nerve,* for the plantaris tendon, and discovers that a *pearl* is a medical maxim, always concise and sometimes true. The physician in private practice picks up such terms as *script, tab, cap,* and *legend drug* from pharmacists.

The laboratory researcher has his own brand of jargon. When he writes that his experimental animals were *sacrificed by cervical dislocation*, he means that he 'killed them by wringing their necks'. Instead of bluntly referring to the mating of laboratory animals, he borrows the lawyer's stuffy circumlocution, *cohabitation*.

Words and phrases from the jargons of commerce, government, and technology have been borrowed or adapted by physicians in recent years, as medicine forms increasingly close ties with these fields. It is often objected that terms like *health industry, health services consumer, health maintenance organization,* and *delivery of care* degrade the practice of medicine from a professional activity to a commercial enterprise. Computer technology has contributed *feedback, input, interface,* and *software*. Other terms like *marginal, module, protocol,* and *profile* have entered medicalese from related sources. Though some of these borrowings prove apt and succinct (lipid *profile*, broad-*spectrum* antibiotic), others degenerate into mere doubletalk (*scope, factor, orientation, parameter*).

Medical speech and writing have not altogether escaped the taint of gobbledygook, the tangled gibberish of politics. Characterized by studied imprecision, unrestrained verbosity, and an implicit denial of human involvement in anything, gobbledygook is an alarmingly contagious disorder of language and thought. Medical writing is often encumbered with snatches of gobbledygook, as when one reads that something happened *on a daily basis* instead of *daily*, or was done *at weekly intervals* instead of *weekly*, or that a rash was *pruritic in nature* instead of just *pruritic*. Brief and pithy English words are scrapped in favor of long-winded and often nebulous phrases, so that *neck* becomes *cervical region* and *bones* masquerade as *osseous structures*. Some of these inflated terms have been adopted as euphemisms, for instance, *purulent material* for *pus* and *inguinal area* for *groin*.

Schoolmarms and editors may rage against these and other objectionable features of medicalese, but their impassioned diatribes and efforts at reform will probably have no lasting effects. Even though physicians may be compelled to accept external controls on their training and licensure, professional activities, and fee scales, it is unlikely that they will ever submit to having their shoptalk amended or regulated by outsiders.

Medicalese II

Some shrewd old doctors have a few phrases always on hand for patients that will insist on knowing the pathology of their

complaints without the slightest capacity of understanding the
scientific explanation. I have known the term "spinal irritation"
serve well on such occasions, but I think nothing on the whole
has covered so much ground, and meant so little, and given such
profound satisfaction to all parties, as the magnificent phrase
"congestion of the portal system."

Oliver Wendell Holmes
"The Young Practitioner," in
Medical Essays

The physician who spends much of his time working directly with adult patients usually develops a hybrid jargon for discussing diagnoses and treatments with them. For example, he may refer to a diuretic injection as a *water shot,* gastroenteritis as *stomach flu,* and a vaginal examination as an *internal.* In most instances a slight sacrifice of scientific accuracy is more than justified by the gain in intelligibility. Sometimes, indeed, insistence on precise terminology is undesirable.

Using lay terms does not, of course, guarantee comprehension by a layman. It is true that *spinal tap* may be more meaningful, and sound less painful, than *lumbar puncture* and that *hardening of the arteries* is a literal rendering of *arteriosclerosis* into plain English. But the *walls of the heart,* the *lining of the chest,* and the *neck of the womb* can convey little more information to the anatomically unsophisticated than *myocardium, pleura,* or *cervix.*

Some of the words commonly used in this form of medicalese are not lay terms at all but technical ones vaguely or incorrectly applied. Thus, *colitis, kidney infection,* and *low blood pressure* often serve as convenient labels for conditions widely different from those named. Informing a patient that his joint pains are due to *arthralgia* or diagnosing a sore throat as *pharyngitis* is playing at word games, not practicing medicine. One is reminded of Kant's observation that physicians think they have done a great deal for the patient when they have given his disease a name.

No doubt we are all guilty from time to time of evading unpleasant issues by using ephemisms like *growth* for 'malignancy' or noncommittal words like *weight* for 'obesity' and *problem* for 'alcoholism'. Certainly it is only common decency to avoid, when possible, such emotionally charged words as *cancer, epilepsy, underdeveloped,* and *senile.* But there are also good reasons for not adopting substitute terms that are nebulous (*the beginnings of an ulcer*), elusive (*a blood condition*), or so inaccurate that they actually mean something else (*excess acid in the system, heart spasms*).

Medicalese III

Subtle: *Infuse vinegar,*
    To draw his volatile substance and his tincture:
    And let the water in glass E be filt'red,
    And put into the gripe's egg. Lute him well;
    And leave him closed in balneo.
Face: [within]   *I will, sir.*
Surly: *What a brave language here is! Next to canting.*

                        Ben Jonson
                      The Alchemist

Besides the special jargon that physicians use when they speak to patients about technical matters, there is yet another patois in which physicians converse among themselves about these matters when they must do so in the presence of the patient. The former idiom is intended to make complex ideas intelligible, the latter to make simple ideas opaque. Most clinical teaching is done in the patient's presence (and often within earshot of several of his ward mates). Even the uneducated and incurious patient might be expected to make some sense out of plainly spoken references to unwelcome diagnoses or impending catastrophes. Hence physicians customarily veil embarrassing or disagreeable subjects in a cryptic double-talk that has meaning only within the medical fraternity.

For instance, one does not speak of a tentative diagnosis of syphilis before the patient; one uses the archaic *lues.* If the patient's heart is his weak spot, one talks of his *cor;* if one thinks he has something wrong with his liver, one discusses his *hepar.* If, further, one attributes that liver trouble to the chronic abuse of alcohol, one may refer to *ethanolism* or *chronic overexposure to EtOH.* A malignancy may be called a *neoplasm* or a *space-occupying* or *mitotic lesion. Hemoglobin, heme, red cells, erythrocytes,* and *RBCs* may all be used as oblique references to blood; *panniculus* and *signet-ring cells,* to obesity; *acid-fast disease,* to tuberculosis; *motor disorder* or *dysrhythmic episodes,* to epilepsy; *ketogenic disturbance of carbohydrate metabolism,* to diabetes mellitus.

If the patient's death seems imminent, it may be suggested that the exact nature of his trouble will soon be made clear by Dr. MacTavish, or Schultz, or Paglioni, or whoever is the hospital pathologist. Or one may refer to an imminent transfer to *Room 301* (if that is the number of the morgue) or to the *thirteenth floor*, a veiled allusion to heaven, also known as the *Eternal Care Unit*.

A patient whose complaints seem largely imaginary, or at least unrelated to any organic disease, is said to have a *supratentorial* problem. This term may also refer to mental illness or incompetence. Extreme stupidity may also be dubbed *Betz cell atrophy*, not very aptly since Betz cells are found in the motor cortex. The slang term *crock*, meaning 'a person with many complaints for which no organic basis can be found', has spawned such derivatives as *a high serum porcelain* level and *psychoceramic medicine*.

While carefully avoiding frightening or derogatory terms in their bedside discussions, physicians may use terms that seem perfectly innocent to them but that offend or alarm the patient because he misinterprets them. Every medical student has heard the story about the attending physician who put his hand on a female patient's chest, dryly remarked that he felt no *thrill,* and was rewarded with a slap in the face. What must a patient think who learns that his physicians plan to *get a liver panel on him* or to *look for light chains in his urine* or who hears himself characterized as a *possible chronic brain*?

Patientese

The doctor contributed everything to my gall, and gave me a subscription to strengthen my kidneys.

Anonymous

Physicians do not have a monopoly on the use and abuse of medical terminology. The language of medicine, with its resounding polysyllabic words and its aura of drama and mystery, has always exercised an irresistible fascination on the lay mind. From the Middle Ages almost to our own day, any mountebank with a few scraps of Latin at his command could convince the gullible of his medical learning and skill.

Patients themselves delight in exchanging exotic-sounding diagnoses and comparing drug names. Their inability to remember such words accurately can be used as an argument both for and against labeling prescription packages with drug names. The patient cannot go far wrong as long as the label is in front of him, but when it is not his recollection of the name of the drug is apt to undergo astonishing metamorphoses.

Lay medical language is based largely on misconceptions and misunderstandings of human anatomy, physiology, pathology, and pharmacology, on scientifically invalid groupings and distinctions of facts and phenomena, on folk medicine and superstition. Insofar as this language varies from that of the physician, it can be considered under the fourfold division of standard English, dialect, conscious slang, and error.

The medical English discussed in Chapter 2 consists of words and phrases used by the medical profession as part of its technical vocabulary. A great many other lay expressions never find their way into the speech of physicians. The patient may say that he has *stoved* a finger, or feels a *stitch* in his side, or a *crick* in his neck, or that his eye is *mattering*, or that he has a *bum* ankle, or a *gimpy* leg, or a *trick* knee. If these terms get into medical records at all, they will probably be put in quotation marks. Some common vernacular expressions are avoided by physicians because they are misleading or inaccurate: *heartburn* has nothing to do with the heart, *hay fever* does not cause a fever, and *poison ivy* is a plant, not a skin eruption.

In lay use the name of a symptom or disease is often preceded by the definite article: *the flu, the gout, the hiccups, the measles*; the indefinite article is usual with words for isolated events or intermittent troubles: *a fever, a migraine, a hemorrhage.* (In German, *Diarrhöe* is sometimes cut down to *'Arrhöe* by uneducated speakers, who take the first syllable to be the definite article *die*; so also *'Abetes* for *Diabetes*.) In contrast, physicians are more likely to use the indefinite article with disease names (*an encephalitis, a pneumonia*) and the definite article with anatomic terms (*the intestine, the kidney*) where the layman omits the article and pluralizes the noun (*intestines, kidneys, brains*). Even *appendix* is apt to be regarded as a plural ("My appendix? They're out".). Here may be mentioned also the lay solecism *double hernia* when *bilateral inguinal hernias* are meant. Other lay plurals not used by the physician are *aspirins, guts,* and *ulcers*; but the physician has his own set of irrational plurals, including *salicylates, steroids, chlorides,* and *antibodies.* (The latter is now common in foreign literature even when only one antibody is meant; cf. Italian *anticorpi* and Spanish *anticorpos*.)

Standard medical English fosters many euphemisms such as *period* 'menstruation', *cramps* 'dysmenorrhea', *passage* 'defecation', *irregularity* 'constipation', and *expire* 'die'. It also preserves a host of old-fashioned terms that were once used in medicine but have now died out: *wen* 'sebaceous cyst', *physic* or *cathartic* 'laxative', and *rheumatism* 'aches in joints or muscles'. Certain lay terms have been created, or at least perpetuated, by journalists and "science writers", among them *birth canal, rib cage* (cf. German *Brustkorb* 'chest basket'), and *voice box*. We have the journalists to thank also for *miracle* and *wonder drug, scientific breakthrough, guarded condition* (for 'the prognosis is guarded'), and *truth serum*.

Many of the numerous ethnic and regional dialects spoken in the United States share a core of medical expressions that may be heard almost anywhere in the country. A *raising* or *rising* (often pronounced *raisin'* and hence apt to be confused with the dried fruit) is any swelling on the surface of the body. It may also be called a *kernel* or a *knot*. *Beal*, a variation on *boil*, is often used in an adjectival sense ("a bealed ear"). This is an ancient dialectal word that was in use in English as early as the fourteenth century. Much older still is *gathering*, noun and adjective, referring to suppuration, as in *gathering* ('infected and draining') *ears*. Irritation of the skin due to friction is called *galding*, and skin so affected is said to be *galded*. These are popular corruptions of *galling* and *galled*.

Syncope is *falling out*, and diarrhea is *running off*. A urethral discharge is called a *strain* unless it is due to gonorrhea; then it is *the clap* or *claps*. The primary chancre of syphilis (*blood disease, bad blood*) is known as a *haircut*. *Water* may mean tissue fluid, as in *water on the knee*, but more often refers to urine. *Bowels* can mean either the intestine or its discharges. *Cold* (often *col'*) is mucus, originally nasopharyngeal but by extension any other kind, as in, "My baby is passing cold with her bowels."

Smarting (usually, 'stinging of eyes or skin') is akin to Middle English *smerte*, Dutch *smart*, and German *Schmerz*, all words for 'pain'. Compare also, "It hurts right smart." *Sleep* is inspissated mucus in the corners of the eyes. A *hickey* is an ecchymosis of the kind described by Tibullus as *livor . . . quem facit impresso mutua dente venus*.

Deliberately formed slang expressions for medical matters are partly the result of patients' inability to reproduce accurately the pronunciation of "big" medical words, partly a reflection of their efforts to keep up their spirits in the face of suffering. Among teenagers, acne pustules are commonly known as *zits*, despite the cosmetic manufacturers' insistence on the genteel euphemism *blemish*. Vomiting has a number of colorful slang designations, including *barf, heave, toss, pitch, urp,* and *up-chuck.*

Lay medical slang includes many of the unprintable words in the common speech connected with excretory and reproductive functions. Socially acceptable synonyms for these "gutter" words may be expressions borrowed from the nursery and the schoolroom, like *weewee, bottom,* and *number two.* Diarrhea is known by a variety of bitterly humorous epithets such as *the runs* and *the trots.* Most of the numerous names for tourist diarrhea include geographic references: *Aztec two-step, Casablanca crud, lower Burmas, San Franciscitis, gyppy* (or *Egyptian*) *tummy, Basra belly, Hongkong dog, Montezuma's revenge, Delhi belly, Poona poohs, squitters,* and *tourist trots.*

Lay terms for doctors are usually jocular and often pejorative: *sawbones,* ingeniously but doubtfully derived from *Sorbonne; pill peddler; croaker;* and (for a psychiatrist) *shrink,* from *headshrinker.* The verb *to doctor* (a drink, a report) usually implies craft or dishonesty ("Doctor my drink and I'll nurse it all evening").

Military medical slang has contributed *GI gin* ('elixir of terpin hydrate') and *blackout* (noun and verb), referring to 'transient loss of consciousness', first used by World War II aviators for brief syncopal spells during powered dives. *Paramedics* once referred to 'medical corpsmen ("medics") trained as parachutists', though its current sense is of course based on a different etymology.

Laymen's language has also been enriched by borrowings from the argot of athletics (*Charley horse, shin splints,* and such nicknames for muscles as *lat* 'latissimus dorsi' and *quad* 'quadriceps femoris') and drug abuse (*uppers, downers, yellow jackets* 'Nembutal' and its generic impersonators, *dexies* 'Dexedrine', and *bennies* 'Benzedrine').

Abbreviated forms of medical terms are as popular with laymen as with physicians: *mono* for *mononucleosis, polio* for *poliomyelitis, trich* (or *trick*) for *trichomonal vaginitis,* and *flu* for *influenza.* The latter term has a variety of meanings to nonphysicians, including

gastroenteritis, acute viral syndrome, and indeed any illness whatsoever characterized by fever and malaise.

Patients occasionally fabricate their own unconventional forms
of speech. A diabetic who tells his doctor that he has been "blue for
two weeks" may be reporting a bout of depression but is more likely
indicating that his urine has been consistently negative for sugar when
tested with Clinitest tablets. Lay terminology can be just as be-
wildering to the physician as technical terms are to the patient. *Bone
bruise, growing pains, sun poisoning,* and *walking pneumonia* do not
admit of precise definition, a fact to which patients may react with
incredulity or annoyance. Folk etymology is nowhere so active as on
folk terminology. Thus, *seed warts,* so called because they look like
(?poppy) seeds, are often believed to be capable of "seeding" the body
surface with their offspring (as indeed they are, but no more so than
other warts). *Liver spots,* named for their color, are often assumed to
be signs of liver disease. *Gangrene* is often expected to appear
green.

Pronunciations that are regionally acceptable (*gooms* for *gums* in
the Dakotas and the Ozarks, *fleem* for *phlegm* in Appalachia) may
not seem quite appropriate in standard medical English. Errors in
pronunciation may be simple phonetic blunders, such as *bronichal,
chicken pops, clog* (for *clot*), *dip'theria, infantigo, prostrate* (for
prostate), *vomick,* and *wound* (for *womb*). But they may also betoken
complete misunderstanding of the purport of a word or phrase, as in
high anus (*hiatus*) *hernia, very close* (*varicose*) *veins,* and *purple*
(*puerperal*) *fever,* perhaps by analogy with the scarlet and yellow
varieties. (French *émeraudes* 'emeralds' for *hémorroïdes* may be a
phonetic error or deliberate slang, depending on the educational level
of the speaker.)

Lay errors in terminology often arise from confusion about
anatomy. *Stomach,* to perhaps a majority of nomedical people, means
the lower two-thirds of the ventral body surface. The *anus* is generally
referred to as the *rectum* and the *vulva* as the *vagina.* The *gallbladder*
is frequently confounded with the *urinary bladder* and the *spinal cord*
with the *spinal column.* When the patient speaks of his *system,* he
may mean his digestive system in general, or its nether reaches in
particular, or again he may be indulging in an abstraction of about the
same degree of vagueness as the physician's *metabolism.*

Schizophrenia is almost universally taken to mean a 'dual or split personality'. *Psychosomatic* is often truncated to plain *somatic*, which means just the opposite. *Hypertension* (by confusion with *tension*) signifies a 'chronic anxiety neurosis' to many and *bandage* (through the influence of Band-Aid), a 'dressing or compress'. Any laboratory test may be called a *count* ("My uric acid count was high"); any headache, a *migraine*; and any chronic upper respiratory complain, *sinus* ('I've had sinus for years"). Physicians may disparage the lay use of *temperature* to mean 'fever', but it is likely that this practice began within the medical profession. A thorough misunderstanding of the term is evident when a person asked whether he has *diarrhea* replies that he doesn't know because he hasn't been to the bathroom for several days. *My back went out* is an echo of chiropractic drivel. *Complex*, introduced in the psychiatric sense by Neisser in 1906 and soon afterward popularized by C. G. Jung, by the 1920s had become a much-abused fad word.

Sulfonamides are often called *sulfur drugs*, and *barbituate* is an extremely common error both in spelling and in pronunciation. Antibiotics are lumped together as the *mycins*, which more often than not is given an extra syllable, perhaps by attraction to *niacin*. Many laymen take *medical ethics* to mean not the whole body of moral principles regulating the practice of medicine but specifically a physician's reluctance to discuss his patients or to defame his colleagues.

Nursese

Nurses are wonderful women and dedicated ministering angels, and they have no time to fritter away on the trivia of spelling and pronunciation.

James Thurber
"The Tyranny of Trivia"

Between the patient, whose lack of professional training excuses even the most flagrant garbling of medical terms, and the physician, who arrogantly believes that his own usage of these terms should set an inviolable standard, the nurse is trapped in a kind of linguistic limbo. On the one hand, she is expected to understand the physician's argot no matter how far it diverges from formal terminology; on the other, she is frequently called upon to interpret his cryptic utterances to the patient. Small wonder if her use of technical language sometimes hovers between professional and lay.

For instance, if you ask a nurse whether a razor blade can cause a laceration, or whether tracheal aspiration can relieve congestion, you will probably get an affirmative answer. But a physician would reply that a *laceration*, literally a 'tear', is the result of blunt trauma, whereas a razor blade inflicts an incised wound. He would also say that *congestion* is a vascular phenomenon and has nothing to do with the presence of excessive secretions. Similarly, the meanings attached by the nurse to *concussion, constipation,* and *paranoid* are apt to be closer to the popular definitions of these terms than to the much more specific ones cherished by physicians.

Nursing has a voluminous argot of its own. *Confused* and *involuntary* are the nurse's versions of the physician's *disoriented* and *incontinent.* Certain trade names (*Gurney, Posey*) and abbreviations (*TPR* 'temperature, pulse, and respirations'; *FOOB* 'fell out of bed') get more use from the nursing than from the medical profession. Helping a patient to sit on the side of his bed with his feet dangling is called simply *dangling*, a term that has flabbergasted many a neophyte physician. *Grafting* (of temperature readings) is just *graphing* with a parasitic consonant.

Nurses also have their own exotic brand of Latin in which *noc* means 'night' (even forming the compounds *midnoc* and *tonoc*), and $\bar{c}$ is used not in the sense of Latin *cum* (of which it is an abbreviation) but in the broader Germanic sense of English *with*: "Area cleansed $\bar{c}$ soap and water": "Patient very angry $\bar{c}$ orderly"; "Five mL blood $\bar{c}$drawn."

Typistese

Phantom word: *A word that came into being through an error of a lexicographer or printer.*

Mario A. Pei and Frank Gaynor
A Dictionary of Linguistics

Even with all its variety and vigor, the language of medicine might be a rather stodgy and sterile idiom were it not for the delicious element of absurdity introduced by the medical records typist. What a boost she can give to the dramatic interest of an operative report by starting it off with the statement, "The patient was prepped and raped in the usual manner"! What zest she can add to an otherwise prosaic and tedious medical history by inserting a statement like, "The patient experienced weakness and a pair of seizures in the left lower leg"!

There is a subtle difference between these two examples. The first is probably a typing error, like the recurring ribtickler *extra ocular muscles*. But *a pair of seizures* roughly and somewhat naïvely reproduces the phonetics of *paresthesias* with wrong but still legitimate words. Phonetic misspellings much commoner than this one are *sinus track* (for *tract*), *shoddy* (for *shotty*) *lymph nodes*, and such dissociations as *serous sanguineous* and *normal tensive*. Inevitably, *Roth's spots* sometimes become *raw spots*, and *hypesthesia* turns up as *hip esthesia*.

With disturbing frequency, transcription errors reverse the meaning of the original: *had no carcinoma* for *adenocarcinoma, an ovulatory cycle* for *anovulatory cycle, no degenerative joint disease* for *known degenerative joint disease*. More elaborate reworkings of what the physician dictated are less often serious than ludicrous, such as *cannot rule out brain absence*. A surgeon was staggered to read that he had incised a cyst with *a sharp and clean borrowed pocketknife*. What he had actually mumbled into the dictating machine was: "a size fifteen Bard-Parker knife."

Careless dictating habits and the limitations of recording systems are no doubt at the root of most of these errors. Whatever their source, they enrich and enliven typewritten clinical records with an unfailing and unpredictable stream of absurdity.

References and Readings

Barkley D: Hospital talk. *Am Speech* 1927;2:312-314.

Berney LV, Van den Bark M: *American Thesaurus of Slang*, 2nd ed. New York, Thomas Y. Crowell Co., 1953.

Farmer JA, Henley WE: *Slang and Its Analogues*. New York, Arno, 1970.

Hardy RE, Cull JG: *Drug Language and Lore*. Springfield, Illinois, Charles C. Thomas, 1975.

House DE: Hospital lingo. *Am Speech* 1938;13:227-229.

Hukill PB: The spoken language of medicine: argot, slang, cant. *Am Speech* 1961;36:146-148.

Hyde LS: *A Discursive Dictionary of Health Care*. Washington, D.C., U.S. Government Printing Office, 1976.

Kolin PC: The language of nursing. *Am Speech* 1973;48:192-210.

Mencken HL: *The American Language*, 4th ed. New York, Alfred A. Knopf, 1937.

Partridge E: *Slang To-day and Yesterday*, 4th ed. London, Routledge & Kegan Paul, 1970.

Peanuts and Tea. A Selected Glossary of Terms Used by Drug Addicts. Lexington, Kentucky, National Institute of Mental Health Clinical Research Center, 1972.

Sandry G., Carrère M: *L'Argot Moderne*. Paris, Éditions du Dauphin, 1974.

CHAPTER 7

Diseases of the Tongue

This final chapter attempts not simply to catalog ways in which physicians mishandle language but also to show some of the reasons for this mishandling and to distinguish harmless linguistic evolution from changes that prevent language from transmitting thoughts clearly and coherently. The perpetual drive toward change, a vital, creative, and essential force in language, is held in check by an opposing drive toward stability, a conservative force arising from the need for language to remain generally intelligible. The product of the endless give-and-take between change and stability is that abstraction that is called *a language*.

Meaning is primary in language—indeed, what has no meaning is not language. Hence I shall talk first about change of meaning.

A Digression on Semantics

Men converse by means of language, but words are formed at the will of the generality, and there arises from a bad and unapt formation of words a wonderful obstruction to the mind. Nor can the definitions and explanations with which learned men are

> *wont to guard and protect themselves in some instances afford a*
> *complete remedy; words still manifestly force the understanding,*
> *throw everything into confusion, and lead mankind into vain*
> *and innumerable controversies and fallacies.*
>
> Sir Francis Bacon
> *Novum Organum*

In everyday speech the term *semantics* is often used in an imprecise and derogatory sense to denote futile quibbling over the meaning of words or to refer to the verbal trickery of advertisers and politicians. Actually there is nothing frivolous or disreputable about semantics, a valuable branch of linguistics from which all users of language have much to learn. In the next few pages I shall examine selected aspects of semantics that may be of interest and worth to the physician.

Semantics 'the study of word meanings' belongs to the broader science of *semiotics*, which deals with the origin and meaning of signs. A *sign* may be defined as 'anything that points to something outside itself'. Generally a sign is related to the thing signified as effect is related to cause. That is, a sign does not actually determine, much less call into being, the thing signified. Naturally occurring signs include the turning of leaves in autumn, thunder and lightning during a storm, bloody fingerprints at the scene of a murder, and burrows and scratch marks in scabies.

A man-made sign may depend on some natural relation, as when a picture of a lion indicates the lion house at the zoo or a skull and crossed bones indicates a poison. A chain across a park entrance serves more as a sign that entry is prohibited than as a physical means of enforcing the prohibition. But most often, man-made signs are arbitrary, like the red light that means 'stop' and the green color that identifies a cylinder of oxygen. Language began as a system of arbitrary audible signs (speech) that is now represented by a second set of arbitrary visible signs (writing).

The semanticist does not waste his time in unprofitable searches for the origins of language and meaning but concerns himself with the actual behavior of words under conditions of use. The forces responsible for changes in the sense and application of words are far more diverse, complex, subtle, and unpredictable than those that affect the pronunciation and spelling of words. In fact, it is a general linguistic law that we tend to preserve form at the expense of meaning. That is, we would rather keep an old word and change its meaning or reference than invent a new word.

For example, *umbilical tape*, which is used nowadays for tying just about everything except umbilical cords, retains its old name among a generation of doctors and nurses who have never seen a cord tied. *Flat plate* continues in use more than 50 years after plates were superseded by film in diagnostic radiology. *Lordotic films* of the chest are still so designated even though for decades they have been made by angling the x-ray machine rather than the patient.

In *umbilical tape*, a name has been kept even though it has been made inaccurate by a change in the use of the *referend* ('the thing named'). *Flat plate* and *lordotic film*, however, have been transferred from one referend to another in outright contradiction of their obvious literal meanings. In all such cases, words have remained in uninterrupted use despite substantial changes of reference.

In this connection I might also note the survival of words that have been left without referends by the advance of science. Such terms as *cachexia, dyscrasia,* and *marasmus*, relics from the infancy of medicine, still flourish as covers of confusion and ignorance. As mentioned in an earlier chapter, terms referring to long-exploded myths, like *hysteria* ('womb trouble') and *influenza* ('influence of the stars'), continue in use although one might have expected them to repose by now on the junk pile along with the once-popular *chlorosis* ('the green sickness', an anemia of adolescent girls often mentioned by Shakespeare) and *sideration* ('star-stroke', used for both erysipelas and sudden paralysis). Near relatives are such durable misnomers as *retinitis pigmentosa* (atrophic, not inflammatory), *biliuria* (more accurately, *bilirubinuria*), and *cervical erosion* (actually *adenosis*).

I have spoken thus far about words kept in use despite changes of referend. A much commoner semantic phenomenon is a gradual or sudden shift in the application of a word even though there has been no discernible change in the thing referred to.

From the tenth to the fifteenth century, the sense of the English word *deer* gradually narrowed from 'animal in general' (Greek *ther*, German *Tier*) to a particular kind of animal. At the same time *venison* (from Latin *venatio* 'hunting'), which at first meant any kind of game, became restricted to just one kind. If a historian tells you that it was no coincidence that both of these cases of semantic narrowing concerned the same animal, his use of *coincidence* to mean 'a chance concurrence' itself implies semantic narrowing, since the etymologic sense of *coincidence* is simply 'happening together'.

Specialization or narrowing of meaning often occurs when a word moves from one language to another. Thus, although Greek *aphtha* means simply 'ulcer', our modern medical adjective *aphthous* refers so consistently to a certain kind of lesion that the etymologically redundant phrase *aphthous ulcer* is in common use and acceptance. Similarly, *skeleton* classically means 'something dried up', but the use of the word in English for 'all of the bones of an animal or human (living or dead)' forces us to indulge now and then in another redundancy, *dried-up skeleton*.

A specialized language, such as that of medicine, readily takes words from lay speech or from other disciplines and attaches specialized meanings to them. In clinical parlance the *reaction* of a urine specimen refers exclusively to its effect on litmus paper or some more sophisticated indicator of hydrogen ion concentration. A *traumatic* lumbar puncture is, quite specifically, one that causes blood from outside the dura mater to appear in the specimen of spinal fluid. *Eclampsia*, from Greek *eklampein* 'to shine forth suddenly', meant 'any sudden convulsion' when first coined in the eighteenth century; only in the past few decades has it come to refer to 'toxemia of pregnancy'.

Narrowing of meaning within a particular context often occurs in lay language also. Thus, *change* serves as a euphemism for 'show signs of aging', as in, "You haven't changed a bit; in fact you look younger." (*To look younger* would certainly imply a change in the more general sense of the word.) *Change* may also connote alteration to a particular end point, as in the deepening of the male voice at puberty. Hence one may say, "His voice hadn't changed completely," although the adverb would in another context be irrelevant and enigmatic.

Broadening of meaning occurs when, for example, a word becomes a generic term for all members of a class to which its referend belongs. *Electrocution*, a late nineteenth century coinage from *electric* and *execution*, logically refers only to capital punishment. Yet in modern textbooks of pathology and forensic medicine, it means 'any lethal electric shock', as it has in demotic American English and journalese for the past 75 years. Although the literal meaning of *colic* is '(a pain) in the colon', the term has been extended to include any cramp in the abdomen—hence the etymologically contradictory *renal colic*. Similarly, one may speak of *digitalization* with ouabain and of *oxidation* in which oxygen does not take part.

Words may also undergo shifts of intensity or vigor. Examples of weakening are seen in overworked hyperboles like *massive, fulminant*, and *florid*, and of intensification in habitual understatements like *considerable, substantial*, and *marked*. Jargon words used over and over in widely varying senses (*aspect, factor, involve*) eventually lose both force and specificity. A word may take on a particular flavor or bias from the settings in which it is customarily used. Thus *manipulate, maneuver, contrive, scheme*, and *plot* all have slightly derogatory and sinister overtones not inherent in their literal meanings. Many words in common use have an emotional coloring that expresses, often with great subtlety, the attitude of the speaker or writer.

In medical language as in lay speech, slang terms sometimes become respectable. Thus, the jargon phrases *high index of suspicion, varus deformity, falciparum malaria*, and *coliform bacteria* are now acceptable in formal medical writing. Conversely, formal terms may take on unofficial slang meanings in workaday speech. The anatomic term *supratentorial*, when used correctly, implies an organic lesion, but in medical argot it has the derivative sense of 'psychogenic'. When urine or stool is said to be positive for *heme*, the term is less likely to be used in its strict chemical sense than as a euphemism for 'blood'.

Besides undergoing changes in the scope of its meaning, a word may take on related but distinct meanings through *metonymy* or *metaphor*. When the relation between the established and the added meanings is close and fairly concrete, as when *oil immersion* becomes synonymous with *1000✕*, or when one says *in Sutton* to mean 'in Sutton's textbook', it is called *metonymy*. When the relation is accidental, abstract, or tenuous, as when one speaks of the *bridge* of the nose or the *peak* flow rate, one has a metaphor. But in fact no sharp distinction can be drawn between these two, even though rhetoricians have been telling themselves otherwise for 25 centuries.

The point cannot be made too strongly that a metaphoric meaning may have only the slightest relation to the literal meaning. Many common and perfectly serviceable medical expressions are warped metaphors. Using *aspirate* to mean 'withdraw fluid from a cavity by suction' is stretching the original meaning, 'breathe in', rather far. The biochemist's *thresholds* and *plateaus* bear little conceptual resemblance to their counterparts in the real world.

The history of a word or root is often largely the record of its metonymic progressions. Indo-European *bhogo* and its Greek descendant *phogo* had a single, concrete meaning: 'to cook'. But the related Latin noun *focus* referred to both the kitchen hearth and the fire, whence modern Spanish *fuego* and Italian *fuoco* 'fire'. By a further extension, *focus* came to mean a device used to start a fire—'a burning glass'. That is why Johannes Kepler (in 1604) chose the term *focus* to mean 'the point at which light rays converge after passing through a lens'. Soon the word was extended to a broad range of other applications in geometry, astronomy, and optics, and the verb *to focus* was born.

By yet another extension, this verb began to be used with instruments in which there was no convergence of rays (as in a slide projector) or even no lens (as in a television set). Nowadays it often has a purely abstract sense, as when one says, "We are focusing our attention on the liver" or " . . . our efforts on prevention." Meanwhile, the sense of the original Latin noun has evolved, along another track, to mean 'center' or 'source', as in *focus of infection* and *unifocal PVCs*.

It is worth pausing here to distinguish two patterns by which metonymy can generate new senses for a word. One of these is extension, exemplified by *focus*, whose meaning has advanced step by step from one referend to another. In contrast, the various meanings of *organ*—a musical instrument, a complex bodily structure with a particular function, an official publication, a functional division of an institution—are not interrelated. Each of these metaphorical senses has arisen directly and independently from Greek *organon* 'tool' by a phenomenon called *radiation* or *polysemy*.

Among the most primitive terms in any language are the metaphors it uses to denote basic abstractions or qualities. Words for *mind* or *soul* often stem from earlier terms for the breath or for some part of the body where the soul was thought to reside. Similarly, in modern English *body* means 'thickness' or 'solidity' when applied to a coiffure or a stew. In common parlance *sore throat, upset stomach,* and *stiff neck* can either have their literal and concrete meanings or stand for the abstract concepts 'soreness', 'upsetness', and 'stiffness' ("My sore throat is gone").

The reverse process, naming a concrete thing with an abstract term, gives us such expressions as *That is another kind of cabbage* (meaning, 'that is cabbage of another kind') and certain euphemisms (*bowel movement*). But the practice of using abstract for concrete is less common in natural, spoken language than in scientific jargon and in overblown, pretentious, or legalistic writing, where it flourishes exuberantly. There one often finds vague abstractions substituted for more explicit terms: *a malignancy* instead of *a malignant tumor; the circulation* instead of *the circulatory system,* itself an abstraction standing for the heart and blood vessels. Failure to distinguish concrete terms (*neoplasm, gallstones*) from corresponding abstract ones (*neoplasia, cholelithiasis*) frequently leads to confusion in thought and obscurity in speech and writing.

When a word gains one or more new meanings by extension or radiation, the old ones usually persist at least for a time. If they eventually die out, the word may be found to have undergone a complete shift of reference. When a figurative sense replaces a literal one, the word is called a *dead metaphor.* Once immunization against smallpox by induction of cowpox (vaccinia) had become generally established, the terms *vaccine* and *vaccination,* literally referring only to cowpox, were extended to virtually all other immunizations. Now that induction of vaccinia is no longer practiced, the still-active term *vaccination* can be viewed as a dead metaphor.

It would be hard to imagine a more obvious metaphor than *nutmeg liver,* or the *sulfur granules* of actinomycosis. But is *polyp* a metaphor or just a queer old relic of Greek? The answer lies in the etymology of the word. The full noun *polypus* (Greek *polypous),* meaning 'many-footed', hence 'octopus', was applied by Hippocrates to a soft mass in the nose with footlike projections. Since an octopus is no longer called a *polyp*, the pathologic term is a dead metaphor. Dozens of Greek and Latin medical terms may be numbered among dead metaphors of this kind. Moreover, many common English words borrowed or modified from classical languages are likewise dead metaphors because their original meanings are not known to modern speakers: *develop* 'unwrap'; *program* 'written before'; *reflect* 'bend back'; *remorse* 'biting again'.

Loss of the etymologic sense of words results in redundancies such as *yellow jaundice, foot pedal, bottomless abyss, wall mural,* and *audible click,* all of them indefensible. By contrast, modern usage permits or even demands repetition of a buried meaning in the phrases *manual dexterity, index finger, several different,* and *outlandish foreigner.* If one considers the literal meanings of such expressions as *solitary inmate, comfortable patient, retrograde ejaculation, palpable crepitus, cider vinegar, endorse on the front, quarantine for 7 days, a siesta at 3 o'clock,* and *a bishop preceded by his acolytes,* one finds every one of them self-contradictory. But in modern usage they are all more or less acceptable because one of the words in each phrase is no longer taken literally.

The portal vein takes its name from Latin *porta* 'gate', referring to the unperitonealized cleft on the undersurface of the liver where the portal vein and the hepatic artery enter and the common bile duct leaves. For centuries students of anatomy were taught that the portal vein is the only vessel in the body that begins in capillaries and ends in capillaries. The fading of the Latin terminology helped along the notion that *portal* somehow meant 'starting and ending in capillaries'. Hence it is not surprising that when another such arrangement was discovered in the pituitary, the vessels in question were named *pituitary portal vessels.*

Now and then the meaning of a word changes because its etymology has been not simply lost but replaced by a false one that seems plausible to the present generation of speakers. Thus *insolence* 'something unusual' took on a special sense by being mistakenly associated with *insult,* and *apocrine* by being mistakenly derived from *apex.* False etymology does not always change the reference of a term. Thus, *stucco dermatitis* means the same thing whether one believes, with one dermatologic writer, that Italian *stucco* is somehow related to English *stuck on* or knows of its origin from Old High German *stucki* 'crust'. Sometimes a false semantic analogy is forced by the promoter of an idea, as in the case of *acupressure,* touted as 'acupuncture without needles' even though Latin *acu* means 'with a needle'. Similarly, a test of prostatic acid phosphate is called acronymically *the male PAP test* to create a spurious link with the Pap (Papanicolaou) smear of the cervix.

Shifts in meaning undergone by dead metaphors and other words whose origins have grown obscure are part of a larger pattern of change that is called *formulization.* Everyday usage can impart values to words and phrases that bear little relation to their etymologic or literal values, even when these remain perfectly obvious. The tendency to ignore the literal and often palpably evident sense of a word or phrase, mechanically using it as a formula, has been seen already in the examples of *umbilical tape* and *flat plate*. The same tendency may lead even the careful speaker into redundancies (*traumatic injury, two-wheel bicycle*) and contradictions (*rusty tin, tight slacks*) or prompt him to overstrain metaphors (*a bird's eye view of anaerobic glycolysis*) or mix them with ludicrous effect (*He's tired of playing second fiddle to visiting firemen*).

A word used often enough to become a formula is apt to undergo a semantic drift in the direction of some associative meaning. Since *decompensation* plainly implies a 'failure or cessation of compensation', it makes no sense to use this term for 'acute cardiac failure' where there has been no prior compensation for cardiac overload. Even more objectionable is an expression like, "The sensorium was *decompensating*," that is, 'deteriorating'. The phrase *interrupted sutures* is specific, logical, and able to be taken at face value. Not so the statement, "The catheter was held in place with one interrupted suture." Explaining to a nonphysician that a *closed wound* is one that was never open is almost as hard as explaining why dermatology is considered a branch of *internal* medicine.

Those who have only imperfectly learned the lessons of semantics sometimes imagine that every word has a "true" or "literal" meaning that can be found in the dictionary and that has a much stronger title to existence than extended, imposed, or metaphorical meanings. This is an ancient myth indeed, embodied in the very word *etymology* (Greek *etymon* 'true, genuine'). Extreme adherents of this view argue that any meaning of a word that is at variance with the literal meaning is at least somewhat incorrect.

One can readily excuse the annoyance of an educated person who sees meanings changed, through carelessness or ignorance, in open defiance of origins that are plain. But it is a fallacy to suppose that the meaning of a word is, or ever can be, anything other than what the generality of speakers take that word to mean. If I wanted to insist upon literal meanings for all words, I would have to discard all metaphors living and dead, including a large part of anatomic nomenclature. I would have to find new words for a soldering iron that is made of copper and a marble that is made of glass. I could no longer speak of *discovering* anything unless it had previously been concealed by a real cover, and I would have to limit use of the expression *a bit* to things that had actually been bitten. Even if this preposterous renovation of language could be put into effect, the only result would be to move language back a few thousand years to the time when writing began to record the meanings of words—a very inconsiderable period in the overall history of language and a degree of change that seems hardly worth the effort.

Another popular misconception about the reference of words may be called the *myth of the real name*. According to this idea everything has a proper or correct designation, and other words for it are wrong: "Everybody calls them buffalo, but they're really bison." How can the word by which "everybody" calls a thing not be its name? The speaker means to say that *bison* is preferred by a learned minority, while *buffalo*, though in wider use, is a misnomer from the viewpoint of official terminology.

The scientist must carefully guard against the delusion that one label is inherently more correct or less arbitrary than another. Otherwise he can boast of no more intellectual sophistication than the planetarium visitor who marveled that astronomers had been able to learn the names of stars millions of light years distant.

Arguments against language change based on the myths of literal meaning and real name must be dismissed as nonsense. Yet undeniably, some forms of semantic evolution do weaken and muddle the orderly structures on which the usefulness of language depends. Adding new meanings to a word creates *homonyms*—imperfect homonyms, since they all have the same origin. Sometimes the convenience of using an established word or root for a new referend is overbalanced by the vagueness or ambiguity that results when a word has several divergent senses. Synonymy, the process by which a thing acquires several historically unrelated names, occasionally leads to difficulties also, for in time each synonym goes its separate way as convention qualifies or specializes its meaning. But homonymy threatens intelligibility to a far greater degree.

One seldom pauses to consider the fundamental incongruity of using the same word, often in the same setting, to mean radically different things. *Normal saline* is not *1 N NaCl*. A *keratolytic* does not dissolve the tissue that is inflamed in *keratitis*. *Malignant hypertension* is not induced by a *malignant tumor*. *Steroid-dependent asthma* and *insulin-dependent diabetes* are dependent in an entirely different sense than *estrogen-dependent adenocarcinoma*. If the reader finds these remarks banal platitudes, it is not because they are self-evident but only because he has learned the meanings of the words by rote and has learned at the same time to disregard the misleading cues that they contain.

The use of one word for two or more unrelated concepts inevitably forges a spurious intellectual link between these concepts. Metaphors and abstractions acquire the same force and weight as literal, concrete senses of a word. Formerly oblique and tenuous connections between two things are ratified and strengthened when the two things share the same name. Here I verge on the field of psycholinguistics and encounter issues whose exploration would carry me far out of my way.

Semantics is not primarily a practical science. Its purpose is to investigate the meanings of words and the ways in which they change, not to determine what is right or to guide the user of language in choosing his words or deciding how to arrange them. But a knowledge of semantics can benefit every speaker, writer, and reader by making him more aware of the dangers of obscurity and misrepresentation inherent in the use of metaphors, homonyms, and formulas; by shaking his faith in the power and immutability of words; by exploding myths about etymologic meanings and "real" names; and indeed simply by drawing his attention to the language he uses.

Meanings and their transmission are what language is all about. The meaning comes before the word: the intellectual concept exists before the sign by which it is marked. But meaning cannot be directly perceived and learned as a word or phrase can. Meaning is fugitive, intangible, spiritual, and it exists only for those who understand it. Language, by contrast, is durable—indeed, almost indestructible— and can readily be used by those who but vaguely understand it.

When one uses language, attention is on meaning, not form; on the message, not the means by which it is transmitted. When attention is turned toward the means, one begins to use language more rationally, skillfully, and effectively.

Bad Pennies

Vague and insignificant forms of speech, and abuse of language, have so long passed for mysteries of science: and hard and misapplied words, with little or no meaning, have by prescription, such a right to be taken for deep learning and height of speculation, that it will not be easy to persuade either those who speak them or those who hear them, that they are but the covers of ignorance, and hindrance of true knowledge.

John Locke
An Essay Concerning Human Understanding

The efforts of lexicographers, editors, official boards, and international committees to put technical terminology on a strictly rational, coherent, and consistent footing and keep it there have only partially succeeded. Systems of technical terminology are seldom truly systematic. Language, even the deliberately fabricated language of science, is after all a form of human behavior, and as such it obeys many complex and interacting psychological laws. Certain old words from dead languages are retained and used alongside brand-new ones. Argot and corruptions are gradually elevated and so absorbed into formal technical nomenclature, while useful terms are allowed to degenerate into vague abstractions or to slip into oblivion.

But despite its flaws, our modern medical terminology is a remarkably serviceable, viable, and durable tool. Objections to certain of its peculiarities spring less often from legitimate concerns about lack of intelligibility or usefulness than from the vain pursuit by editors of an elusive and worthless uniformity or from the idle theorizing of pedants and purists.

Logan Pearsall Smith expressed the view, in 1928, that the practice of compounding new technical words from classical elements has not only weakened our "powers of native composition" but promoted a false ideal of nomenclature, according to which scientists expect that the meaning of a new term shall be evident from its components. Smith's remarks seem to have carried little weight with the scientific community of his day, perhaps because he prefaced them with the observation that the task of making technical terms had been left to those least fitted to fulfil it—the scientists themselves.

But Smith's strictures contain more than a grain of truth. Most new terms proceed not from the thoughtful deliberations of official bodies but from the fevered brains of individual scientific researchers and writers who are eager for eternal fame through association with some novel and arresting neologism but who have little interest or competence in linguistics. The unbridled proliferation of ambiguous, unorthodox, and unpronounceable scientific words is not progress but decadence, not science but senselessness.

Certainly a stronger case can be made nowadays than in Smith's time against the continued coinage of new terms from Latin and Greek. Because the typical physician of today has not acquired even a smattering of either language in the course of his studies, he absorbs what little he knows of the classical roots and affixes by inference from words containing them. He thus learns Latin and Greek backward, in fragments, and largely wrongly. For this reason, coiners of new words from classical material are more likely today than ever before to botch the job.

There would seem to be no objection to the continued use of stems whose meaning is familiar because they already appear in words of wide use. Thus, no physician has any difficulty in deciphering *hypomagnesemia* or *lipophilicity* the first time that he sees it. But who recognizes or remembers that *fulguration* comes from Latin *fulgur* 'lightning', or that *botulism* is derived from *botulus* 'sausage'?

Even among the more familiar stems, many have become ambiguous by being used inconsistently. Consider, for instance, the family of *-philias*, a variegated collection of terms formed on several distinct models. In *necrophilia* one sees the Greek word in its literal meaning, 'love or attraction'. *Hemophilia*, though, could not be called an analogous use except by the exercise of considerable imagination. *Argyrophilia* and *basophilia* metaphorically extend the notion of attraction to include chemical affinity. But *eosinophilia* and *neutrophilia* refer, in current use, not to the affinity of certain cytoplasmic granules for eosin or for neutral stains but rather to increases in the numbers of cells containing such granules.

Medical dictionaries contain whole dynasties of *-emias*, *-penias*, *-urias*, and *-algias*; in each of these dynasties the operative suffix bears several loosely related meanings. *-Uria* refers to the 'urine' in *hematuria* and *pyuria* and to the 'act of voiding' in *nocturia* and *dysuria*. *-Penia* denotes 'fewness' in *leukopenia* and 'reduction of mass' in *osteopenia*. Among twentieth century inventions are the large and motley family of *-pathies*. *Adenopathy* means 'something wrong with the glands'; *neuropathy*, 'something wrong with a nerve'; and *uropathy* 'something wrong with the excretory system'. Each of these terms labors under the double disadvantage of vagueness in meaning and an illusory flavor of specificity.

But for that very reason they are handy words for the intellectually indolent, and the *-pathy* clan shows no signs of dying out. Indeed, we now have *vasculopathy, cardiomyopathy* (alias *myocardiopathy*), *coagulopathy, endocrinopathy, gammopathy* (referring to gamma globulin), and *consumptive opsoninopathy*. *Empathy* has become a fad word for *sympathy*, though it was adopted expressly to mean something different from sympathy: 'intellectual insight into another's emotional state without sharing in it'.

A distant cousin of the *-pathy* family is the adjective *idiopathic*. Galen applied the original Greek word, from *idios* 'personal, private' and *pathos* 'disease', to any disease that arises of itself in the part affected. Although modern scientific medicine tells us that there is no such thing, the word continues to be used for conditions whose origin modern scientific medicine has yet to explain. In this context some physicians, perhaps finding *idiopathic* uncomfortably reminiscent of *idiot*, prefer the equally unscientific and noncommittal adjective *essential: essential hypertension, essential hypoglycemia.* (When this term first came into use, however, it meant not 'idiopathic' but 'necessary'. Thus, *essential hypertension* implied that the abnormally high blood pressure was needed to maintain flow through sclerotic arteries.) Before leaving the trail of *path*, I might mention that *pathognomonic*, as used by Galen, meant 'skilled in diagnosis' and not, as at present, 'surely indicative of a certain disease'.

Many of the living stems and affixes used in making technical terms have lost their original meanings and acquired new ones by association or analogy. *Autopsy* means 'a personal inspection, seeing for oneself', from *autos* 'self' and *opsis* 'view'. After the word had come to refer specifically to the dissection and pathologic examination of a dead body, it seemed proper to form a new term for removal of tissue from the living by introducing the stem *bi-* of *bios* 'life': *biopsy*. This works well in practice, though classicists may object to the lopsided antithesis between *autos* and *bios*, and we are all free to question how a biopsy can be taken during an autopsy, as it often is.

Macroscopic, which has entered the language as the antonym of *microscopic*, was no doubt formed by analogy with that word, even though there is no such thing as a *macroscope*. The latter part of *hemorrhage* (*haimorrhagia*) has absorbed the connotation of 'bleeding' from the former part and appears with that sense as a kind of suffix in *menorrhagia* and *metrorrhagia*. The classical meaning of *rhagia* (which is essentially the same word as *rhexis*) is 'bursting'. *Sternebra* includes the instrumental suffix *-(e)bra* of *vertebra*, as if this meant 'one of a linear series of similar bones'. *Scoopula*, the name of a familiar chemical laboratory implement, is formed from *scoop* and the diminutive suffix *-ula*, as if this represented the semantic core of *spatula*.

In contrast to these rather harmless cases of semantic shift, a few stems, words, and phrases have undergone such violent metamorphoses under the influence of usage and analogy that they are as ambiguous as homonyms. Here might be mentioned the term *cardiospasm*, which derives its significance from an ill-advised figure of speech—*cardia*, referring to the part of the stomach nearest the heart. Terms containing negative particles sometimes take on operational meanings that contradict their literal ones, or at least sharply diverge from them. Thus, upon reading, "The modern consensus is that in acute gouty arthritis a nonsteroidal agent is preferable to colchicine," the intelligent lay person would conclude that colchicine is a steroidal agent. To interpret the sentence correctly one must be in on the private joke that *nonsteroidal agent* in the jargon of medicine refers to a specific group of newer anti-inflammatory drugs and excludes not only steroids but all other drugs not in that pharmacologic group. Similarly, one must appreciate the special, narrowed sense of *antithyroid drug* to understand why the class so designated does not include radioactive iodine.

Besides ambiguity of semantic content, modern medical terminology suffers from an ambiguity of structure. Grammatical lawlessness is, of course, the very essence of word making. A compound coinage is not only a fused phrase but a mutilated one in which grammatical relations are left to be guessed at or learned by rote. In a few kinds of compound word, the sequence of elements offers a clue as to their relation—for example, in the large class of words meaning 'A in B' (*pyosalpinx, pneumothorax, hydrocephalus*). Sequence may also help to differentiate between a concrete concept (*megaureter*) and an abstraction (*ureteromegaly*). But even in unfused phrases the sequence of elements may not give reliable clues to their syntactic relations. In *broken cast shears* and *old brown suit* the first adjective modifies the noun, whereas in *broken bottle injury* and *dark brown suit*, the first adjective modifies the second one. So in many terms of modern manufacture, the apparently arbitrary order of morphemes is as likely to mislead as to enlighten.

This leads me to the subject of degrees of juncture in compounds. When more than two morphemes or lexical elements apper in a word, the bonds or seams that join them will usually vary in tightness or closeness, somewhat like the strong and weak bonds in chemistry. A few simple examples will make this immediately clear. In *uninterrupted* it is evident that the joint between the base verb *interrupt* and the participial ending *-ed* is closer than that between the verb and *un-*.

Put differently, *interrupted* can be thought of as having led an independent existence before the addition of the negative prefix *un-*, whereas *uninterrupt* is not a word at all.

By contrast, in *unearthed* one naturally places the tighter seam between *un-* and *earth*, since the verb *unearth* existed before the addition of the ending *-ed*. There is no such word as *earthed* in general use. I might symbolize the differences between these two degrees of juncture as follows.

$$[un + earth] + ed \qquad un + [interrupt + ed]$$

Although the *un-* that is used to make reversive verbs like *unearth* is etymologically different from the negatively adverbial *un-* of *uninterrupted*, for practical purposes the two long ago became one. Thus it happens that a majority of words formed on the pattern *un——ed* can be interpreted in two ways. *Untied* may mean either 'never tied' or 'tied and then released'. Both an article that has never been wrapped and one that has been wrapped and then had the wrappings removed may be said to be *unwrapped*. These variant structures are shown below.

$$un + [tie + (e)d] \qquad un + [wrap(p) + ed]$$
$$[un + tie] (e)d \qquad [un + wrap(p)] + ed$$

The ambiguity arising from this dual way of forming common English words is mirrored in many technical terms containing negative particles. *Nonparenteral* has been the subject of much published semantic debate. *Parenteral* means literally 'other than by the digestive tract'. Does the *non-* in *nonparenteral* negate *other than*, making the word synonymous with *oral, alimentary, and enteric*? Or must one assign to *parenteral* a specialized, nonliteral meaning, 'by needle'? (After all, *off-Broadway* does not mean just anywhere besides Broadway.) In this example, the buried prefix *para(a)-* exerts a negative force of its own, like *extra-* in *nonextrapyramidal* and *a-* in *nonatopic*, two other modern semantic enigmas.

Even without the complexity arising from double negation, a term like *anticoagulant* lends itself to a range of interpretations (unless and until one has been apprised of its accepted meaning). If one chooses to believe that *anticoagulant* belongs to the same class as *antihistamine* and *antilewisite*—in which the prefix negates the whole rest of the word and the suffix is simply retained from that word—an *anticoagulant* must be something acting 'against a coagulant'. But if one decides to interpret *anti-* in the sense that is has in *antibody* and *antidote*, an adverbial one implying opposition, an *anticoagulant* is a 'coagulant acting against something unspecified'. Finally, if one takes the suffix to be working in league with *anti-*, as in *antipyretic* and *antihypertensive*, and to have no prior connection—no strong bond— with the stem *coag(ul)-*, our understanding of *anticoagulant* will be 'an agent working against clotting'. Even after learning that this last sense is the right one, one is not particularly well prepared to interpret correctly the derived verb, *to anticoagulate*.

Many other examples could be offered of ambiguity arising from inconsistency in the use of structure to convey meaning. A *hypo-glycemic* drug is used neither to induce hypoglycemia nor to treat it. *Antiatherogenic* does not fit cleanly into any of the three classes of *anti-* words mentioned in the preceding paragraph. As a result of reckless coinage, many suffixes have lost their precise meanings and been turned into mere plugs or fillers to denote parts of speech, so that roots derive little benefit from being yoked to them. In fact, many compounds at present show a tendency to revert to the status of roots.

Thus, we are losing the notion of contrast between active and passive once plainly expressed in the suffix series *-ant*, *-ent*, and *-ive* versus *-ate* and *-ee*. The first two, from Latin active participles, properly connote action (agency): *agent, disinfectant, propellant, solvent*. But in practice these active suffixes often displace the gerundive (passive) endings *-and* and *-end*, used correctly in *agenda, memorandum*, and *proband*. Hence an *inhalant* poison is one that is inhaled, and a *receptant* is supposed to be something received by a receptor. The adjectival suffix *-ive* likewise implies agency or action, as in the very word *active*. Yet one now finds that *selective* has somehow become synonymous with *selected* ('a review of selective case histories'), while *corrosive* can apparently mean-either 'corrod-ing' or 'being corroded'. In any event, *noncorrosive* glassware is glassware that is not etched or clouded by laboratory chemicals. Meanwhile, a *perforated* IUD is not one with a hole in it but one that *has perforated* the uterus.

The passive participle ending *-ate* may either retain its passive sense, as it does in *hydrolysate* and *leachate*, or supplant *-ant* and *-ent* as in the increasingly popular but nonexistent adjective *predominate* and the widely accepted substantive *infiltrate*, meaning 'that which [actively] filters in'; contrast *filtrate* 'that which [passively] is filtered'. The French equivalent of *-ate*—strictly an accented final *e* but in modern English nearly always represented by the feminine *ee*—has also begun to lose its passive connotation. Alongside *payee, employee,* and *parolee,* where it preserves this passive sense, it now usurps the role of the agent suffix *-er (-or),* as in *attendee, returnee,* and *standee.*

There appears to be a widespread notion that a new, unfamiliar, long, unorthodox word is somehow preferable to a phrase whose component words are well known and whose meaning as a whole is self-evident. At times the natural tendency to fuse two or more concepts in a single word flares up into a raging passion and engenders superfluous and often ludicrously irregular neologisms like *copro-examination* ('stool examination'), *chenotherapy* ('treatment with chenodeoxycholic acid'), *immunocompromised, megavitamin,* and *serumcidality.*

Many such terms have evidently been formed by analogy with others already in use. Word families sometimes show an alarming tendency to self-propagation, the mere presence of a root in one compound inviting the formation of other words on the same pattern. Once three or four of these are in use, there is no stopping the process, and in time virtually any stem may be reduced to the status of a mere affix. *Thermophilic* invites *thermotolerant; cholinergic* and *adrenergic* pave the way for *dopaminergic; saluretic* (an eccentric variation on *diuretic*) leads inevitably to *kaliuretic* and *natriuretic; urinalysis* prompts *synovianalysis; alcoholic* calls up *workaholic* (with spurious connecting *a*); and *menarche* spawns *thelarche, pubarche, adrenarche* and *semenarche.* There is little to recommend the steadily expanding groups of terms formed with *bio-* (*biocompatibility, biodegradable, biofeedback*) and *immuno-* (*immunocompetent, immunocompromised, immunodeficient, immunofluorescence, immunosuppressed*). The lists of *-manias* and *-phobias* named to date are nearly endless.

The ceaseless manufacture of new technical words generates gangs of synonyms, of which one would suffice. Though one may still speak of *yellowness* of the nails, one is expected to select a learned-sounding synonym for *yellowness* when it affects the skin (*icterus* if due to hyperbilirubinemia, otherwise *chrysoderma*), spinal fluid (*xanthochromia*), teeth (*xanthodontia*), cartilage (*ochronosis*), or urine (*normochromia*). And yet the multiplication of words has not in the least remedied the redundancy of technical speech and writing— quite the reverse. In *antinuclear antibody* the prefix is tediously repeated. In *the head is normocephalic* (the degenerate modern version of *the patient is normocephalic*) the Greek stem needlessly echoes the sense of *head*.

It is not surprising that many modern terms are both superfluous and obscure, since they owe their existence not to any genuine need but rather to a craze to attach labels ("Unlike propranolol, metoprolol chiefly blocks β_1 receptors and is thus highly *cardioselective*"), an obsession to manufacture jargon (*atraumatic normosis*), or a weakness for novelty (*pseudopseudohypoparathyroidism*), euphemism (*chemical dependence*), or circumlocution (*erectile dysfunction*). Ignorance of English has led to the creation of *fecundability* and *obtundation*, even though *fecundity* and *obtusion* are already in the language, and of *orthograde* as an antonym to *retrograde* (cardiac conduction), though *antegrade* is already available and somewhat more apt.

To the extent that medical terminology is the workaday medium of communication for busy professional people, its fertility and flexibility cannot and probably should not be curbed. But this medium could serve its purpose much more smoothly and efficiently if those who bring new technical words and phrases into being would exhibit more intelligence and foresight; at least try to preserve established phonetic, semantic, and structural traditions; and, above all, exercise a little restraint.

Latin and Greek

Besides, 'tis known he could speak Greek
As naturally as pigs squeak;
That Latin was no more difficile
Than to a blackbird 'tis to whistle.
Being rich in both, he never scanted
His bounty unto such as wanted
But much of either would afford
To many that had not one word.

Samuel Butler
Hudibras

Unlike diplomatic and ecclesiastical Latin, which strove with some success to preserve a Ciceronian elegance down through the centuries, academic and scientific Latin was never distinguished by grammatical correctness or purity of vocabulary. As a medium of medical communication the classical language has suffered many changes through phonetic attrition, deliberate variation, and error. Nowadays, of course, Latin is no longer used as a *language*: it survives in medical parlance only as a disjointed collection of stems, affixes, words, and phrases. Still less does classical Greek endure as a system of speech. Except for a small number of un-Latinized freestanding words, the only remnants of Greek in the language of medicine are roots and affixes.

I have dealt elsewhere with English terms derived from classical languages by phonetic modification (*clavicle, pleurisy*) or through derivation or composition (*retrosternal, cystoscope*). Here I am concerned with words and expressions that preserve the original form of the Latin or (usually Latinized) Greek: *serosa, rhonchus, femur, syncope, asterixis, flexor digitorum profundus, pulsus rarus, parvus, et tardus*. Though many of the terms in this class have been thoroughly naturalized, so that they are treated just as if they were English words born and bred, others preserve a distinctly foreign character. One can, for instance, speak of *adductors* or *fistulas*, adding the English plural suffix -*s*, but it is hard to imagine that any professional person, even one totally ignorant of Latin, would dare to say *corpus cavernosums*.

This example pinpoints two of the major challenges that the modern physician must meet in using terms that retain their Latin or Greek form: the proper formation of plurals and the correct handling of phrases. (I am speaking here of proper Greek and Latin phrases, not groups of classical words governed by English grammatical principles, such as *stasis dermatitis, posterior septum,* or *lentigo maligna melanoma*.) A dwindling number of physicians use correct forms because they know Latin; many others, because they habitually reproduce spellings accurately. For the rest a few explanations may make matters easier.

Persons whose mother tongue is English are likely to be impatient with the grammatical rules of inflected languages and inept at learning and applying them. A common error is the ungrammatical combination of a noun and an adjective. False concords such as *pyoderma gangrenosa, Treponema pallida,* and *lymphedema tarda* abound in modern writing, and some have even found their way into medical dictionaries. The nouns in these examples are neuter in gender and therefore need neuter adjectives: *gangrenosum, pallidum, tardum.*

The linguistically naïve, misled by such everyday expressions as *vena cava, situs inversus,* and *stratum corneum,* often conclude that matching nouns to adjectives in Latin is merely a matter of rhyming. Unfortunately, it is not so simple as that. The gender of a given inflectional ending is not absolutely fixed. For example, though most Latin nouns ending in *-us* are masculine, *corpus* and *pectus* are neuter, while *manus* and, of course, *Venus* are feminine. The adjectives *planus* and *sclerosus* are masculine, but *minus* and *majus* are neuter. (Hence *ecthyma minus,* not *minor; labium majus,* not *major.*)

Perhaps the most prolific source of error and confusion regarding adjective concord is the large and heterogenous group of classical terms ending in *-a.* Though most Latin nouns ending in *-a* are feminine, some that have been borrowed from Greek are neuter (*carcinoma, condyloma, stoma*), while *strata* and *milia* are plural forms of neuter nouns whose singulars end in *-um.*

Since the adjectives *varus* and *valgus* change their terminations to agree in gender with the noun modified (*pes varus, genu varum, coxa vara*), it is not strictly correct to speak of "varus deformity of the knee." Another kind of false concord results when a taxonomic species name is appended to a disease name that is derived from the corresponding genus: *schistosomiasis haematobium.* Even when the genders chance to match, as in *entamoebiasis histolytica,* such usage is little better than argot. Still, the example of conceptually disjointed terms like *otitis media* exerts a strong influence.

The erroneous phrases *sinus tarsus* and *vasa vasora* owe their origin to the rhyming fallacy coupled with the notion that their second members are adjectives. In *sinus tarsi* 'cavity of the ankle' the second word is not an adjective but another noun, in the genitive case. *Vas vasorum* 'vessels of vessels' also consists of two nouns, or rather of one noun in two different forms, the second again a genitive. Other cases of missed or dropped genitive are *abruptio placenta* (for *placentae*), *chondromalacia patella* (for *patellae*), *tendo Achilles* (for *Achillis*), and *Haemophilus influenza* (for *influenzae*). Many of these dropped genitives come about through mistaken analogy with phrases containing genitives that are identical to the corresponding nominatives, such as *appendix testis* and *corpus cavernosum penis.*

It is considered good English usage to say and write *fetuses*. The incorrect Latin plural *feti* only betrays the ignorance of the speaker. But there are objections to forming the plurals of all "foreign" words by adding -*s* or -*es*. This practice would sorely disappoint those pedants who glory in such plurals as *encephalitides* and *enemata*. Moreover, everyone recoils from expressions like *analysises of renal calculuses* and *neurosises and psychosises*. But if the correct plurals are to be used, physicians need to know enough Latin and Greek to avoid such blunders as *decubiti* and *pruritides*.

Latin nouns ending in -*a* in the singular quite consistently form their plurals in -*ae: fossae, scapulae.* Many Greek nouns ending in -*a* have joined this class on becoming Latinized: *pleurae, tracheae.* But when the final -*a* of a Greek noun is preceded by *m*, the word is nearly always a third-declension neuter, which forms its plural in -*ata* (*stomata, condylomata*). The sole exception in medical language is *drachma,* Greek *drachme* 'dram', whose plural is *drachmae*. *Mamma, rima,* and *struma* are Latin and form their plurals in -*ae*. Although *gumma* is also Latin, it is a corruption of Latin *gummi* (from Greek *kommi*) and has been absorbed into the neuter group forming its plurals in -*ata. Hydroa,* a neuter plural for which no singular form is known, is usually treated as a singular—sometimes neuter (*hydroa aestivale*) and sometimes feminine (*hydroa aestivalis*).

Most Latin and Greek nouns ending in -*is* or -*es* have plural forms in -*es: paralyses, pelves, facies.* Many of these, however, insert an extra syllable containing a dental consonant: *arthrit*(*id*)*es, pari*(*et*)*es, com*(*it*)*es.*

A Latin noun ending in -*us* may belong to the second, the third, or the fourth declension, each of which forms its plurals in its own way. Nouns of the second declension, such as *villus* and *limbus*, form the plural in -*i: villi, limbi.* Most Greek nouns ending in -*os* have joined this group: *bronchus, borborygmus, canthus.* A few Greek compounds ending in -*pous* 'foot' have joined it also, and although *polypus* has been anglicized by cutting off the Latin termination -*us*, one still sometimes hears the plural *polypi*, which is perfectly correct if a little archaic. (*Octopi*, however, is a variant that the dictionaries will not tolerate in place of the classical *octopodes*, though most of them permit *octopuses*.) Latin nouns of the third declension that end in -*us* form their plurals by changing *s* to *r* (often changing the preceding vowel as well) and generally ending in -*a: corpus, corpora; pus, pura; viscus, viscera.*

A substantial number of Latin nouns ending in -*us* belong to the fourth declension. Most of these have been formed from verb stems: *apparatus, coitus, crepitus, decubitus, ductus, fetus, fremitus, hiatus, ictus, introitus, meatus, plexus, pruritus, risus, spiritus, tinnitus, vomitus.* The plurals of nouns in this group are spelled exactly like the singulars. The ancient Romans distinguished the two forms in speech, but exactly how they pronounced either form is and will always remain a puzzle. A more practical question is how the correct spellings can be retained and yet misunderstandings be avoided. *Decubiti* and *plexi* are out of the question, being mere blundering innovations. Probably the best solution is to form the plural of a fourth-declension Latin noun by adding -*es*, as in *fetuses.* Fortunately, the occasion seldom arises to use words like *pruritus* and *tinnitus* in the plural.

Singular Latin nouns ending in -*s* without a preceding *u* (*ascites, biceps, herpes, lues, scabies*) are sometimes mistaken for plurals through the influence of the English practice. Even when such a word is widely recognized and treated as a singular, it is often used unchanged as a plural: *both abducens, both quadriceps.* Admittedly, the plurals formed for these words by addition of English -*es* are unappealing, and the classically correct plurals *abducentes* and *quadricipites* are perhaps slightly worse. Though grammatically singular, *forceps* has so long been taken for a plural ("a pair of forceps," "these forceps are contaminated") that it may as well be one. It is futile to argue against the example of true plurals like *scissors, pliers, tweezers,* and *tongs.*

In contrast to singulars ending in -*s* that look like plurals, plural nouns ending in -*a* are frequently mistaken for singulars. These include the plurals of Latin neuter nouns whose singular forms end in -*um* (*excreta, milia, strata*) or -*s* (*crura, pectora, vasa*) and the plurals of Greek neuters whose singulars end in -*ma* (*condylomata, stomata*) or -*on* (*lochia, prodroma*). To this group also belong neuter plural forms of Latin adjectives and participles: (*labia*) *minora*, (*vasa*) *deferentia*, (*corpora*) *albicantia*. Perhaps because of the example of these plurals ending in -*a*, certain singulars ending in -*a* are often treated in a plural or collective sense: *the patient developed stria; the lingual papilla are atrophic; the sclera are blue.* When a plural ending in *-a* is mistaken for a singular, it may be subjected to an illicit further pluralization: *adnexae, diverticuli, labiae, prodromata, speculi, septae.*

Those who have trouble keeping the *-a* singulars and the *-a* plurals apart may be consoled to learn that long ago the two classes were one. The distinction between them arose, around the dawn of recorded history, by a quirk of linguistic evolution. In primitive Latin all nouns ending in *-a* were singular and grammatically feminine. This class included a number of abstract or collective words (for example, *opera* 'help, assistance, activity'), and it happened that some of these corresponded to neuter nouns from the same roots (for example, *opus* 'work'). By a kind of amalgamation of categories, the feminine singulars were taken over as neuter plurals (*opus* 'work'; *opera* 'works'), replacing an older set of plural forms whose traces are so scanty that it cannot be reconstructed. A parallel metamorphosis in Greek was only partial, for in classical Greek a plural neuter noun still took a singular verb. Hence the famous dictum of Heraclitus, *panta rhei*, means literally 'all things flows'. In English, too, one sometimes finds words of collective or generic import hovering between singular and plural: *a woods; the barracks is on fire; a means of prevention; the waterworks belongs to the city; measles is contagious; counsel are undecided; the band are arguing about uniforms.*

This peculiar conflict of forms has generated confusion in every age. In medieval Latin one repeatedly finds nouns ending in *-a* paired with the "wrong" form of the verb. Many Late Latin neuter plurals were changed back into feminine singulars. Thus *folia* 'leaves' (from neuter *folium*), taken for a singular, evolved into French *feuille*, Spanish *hoja*, and Italian *foglia*, all feminine. Similarly *gaudia* 'joys', from *gaudium*, gave rise to Italian *gioia* and French *joie*. Late Latin and modern Romance *biblia*, a feminine singular noun meaning 'the Holy Scripture', is historically a Greek neuter plural meaning 'books'. *Propaganda, stamina,* and *insignia* are plural in Latin, singular in English.

Modern Romance languages have no neuter gender. Most Italian words derived from neuter Latin nouns are masculine, and many have irregular plurals. Thus Italian *uovo* 'egg' (from Latin *ovum*), though masculine, forms its plural with *-a* rather than the expected *-i*, and, moreover, this *uova* is considered feminine. *Dito* 'finger', *ginocchio* 'knee', *osso* 'bone', and several other anatomic terms in Italian have both regular masculine plurals ending in *-i* and irregular feminine ones ending in *-a*. The summit of irregularity is reached when the singular masculine noun *orecchio* 'ear' (from Latin *auriculum*) takes an anomalous feminine plural ending (*orecchie*) and then by back-formation generates a superfluous feminine singular, *orecchia*.

A common error in modern Latin is faulty back-formation of a singular from a word that is usually used in the plural (*nare, varice*) or from a singular that looks like a plural (*bicep, forcep*). Examples from nonmedical language are *a hot tamale* (the correct singular of Spanish *tamales* is *tamal*) and *another kudo* (Greek *kudos* 'honor' is singular). Compare also the now legitimized subtraction singulars *eave* and *pea* from formerly singular *eaves* and *pease*. Medical plurals ending in *-es* may generate false singulars ending in *-e*, which is sometimes pronounced (as in *phalange* for *phalanx*, *meninge* for *meninx*) and sometimes mute (*comedone* for *comedo*, *fomite* for *fomes*). *Fauces* and *feces* are plural in form though generally singular in sense; the classical singulars *faux* and *faex* are seldom seen. In contrast, several anatomic terms, such as *cervix* and *praecordium*, are singular only by exception—classically always plural. *Sordes* is both singular and plural; so is *pubes*. The incorrect singular *pubis* often seen is actually a genitive lifted from the phrase *os pubis* 'bone of the pubes'. *Menses* 'months', initially meaning the menstrual periods collectively, now often refers to a single one, though still plural in form: *The menses were just ending.*

One sometimes hears the argument that the rules of a dead language should exercise no influence over English usage. The modern savant insists on his right to say, "This data is inadequate" and "That media is sterile" with utter disregard for the fact that *data* and *media* are plural. But surely it is irrational and absurd to cling to a system of nomenclature as tenaciously as modern medicine clings to its immense hoard of Latin and yet refuse to observe the fundamental principles governing its use. The reader need not be reminded that every living language must change to survive. But since technical terminology must be protected as fully as possible from change, scientific Latin ought not to be allowed to degenerate and corrupt in the hands of those who would streamline, modernize, or simplify it. After all, the stability of Latin, as a dead language removed from the mainstream of human activity, is the very reason why this cumbrous, foreign, and antique system is kept in service.

Modern American printing and editorial practice has begun to gnaw away at technical Latin in the name of meretricious standards of consistency and simplicity. The shortening of diphthongs seen in naturalized classical material (*etiology* for *aetiology, hydrocele* for *hydrocoele, hemorrhage* for *haemorrhage*) has begun to extend to words and phrases that are still Latin in form (*previa* for *praevia*), not even excluding taxonomic terms (*Hemophilus* for *Haemophilus, gonorrheae* for *gonorrhoeae*), whose spelling is internationally fixed. If such meddling can be justified, why not follow the usage of medieval copyists and shorten all diphthongs, writing *erobic* for *aerobic* and *influenze* for *influenzae*? Why not further allow the Oriental races the privilege of changing *l*'s to *r*'s or vice versa to bring taxonomic terms into accord with their respective phonologies— Chinese *Neisselia gonolee*, Japanese *Hemophirus infruenze*? The answer is obvious: Because such regional or national modifications of the system destroy the consistency and universality that it is meant to preserve.

Much of what passes for Latin in modern medical terminology is actually corrupt, the work of inept meddlers and careless writers. Worse than the speaker or writer who knows nothing about the classical languages is the one who mistakenly believes he knows everything about them. He can be recognized easily by his preference for learned terms like *cicatrix, facies,* and *singultus* over plain English *scar, face,* and *hiccup*; by the unction with which he mouths modern jargon like *cor bovinum, status anginosus,* and *dementia dialytica*; and by his propensity to substitute wrong Latin for right English (*pulsus paradoxus pulmonale* for *pulmonalis*). He derives *portal* vein from *portare* 'to carry', though every vein carries blood and the Latin verb never referred to that kind of carrying.

No doubt we are stuck with such dog-Latin phraseology as *gravida 3, para 2, abortus 1*; *status post infarct*; and *premortem* (for *antemortem*). But surely enough is enough. If we must go on fabricating jargon to replace plain English, let us at least have correct jargon. What is the point of calling a disease *keratoconjunctivitis sicca* if 9 physicians in 10 end up calling it *sicca syndrome*? Before pretentiously putting the motto *Lex et Medica* on his letterhead, a forensic pathologist might have been expected to acquire enough

Latin to see that this phrase is gibberish. (It means 'a law and a woman doctor'. Probably *Jus et Medicina* is what he had in mind.) Did the dermatologist hesitate, or blush, as he invented out of thin air a grotesque pseudo-Latin *detergicans*, intended apparently to mean 'caused by a detergent' (as in *acne detergicans*)? Perhaps the same Philistine was responsible for the painfully irregular *nevus depigmentosus* and *incontinentia pigmenti achromians*. Any writer who is unable or unwilling to observe the orthographic and grammatical rules of any language, classical or modern, should leave it strictly alone and not presume to quote it inaccurately, much less augment it with botched and monstrous inventions.

Pronunciation

The pronunciation is the actual living form or forms of a word, that is, the word itself, *of which the current spelling is only a symbolization—generally, indeed, only the traditionally-preserved symbolization of an earlier form, sometimes imperfect to begin with, still oftener corrupted in its passage to our time.*

General Explanations
Oxford English Dictionary

The English language community is so broad and diverse that one must be circumspect indeed in laying down rules for pronunciation or finding fault with the speech practices of others. It is more often proper to speak of regionalisms, variants, or shifts than of downright errors. With spelling as erratic as ours, it would be futile to object to a pronunciation on the grounds that it does not match the letters on the page. That, after all, is rather a shortcoming of the letters. Even the illiterate "disect" for *dissect* and "aceedic" for *acidic* may, like the silly affectations "abscesseez" and "processeez," eventually become preferred forms.

Phonetic shifts are no less common than semantic ones in living languages, but they obey simpler laws and are often perfectly predictable. Many of them result from the natural leaning toward economy and ease of articulation. Thus, phrases are contracted (*isn't, they've, we're; Halloween* from *All Hallow Even*; German *Salmiak* from *sal ammoniac*) and words are shortened by aphesis (*sample* for *example, tend* for *attend, sciatic* for *ischiadic*), by syncope (*append-ectomy* for *appendicectomy, dilation* for *dilatation*), and by apocope (*lab* for *laboratory, exam* for *examination*).

Adjacent sounds are jumbled by metathesis: *comftorble* for *comfortable*; Spanish *cocodrilo* 'crocodile'; French *moustique* 'mos-quito'; medieval Latin *panaricium* for *paronychia*. (Cf. such common lingual lapses as *digilatize* and *intregal*.) Neighboring sounds may also alter one another through assimilation (*annex* from *adnexum, cubboard* for *cupboard*), dissimilation (*pilgrim* from Latin *pere-grinus*, medieval *cephalargia* for *cephalalgia*), umlaut (*child* and *drive* with long *i, children* and *driven* with short *i; thumb, thimble*), or by favoring insertion (*jaundice* from *jaunisse; horehound* from Middle English *horhowne* 'hoary herb') or deletion (*su'prise, Feb'uary*).

Sometimes the sound of a word is shifted by attraction to another word that is felt somehow to be analogous. Thus, Middle English *femelle*, from Latin *femella* 'woman', via Old French, was altered centuries ago to *female* by constant association with *male*, from Latin *masculus*. More recently, *gonadotrophin, somatotrophin*, and other terms formed from Greek *trophe* 'nourishment' and the suffix *-in* have been corrupted to *-tropins* by attraction to words formed from *trope* 'turning'. (Perhaps this shift is behind the semantic confusion responsible for a term like *psychotropic*.) The lay Spanish word for *hemorrhoid(s)*, *almarrana*, is a phonetic corruption of the Greek original due in part to the example of the many Spanish words incorporating the Arabic definite article: *alcohol, álcali, alcalde*.

A word may acquire a deviant sound to point a contrast, as in the sports announcer's "AW-fense" and "DE-fense." Consider also the differing senses of *has* in "the money the committee *haz* to spend" and "the money the committee *hass* to spend." By a mysterious process working directly against the principle of economy, words may be lengthened, as *panderer* for *pander, hypochondriasis* for *hypo-chondria*.

A common source of variations and errors in both pronunciation and spelling is the neutral vowel sound so common in English, represented by *a* in *oral, e* in *liver, i* in *urine, o* in *tumor, u* in *fetus*, and *y* in *analysis*. This nondescript sound, symbolized in the international phonetic alphabet by ə, is called *schwa* after the Hebrew half-vowel of that name. Many word pairs formerly distinguished in speech, and still spelled differently, have become homophones because of the intrusion of the neutral vowel: *council* and *counsel*, *effect* and *affect*, *principle* and *principal*, even *have* and *of*.

When the neutral vowel falls in the middle of a polysyllable, it often virtually disappears, whence such common spelling errors as *anaphlaxis, cartlage, tetnus*, and *staphlococcus*. Consider also the common misunderstanding of *racemate* (from *racemic*) through the mispronunciation "race-mate." A similar blunder with *tuberose* (Latin *tuberosus* 'tuberous') led to the creation of a new kind of rose, the "tube rose."

On the other hand, when schwa has to be inserted where no symbol appears, as in the last syllables of *algorithm, aneurysm*, and *spasm*, an extraneous letter may creep into the spelling. Since the Latin noun ending *-us* and the English adjective ending *-ous* are both pronounced əs, they are often confounded: *mucus membrane, villus adenoma, a callous, a plug of mucous*.

Conversion of liquid consonants (*l, r*) to vowels (a regular feature of Sanskrit) makes it impossible for the ear to distinguish between *oral-pharyngeal* and *oropharyngeal* or between *glomerular nephritis* and *glomerulonephritis*. In these the differences are negligible since both forms are correct, unlike such embarrassing absurdities as *arterial venous* and *normal glycemic*, which occasionally appear in print.

Homophony may demand a special effort from the speaker so that he will not be misunderstood. For example, one may have to exaggerate vowel sounds to distinguish *perineal* from *peroneal*. Only a strained, unnatural pronunciation of *apatite, interpellate, immanent*, and *exorcise* can ensure that these will not be mistaken for *appetite, interpolate, imminent*, and *exercise*. The initial vowels of *afferent* and *efferent* are commonly stretched from short to long to prevent confusion. *Otic* has quite replaced *aural*, which sounds exactly like *oral*. In French one must depart from customary usage and say *une crise du foie* 'an attack of *the* liver', so as to exclude the alternative meaning, *une crise de (la) foi* 'a crisis of faith'.

English phonetic practices, inherently inconsistent and erratic, are nowadays generally imposed on classical words. Greek *ch* usually receives the correct pronunciation (*k* or *kh*) except when it is preceded by *s*, as in *ischium* and *schistosomiasis*, where the influence of German often suggests an *sh* sound. *Schizophrenia* usually escapes this German influence only to succumb to another one, the non-Hellenic *ts* sound of *z*. Greek *g* is often pronounced hard at the beginning of *gynecology* and *gynecomastia* and soft in *meningocele* and *laryngoscope*—just the reverse of the correct ways. Although in classical Greek *g* was always hard, Latinized Greek softens *g* before *e, i,* and *y* (*geriatric, gigantism, gymnasium*), preserving the hard sound before *a, o,* and *u*.

Classical vowel sequences are often fused by syneresis, so that words formed from Greek *oon* 'egg' and *zoon* 'animal' (*oophorectomy, epizootic*) are often heard with the *oo* sound of *boot*, while Latin *rabies, caries,* and *scabies* are reduced to two syllables each. The diphthong *au* in *autopsy, glaucoma, trauma,* and *caudal* is frequently given a classical sound (as in *kraut*), though English usage would prefer the sound in *taut*.

Placement of stress accent in classical words is inconsistent but often correct, apparently by accident. Whereas in *saliva, pruritus,* and *diarrhea* the stress falls where it belongs, on the second-to-last syllable, it has been shifted forward in the American pronunciation of *gingiva, tinnitus,* and *trachea*. Words ending in -*ia* and -*iasis* are almost invariably accented on the third-to-last syllable (*dextrocardia, psoriasis*), though here again the accent belongs one syllable later, as in *hydroa* and *scoliosis*. In contrast, *angina pectoris* should have the accent on the first syllable in each word but seldom does.

Words borrowed from nonclassical languages commonly lose much of their original sound, tending to be pronounced as if they were natives. Borrowings from French are usually treated as exceptions and given something like their original pronunciations, but the effort often goes awry. Moreover, many words are given a quasi-French intonation even though they are pure Latin (*mitrale, ovale, inguinale, annulare, multiforme, sal volatile*) or Greek (*chalazion, raphe*) or are borrowings or coinages from these classical languages owing no fidelity to French (*bacteriophage, centigrade, centimeter, scalpel, vaccine*). *Troche* (meaning 'lozenge'), invariably pronounced as though it were French, is a strictly English corruption of Greek *trochiskos* 'little wheel' and quite unknown in France with any such meaning.

Medical Writing

You must see to it not only that your writing can be understood,
but that it cannot be misunderstood.

Quintilian
The Education of an Orator

Hippocrates may owe his title, the Father of Medicine, principally to his fatherhood of medical writing. He is certainly the earliest writer on medicine whose name and works have survived together to the modern era. This is not to detract from the worth of his contributions to the art and science of medicine. Had he not been a great physician and teacher, his writings would have perished long ago.

In Hippocrates's time, and for many centuries afterward, most of the lore of a trade or profession was handed down orally from father to son or from master to apprentice. Before the invention of printing from movable type in the fifteenth century, books were scarce and expensive. Medicine is not the only science that began to advance by leaps and bounds once there was a simple means of preserving and propagating newly discovered facts.

The saga of medical writing would provide material for a much bigger book than this one. The remarkably durable Corpus Hippocraticum and the scarcely less ancient writings of Celsus, Aretaeus, Dioscorides, and Galen; the contributions of Aristotle; ancient Egyptian, Chinese, and Hindu medical documents; the works of the great medieval authorities, Maimonides, Averroës, and Abulcasis; the radical diatribes of Renaissance reformers like Roger Bacon, Cardano, and Paracelsus; the anatomic drawings of Vesalius and his successors; the brilliant achievement of Osler in his *Principles and Practice of Medicine*; and the stupendous bulk of modern periodical medical literature—all of these compose the rich and varied fabric called *medical writing*.

Given the vital importance of medical writing to the progress of civilization, one might expect the art to be widely cultivated and highly perfected. Such is not the case at all. Modern medical literature is some of the most vapid, obscure, tortuous, and unreadable material in print. In this concluding section, I propose to examine some of the more grievous faults of modern American medical writing. I shall exclude from this discussion faults that are not directly related to language, such as inaccuracy, disorganization, sketchiness, and lack of continuity. Although I cannot claim to have a simple remedy for syntactic incompetence or for an ill-formed sense of style, I say without hesitation that a clear notion of the kinds of error that are most apt to be committed in technical writing is the strongest defense against committing them.

One way to classify faults of writing is to start with the attributes of good writing. Technical literature ought to be correct, clear, exact, and comfortable for the reader. Since correctness, or accuracy, is not primarily a linguistic concern, I shall say nothing about the lack of it here. The remaining faults—obscurity, or the failure to impart a clear message; vagueness, or the failure to be exact; and dullness, or the failure to be interesting and pleasant to read—typically occur together and arise from the same sources: faulty speech habits, ignorance, carelessness, inexperience at writing, and lack of suitable standards. In discussing specific faults, it will be convenient to group them into verbal, phrasal, syntactic, and conceptual.

There could hardly be a more elementary blunder in writing than using the wrong word, and so I shall begin with that. *Malapropism* refers to a confusion between two words of similar form, as when the layman says *prostrate* (instead of *prostate*) *gland*, or when the physician writes that diastolic hypertension *mitigates* (meaning *militates*) against a diagnosis of shock. Though the words in each of these pairs begin and end with the same letters, they have different roots and different meanings. Another kind of malapropism confuses two words that are derived from the same root but have different suffixes, which by convention show a difference of meaning. *Hesitancy* is not the same as *hesitation*, nor *observance* the same as *observation*, nor *selective* the same as *selected*.

Consider the numerous words that can be formed from the stem *sens-* (*sent-*) by the addition of various adjectival suffixes: *sensate, sensational, sensible, sensitive, sensory, sensual, sensuous, sentient, sentimental,* and so on. A well-read native speaker of English readily distinguishes these words and uses them according to conventional patterns. But for the unlettered, most or all of them may run together in an inseparable blur. In reading, he may be able to deduce the meaning of some of these words with fair accuracy from the context.

(Then again, his guesses may lead him far astray.) But in speaking or writing, he will often snatch at the wrong form to express his meaning and so commit a malapropism.

Journalists have been responsible, if not for the creation, at least for the popularization and perpetuation, of many malapropisms, including the hardy perennials *flaunt* for *flout, comprised of* for *composed of,* and *deprecation* for *depreciation.* Medical writers go wrong with ordinary English words like these more often than they do with technical terms. One writes that his patient "responded *refractively* (*refractorily*) to naloxone"; another advises his readers against assuming an *authoritative* (*authoritarian*) manner with adolescent patients; a third states that if the ovum is not fertilized, the corpus luteum gradually degenerates and *scarifies* (*forms a scar*).

Malapropisms arise chiefly from the writer's unfamiliarity with his own language and from the fallacy of false analogy ("Two things that are similar in one way are similar in another"). The objection to malapropisms is that they not only obscure the writer's message to some extent but also damage the integrity of language. The difference between an approximately correct word and an exact one is the difference between articulation and articulateness or, to use Mark Twain's comparison , between lightning and the lightning bug. There are cogent reasons for maintaining a sharp distinction between, for example, *factitious* and *factitial.* The ideas are truly distinct; the difference between the words reflects a difference already perceived by the mind. To blur the distinction by using the words interchangeably is to rob the language of the power of expressing either idea clearly and simply.

Similar to malapropisms, but more flagrant and less defensible, are blunders like the following in which the words the writers used were not even close to the ones they wanted. "The increased incidence of carcinoma in achalasia, Barrett's esophagus, lye strictures, and the Plummer-Vinson syndrome should encourage the high index of suspicion *incumbent* (*essential*) to early diagnosis." "A thromboembolism became *impaled* (*lodged*) within a patent foramen ovale." "Squatting and turning, or simply turning with the knee flexed and the foot planted, is enough to tear a meniscus if it is *impinged* (*trapped, wedged*) between the femoral condyle and the tibial plateau."

Another kind of blunder that is more than superficially related to the classic malapropism is violation of syntactic idiom. This is especially common in those ill-advised passive contructions of which medical writers are so fond (*rats were fasted, the eye was operated*). Reversals of normal idiomatic relations are seen in "Mr. Smith recommended Mr. Jones to the doctor" and "A refund check will be sent to the authorized party that is due the overpayment." An idiomatic phrase that contains a preposition is especially liable to mishandling: *oblivious from* (*of*), *obtunded from* (*by*), *different than* (*from*), *corresponding with* (*to*, unless an epistolary exchange is meant). A medical bureaucrat writes, "When the first and second medical opinions are in dispute," to mean 'when they disagree'. An editor, failing to understand or even recognize the phrase *nothing of moment*, changes it to *nothing of the moment*, which means nothing at all. A surgeon with dim memories of *other things being equal* (Latin *caeteris paribus*) incoherently writes, "The younger the patient, the better the result, all things being equal."

Not only do incompetent writers frequently display a weakness for clichés and foreign, arcane, archaic, and learned-sounding words and phrases (*conspicuous by its absence, erstwhile, far be it from me, stand in good stead, unbeknownst, vis-à-vis*), but they consissistently misunderstand and misapply them. They are apt to crowd their sentences with wildly inappropriate metaphors (*benchmark, hallmark, earmark, cornerstone, capstone, keystone*) and slaughtered idioms (*tow*, for *toe, the mark; a hare's breath* for *a hair's breadth*). Fad terms (*charisma, ecology, Occam's razor, serendipity*) almost always undergo degeneration of meaning upon being taken up by the semiliterate rabble. Once and for all, let it be noted that an *ivory tower* connotes the isolation of the hermit; the traditional symbol for the idealism and impracticality of the academician is the *ivied tower*.

Carelessness with metaphors must sooner or later lead the writer into absurdity. A frequent result of the reckless parroting of figurative expressions is mixed metaphor. Most of us were first exposed to Hamlet's soliloquy at so tender an age that we have never had occasion to perceive the ludicrous tangle of images in his proposal "to take arms against a sea of troubles." This sort of nonsense was brought to its highest development by lady novelists of the nineteenth century ("Jeannie's gentle disposition and gracious manner soon won her a *foothold* in every *heart* and an *open door* at every *table*").

Even dead metaphors, as H. W. Fowler picturesquely remarked, will not lie quietly together if there was repugnance between them in life. Those that are not dead but only a little tattered cannot be mixed without ridiculous effect: "Today's pharmacist stands at a *crossroads*. One *fork* leads to . . ."; "a development that has *crystallized* the *tensions* between the two disciplines"; "During a long illness Dr. Nesbit *polished* his already *well-developed* academic *foundations*." Closely akin to these muddles is the hybrid figure in which elements of two expressions are fused in one meaningless monstrosity: *fill this category, beggars the imagination, cut from the same mold.*

Although pure slang seldom gets into print in a learned journal, many technical terms have two spheres of meaning, one strict and the other loose and colloquial. When the unthinking medical writer uses such a term with its slang meaning, the editor who is not a physician will probably fail to notice and amend the lapse. Bile is the digestive juice produced by the liver. The writer who speaks of *bile in the urine* is either indulging in slang or showing his adherence to medieval physiology.

It may be argued that the errors of a few careless writers and inept editors can have no lasting impact on language. This is simply false. Daily observation shows that every variation, blunder, and ill-conceived experiment in writing is promptly copied with simian fidelity by a dozen scribblers more careless and ignorant than the original perpetrator. Once a malapropism or wrong usage has become nearly universal, the sensible linguist or rhetorician calls it a semantic shift or a homonym and stops grumbling about it. But the prudent writer will avoid using any word that is in transition between an established meaning and a new one, except when the context makes its sense and bearing perfectly unmistakable. To the educated, *nauseous* means 'sickening'; it has not yet been generally accepted as a synonym for *nauseated*. Although *approximate* is coming to mean 'general' or 'inexact', its literal meaning, 'near, nearly correct', is far from defunct. When a writer says that his results are "less approximate than Jones's," does he mean that they are less exact, or more so?

On seeing a sign reading "Dispose of Litter Properly," the perspicacious thinker feels at least a twinge of distress at the semantic distortion: that which is disposed of properly is not litter. Physicians and nonphysicians alike are apt to allow their workaday speech to become so cluttered with formulas and clichés that the validity, accuracy, and precision of every assertion are in jeopardy. Since writing is just an outgrowth of speech, it is not surprising that the careless writer often puts on paper familiar words and phrases that a more thoughtful scrutiny would have told him are altogether foreign to the meaning that he intends.

If repeated often enough, almost any word or phrase can become a formula to which the mind attaches little if any of its literal meaning. The formula then becomes the master and betrays the speaker or writer into one absurdity after another. Language has completely taken leave of thought in sentences like the following: "The urine was grossly bloody and showed four-plus occult blood." "Palpation of the prostate revealed the prostate to be surgically absent." It is hard to put much faith in the diagnostic acumen, or even the intelligence, of a physician who is capable of so expressing himself.

Ordinarily one thinks of a word like *asymptomatic* as having a fixed meaning, not subject to alteration by surrounding words. Yet a writer discussing women who were found to have positive gonococcal cultures in a survey of patients with dysuria finds it reasonable to call them "asymptomatic carriers," even though the symptom of dysuria is what prompted their inclusion in the study. Similar specialization and distortion of meaning have been noted earlier in this chapter with respect to *nonsteroidal* and *decompensation*.

Another example of the careless use of a word in open defiance of its obvious literal meaning is seen in "Chest wall syndrome is a common cause of *undiagnosed cardiac pain*," where the italicized phrase means, not 'pain due to heart disease that has eluded diagnosis', as one might suppose, but rather 'pain that simulates that of heart disease but eludes diagnosis because it is not really due to heart disease at all'. Failure to attend to the patent literal sense of words can betray the writer into self-contradictions like "recurrent sudden death," pointless iterations like "blood serology," and gibberish like "minimal to say the least," "second to few," and "Roger and Kos were one of the first to see the application of Békésy audiometry to clinical work."

Many of the favorite words of technical writers, though not quite incorrect, labor under the disadvantage of undue vagueness and abstractness. Here may be included many of the jargon words of medical literature (*factor, aspect, situation*), which can mean practically anything. The writer who uses vague and noncommittal terms like these seems to consider himself absolved from thinking clearly or nailing down definitions and distinctions either in his mind or in his writings. It is precisely the careless writer's choice of vague jargon and ill-suited metaphors instead of concrete and specific words that makes him most treacherous and unreliable.

Equally objectionable is the pompous practice of cluttering expository prose with long or arcane words when shorter and plainer ones would serve better: thus, *varices* become *varicosities; calluses, callosities*; a *summary*, a *summarization*; and *cautery, cauterization*. The technique often seems to be chosen deliberately to lend an air of scholarship and profundity to pedestrian writing.

Some writers seem compelled to impart to their work a tedious loquacity and roundabout prolixity, swelling out a phrase into a sentence or a sentence into a paragraph. Unbridled verbosity may be just stylistic carelessness, but it often results from ineptness in handling specific words and phrases. Superfluous words come in many varieties. The empty tag, typically found annexed to another word like a parasite, imparts no meaning but only saps the vigor of the host word: disease *entity*, treatment *modality*, receptor *site*, tumor *mass*, crisis *situation*, observations largely subjective *in nature*. A pleonastic word or phrase repeats an idea already fully clear: resort to *other* more potent diuretics; described in five *different* patients; three died, *the rest did not*; the blood pressure decreased gradually *over time*.

The heedless scribbler objects: "As long as all the facts are there, who cares if there are some extra words?" The answer, of course, is that the reader cares very much indeed when useless words slow him down, send him along unprofitable byways, and dilute or bury the writer's meaning.

In an earlier chapter I noted some of the unique properties of the English phrase. The flexibility and versatility of the phrase form invite many abuses. In technical English the typically Germanic practice of linking together several words to form a phrasal noun is often carried to an extreme. *Wellness promotion emphasis* and *sudden onset right upper quadrant pain* may be merely ugly and silly, but *liquid protein diet magnesium deficiency* and *cimetidine postmarket outpatient surveillance program* overtax the capacities of language. By dispensing with prepositions and doing without adjective markers, the inventors of these phrases have produced strings of words whose internal relations and overall significance can only be guessed at. Even when a phrase contains an obvious adjective or two, the meaning may not be clear: *occult foreign-body aspiration, multiple risk factor intervention trial, jejunal gallstone ileus-distorted cholecystoduodenal fistula.*

A similar anomaly is the kind of hyphenated modifier seen in *a several-month period, resistant-bacteria epidemics,* and *learning-disabled children.* Here I may mention also the peculiar tendency of technicalese to invert certain kinds of phrases from the normal word order: *in vivo effectiveness* for *effectiveness in vivo; a growth-suppressing* (often without hyphen) *substance* for *a substance suppressing growth.*

An elliptic phrase, even more abbreviated than a noun phrase, omits—besides prepositions—some crucial lexical element. And unlike the noun phrase, which is apt to be a nonce construction, an elliptic phrase often becomes a standard expression: *gram-negative shock, loop diuretic, dependent edema, DES offspring.* The power of language to influence thought is nowhere more clearly evident than in the way that elliptic expressions generate elliptic thinking. Beyond doubt, the possibility of saying *ski mask, mothball fleet, scratch cake, fungal scrapings, anaerobic antibiotic,* and *negative acute antibody titer* without further effort to define the conceptual relationships within these phrases predisposes speakers of English to sloppy, uncritical, illogical thinking. Writing that bristles with ellipses is typically disorganized, vapid, and obscure.

Another quirk of syntax to which English technical writing is specially liable is hypallage, by which a concept or meaning is shifted to a part of speech that would not ordinarily be expected to carry it. Hypallage often results when an intangible quality is concretized by being absorbed into something tangible: "Auscultation revealed *absent* ['absence of'] breath sounds." "A major disadvantage of propranolol is its ability to cause *decreased* ['decrease of'] cardiac output." "He has had three *broken arms* ['fractures of the arm']." "He complained of painless *decreased* ['decrease of'] visual acuity."

Hypallage may also result from ill-advised experiments at abbreviation—*drug adversity* (adverse drug reaction), *ventricular ectopy* (ventricular ectopic beats). Indeed, many cases of hypallage might also be considered elliptic phrases. Among these I may cite the very common usage, an echo of classical Latin, seen in *right heart, upper tongue, distal ileum, late diastole, middle ear,* and *distal convoluted tubule*, in each of which the words "part of the" have been omitted. Thus, *right part of the heart*, and so forth.

Hypallage may consist in simple jumbling of the words in a sentence: "A mind is a terrible thing to waste" for "To waste a mind is a terrible thing." One often resorts to such devices in showing negation: "I don't think he knows" for "I think he doesn't know," and "She can't seem to absorb vitamin K" for "She seems unable to absorb vitamin K." At its mildest, hypallage contributes a colloquial taint to technical writing; at its worst it introduces variant senses, muddles meaning, diverts and delays the reader, and violates common sense.

I come now to the discussion of syntactic errors. By and large, rules of grammar, syntax, and punctuation are valid only insofar as they protect the integrity of thought and prevent confusion and inaccuracy of expression. Dangling participles, unassigned gerunds, orphan relative clauses, and floating adverbs all have in common a loosening of the bonds that are supposed to hold language together. Whether they engender ambiguity and misunderstanding or only provoke irritation or ridicule, these danglers are objectionable and ought to be kept out of writing.

"Advancing the probe under fluoroscopic control to the opposite margin of the cavity, the patient suddenly complained of a severe, stabbing pain." The participial phrase that begins this sentence creates an altogether false setting for the main clause, which contains nothing that the participle *advancing* can logically qualify or describe. For one brief moment before comprehension dawns, one is struck by the grimly ludicrous impression that it is the patient himself who is advancing the probe. Even when a participle does modify something in the sentence, it may create misunderstanding if it stands too far from its head word, and particularly if it starts the sentence: "Desiring to establish a causal relationship, punch biopsies of ochronotic bone were subjected by Harris and Levis to chemical analysis."

The gerund, a verbal noun that, like a participle, ends in *-ing* but, unlike a participle, does not modify anything, may also be said to dangle if its logical subject is nowhere in sight. That is particularly likely when the verb is passive. "By performing the initial examination with an endoscope adapted for taking biopsies, the patient is spared the trauma of repeated instrumentation." On first reading this sentence, one gets the idea that this patient, too, has undertaken his own treatment, even to the point of performing endoscopy on himself. "Without proposing regimentation or a restriction on innovations, the time has come for health professionals at all levels of training to survey objectively the devices they use." Here it is the editorialist who is not proposing regimentation or restriction, but that becomes clear only on a careful rereading of the sentence.

It may be objected that the meaning of these examples can be determined by a few moment's study, but that is hardly to the point. The reader of technical literature is not supposed to have to stop and figure things out word by word; there are crossword puzzles and murder mysteries for people who enjoy that sort of thing. Moreover, it is not always possible even on careful study to determine just what the writer means in a sentence like: "In explaining further his thinking on the amendment, the director was quoted by Evans as saying . . ." Who was doing the explaining here—the director or Evans? "On flexing the thigh sharply against the trunk, the patient experienced a recurrence of his pain." Did the patient flex his own thigh, or was it once again the invisible examiner?

Nor are dangling verbals the only culprits in midsentence shifts of thought. Here is a tortured muddle of a sentence in which an orphan relative clause is the problem. "He tripped while being pursued by a hornet, which caused a severe deltoid ligament tear." *Which* refers not to the hornet, as one is first led to suppose, but to the act of tripping. "Use of chocolate agar without antibiotics will not diminish the yield of gonococci and will not inhibit the growth of nongono-coccal pathogens, which may occur with use of Thayer-Martin medium." Here the reader is expected to omit the *nots* in applying the earlier clauses to the dependent one. Though not universally recog-nized as an error, the common practice of letting an entire clause stand as the antecedent of the relative *which* so frequently causes confusion that it should be avoided whenever possible.

Medical editors and nonphysicians often accuse medical writers of overusing the passive voice. This objection is generally based on esthetic grounds rather than on the question of intelligibility. More-over, the nature of expository writing sometimes almost forces the writer to choose the passive over the active voice. In the following specimen, however, it must be admitted that the writer has been led far astray by his quest for scientific detachment and objectivity:

"Because of failure of response to conservative treatment, orthopedic consultation was sought." In this sentence, which has to do with the relations among three persons, not one of those persons is mentioned. Instead, they are represented by nebulous abstractions: the primary physician by *conservative treatment*, the specialist by *orthopedic consultation*, and the patient—he for whose sake the science of medicine exists—by *failure of response*.

Notice how, in the following sentence, whenever the opportunity presents itself for the writer to make an honest, straightforward statement about people, he sidesteps it and serves up instead a hash of gerunds and passive constructions: "By initiating two new programs on a pilot project basis and by reemphasizing the use of an ongoing program, it is hoped that the goal will be met of maintaining the same quality of health care while reducing the length of hospital stay."

Not the least objectionable features of this barbarous style of writing are its general air of awkwardness and untidiness and its potential for blurring or even burying the writer's meaning. "On auscultation a murmur was heard" and "At laparotomy the gall-bladder was found to be acutely inflamed" are probably no more clumsy than the melodramatic "Palpation revealed a nodule" or the long-winded "Firm pressure was associated with a marked increase in discomfort." But all four of these expressions are open to the objection that they neither identify the persons whose actions and relations are being described nor give a clear picture of those actions and relations.

In some forms of obscure, ambiguous, or misleading writing, the problems cannot be simply analyzed as verbal or syntactic errors. It may be hard to tell whether the irregularities of language arise from the writer's stylistic incompetence or from his confusion and ignorance of his subject. Errors of this class may subtly and insidiously distort the intended or expected emphasis or point of view, creating a wholly false or illogical impression.

Again, an elliptic phrase omits something critical: *anaerobic antibiotic* for *antibiotic effective against certain anaerobic pathogens*. Provided that the reader or hearer already knows the conventional sense of this phrase, or has sufficient familiarity with the subject, shorthand like this may call up in his mind exactly the intended concept. Nonetheless, with an elliptic expression there is always at least a slight risk of suppressing the concept or relationship for which the suppressed word or words stand. Thus, even an alert and well-trained physician might suppose an anaerobic antibiotic to be one that works only in the absence of oxygen, if he had no prior knowledge of the phrase and had not been tipped off to its right meaning by the context.

When one proceeds to elliptic sentences and even paragraphs, the danger of misunderstanding grows. Not only does it become increasingly difficult to perceive and appreciate what has been left out, but often the reader cannot judge accurately whether the writer has omitted it deliberately or simply failed to consider it. In reading of a case of constrictive pericarditis we are surprised to learn that "triamterene was prescribed to prevent potassium depletion," whereas we would have supposed that it was prescribed to promote diuresis. The grain of truth buried in this misstatement is that triamterene was chosen in preference to diuretics that increase excretion of potassium so as to avoid the potassium depletion that such drugs might have induced. The writer has gone astray by assuming that the medical reader not only knows that triamterene is a diuretic but is familiar with its potassium-sparing property. Though his assumption may be generally valid, the sentence he wrote is false.

"Middle ear effusion as a complication of acute otitis media is usually due to inadequate antibiotic therapy." Is this just a case of hypallage (for *inadequacy of antibiotic therapy*), or does the writer really mean to state that without any antibiotic therapy there would be no middle ear effusions after acute otitis media?

"Under certain conditions, the residual fumes contained in whiskey barrels are potentially explosive." Is this *potentially* pedantry or just carelessness? No matter; it dilutes and weakens the meaning. Why specify "certain conditions" and then describe the danger of explosion as only potential?

Inattention to the business of composition may be responsible for the following circular sentence, but the reader may well suspect the writer's competence and intelligence: "Despite these advantages, when used indiscriminately or in excess, its dangers outweigh its advantages." Is the following bad writing or a typographical error not caught by writer or editor? "Salt retention expands the total fluid volume in the body, increasing the output from the heart and essentially overfilling the circulation that sets off the hypertensive process."

The writer who uses words carelessly and ineptly will be suspected of being similarly careless and incompetent as a scientist and reasoner. Not many years ago, education consisted largely in the acquisition of verbal skills; modern education (more accurately, training or instruction) often neglects these skills. Inevitably, a prejudice exists among the thoroughly educated that unidiomatic English betrays intellectual as well as linguistic deficiencies. The cultivated reader, with his deeper familiarity with the usages of polite literature, his wider vocabulary, and his knowledge of etymology, is apt to despise the writer who violates grammar, idiom, and logic with one crass barbarism after another.

The written word is a tricky and recalcitrant medium. The skillful writer is the one who has learned to work within the limitations imposed by his materials and his tools. The flood of malapropisms, bad grammar, and other forms of gibberish in modern medical writing is clearly the product of unpracticed—not to say unlettered—writers. No one is born with writing skills; they must be acquired through extensive reading and long practice.

A steady diet of technical literature not only narrows one's intellectual horizons but sets a dismally inferior standard of expository prose and offers neither motivation nor example for developing and improving literary skills. The best model of good style is any English prose, regardless of its age or subject, that conveys a clear message in concise, vigorous, readable form. And the best way to form a clear and vigorous style of one's own is to practice writing, painstakingly and persistently, with such models in mind.

References and Readings

Ball CR: Latin or English plurals for anglicized Latin nouns? Am Speech 1927;3:291-325.

CBE Style Manual Committee: *Council of Biology Editors Style Manual.* 4th ed. Council of Biology Editors, 1978.

Day RA: How to write a scientific paper. ASM News 1975;41:486-494.

Dirckx JH: *Dx + Rx: A Physician's Guide to Medical Writing.* Boston, G. K. Hall, 1977.

Dirckx JH, Leider M: A description and directory of plural forms of medical Latin words and terms. Am J Dermatopathol 1981;3:41-53.

Finnegan S: Publishing medical books: advice to authors. J Am Med Assoc 1982;247:1497-1499.

Fowler HW: *A Dictionary of Modern English Usage.* Oxford, Clarendon Press, 1926.

Gordon BL: Welter of words. J Am Med Assoc 1971;218:878-879.

Scientific Publications Division, American Medical Association: *AMA Manual for Authors and Editors.* Los Altos, California, Lange Medical Publications, 1981.

Smith LP: *Needed Words.* Society for Pure English Tract XXXI, Oxford, Clarendon Press, 1928.

Strunk W, White EB: *The Elements of Style,* 2nd ed. New York, Macmillan Co., 1972.

Ullman S: *Semantics: An Introduction to the Science of Meaning.* New York, Barnes & Noble, 1978.

Subject Index

Index of Words and Phrases